The Zampaladus Theory Publishing Group, Proudly Presents.....

"TREASUREZ IN THE SAND VOL I)"

By: Djedefre Memnon KKR 33°/360°

"The True Story of the Glorious Pharaohs" & The Stolen Legacy of the Kushite People....

Disclaimer: The views expressed in this publication are solely those of the author and not the publishing group.

The Zampaladus Theory Publishing Group 2018 ©

Introduction 1: Ba Kuluwm

Initiation:

When the universal mind gave me the flashes of inspiration to write this scroll, I knew instantly that it was going to be my biggest challenge to date. Pondering on how I was going to achieve this gargantuan task, all I knew for sure is that I'd have to stand up to the challenge. I called upon the blood of my illustrious ancestors, to speak through the blood in my veins and assist me in bringing this message from the mists of time into the light of day. I then let the universal forces of the One, guide my pen over the lines of the following pages.

I was forced to put in many days and hours of reading and research, to add to the library of knowledge which was already embedded deep within my psyche. After escaping from the cobra-clutch of contemporary religion and rediscovering the Stolen Legacy of the so called Black man, I became passionate about re-telling 'Our-Story', which is 'Her-Story' – Tamare/Africa – as opposed to, and challenging 'His-Story', (the official history of the European mind as taught in educational institutions today).

My 20 years of research took me on a journey, back tracking through religion and history, back across the burning sands of the Sahara Desert. I began from within the folds of Islam, through Christianity and Judaism, through Roman and Greek theologies and philosophies, studying Kabbalah, Freemasonry and Sumerian Tablets. I was passionate about my research and reading, because a feeling inside always told me that the key to the Riddle of the Sphinx was the African himself, us! And that the bulk of so called scholars was deliberately misinformed. I knew and experienced from the earliest of ages that the racism so prevalent in our world, the so-called 'White Superiority Complex' of the European world would have to be challenged and destroyed head-on, at some point in my life. Subconsciously, it was something I just could not accept and the more I experienced the blatant and subtle racism, I found I needed answers as to why the world so hated my race? I had an urge to discover what we had done to receive so much unexplained hatred, to the point of the most Inhuman 'Trans-Atlantic Slave Trade' of the late 1500's A.D., for which no one has been held accountable. The same can be said for the Arab Enslavers. I was determined to discover the Truth on why the wider world was so silent on addressing the implications, the psychological consequences and the responsibilities it has left, both individually and collectively, because the Racism still exists.

Today in 2K18, the Maatian principles of the ancient people are needed more than ever. And not just for the Africans of the diaspora but also for the wider world in general. The spiritual void created by mankind's materialism has infected each and every race, nation and culture on the planet today. For the love of money, the majority of the planet are more than willing to sell their souls. The youth of the big inner cities today have no positive direction, they are becoming more and more sexualized and criminalized because they don't know that 'Wisdom is better than Silver and Gold', they're not aware that everything that glitters isn't Gold. Look at the state of the Music Industry today with all these effeminate, gay-looking, young lost rappers. Take a look at Hollywood's circus of Celebrity-Clones. Transhumanism. Our ancestors warned us about these realities, these demonic entities incarnate, because the same evil tried to hijack humanity in far ancient times. But you have traded your sacred truths/teachings for myths and unconfirmed beliefs.

Our all the drugs, sex, violence and pleasure-seeking, their melanin, DNA, has become toxic, forcing our people to act barbaric. The glitz and glamour of celebrity has become the most powerful religion. Consumerism and the cosmetic industry long became has made many women superficial, the American Dream, the pursuit of happiness, now embraced by the world, while men think money and status is equal to success. Who is there to tell them and expose the illusion? That happiness cannot be pursued because happiness is a choice not a destination. Who is powerful and influential enough to teach them divine truth? The replaced (Cloned/Droned) Kanye West and Kim Kardashian? No way! How about Jay Z and Beyoncé? No chance, they're all a part of the illusion. The late Tupac Amaru Shakur tried and failed, he tried to go against the Baphomet and paid the price. He had the ear of the youths and they knew it. They saw the potential and it scared those that wish to maintain the climate of mass-mind-control and fear. As a result, (mainstream) Hip-Hop is long dead and unable to produce the same calibre of great minds of the spiritual aspect. The Industry only produces pseudo-rappers, and druggies fulling our children's head with demonic behaviour, a false-reality, and satanic-subliminals.

The challenge today is for others to step up to the plate and present the world with the facts because the facts will eradicate the false beliefs of racism, religion and the unprecedented stereotypes of the fabricated and dated 'Whiteman's Burden'. The time is now. For I Am doing my part. "Not For Ours but For the Glory of the Gods!" – Djedefre Khasekhemre Memnon KKR 360

TREASUREZ IN THE SAND (VOL I)

Djedefre' Memnon 360

Section I: **The Groundwork**

"There is a difference between knowing the path and walking the path"

Morpheus, The Matrix

Chapter One: Sacred Origins

Shadow of the Sphinx:

It has long been the case that Sumerologists, Assyriologists, Archaeologists and the likes persist in their claims that civilization began outside of Africa. Somewhere, anywhere but the Motherland, Africa, which is really called Tamare "Land of the Sun". They teach that the first civilization is the Sumerian civilization which in times far gone was situated in Southern Iraq, between the two rivers of the Tigris and Euphrates. They say that ancient Sumer was established circa 4000 B.C. and Egypt 3100 B.C.

But who were the so called Sumerians "Black Headed People", who sprung up with a civilization, overnight, out of nowhere? Their civilization was fully formed with all its institutions highly developed just as in Kush/Khemet. But How?

What the so called Scholars won't tell you is that the Sumerians were the same ancient Anu people also called Ptah (pronounced 'Twa') people, who came up out of Africa and migrated into the wider world becoming indigenous to every continent. These Anu people were the earliest forms of Homo-Sapiens. These people were Nubians who were the 'New-Beings', ancient Kushites. These Nuwbuns (Ptahites) and Nubians (Kushites) were genetically engineered by a race of woolly-haired 'Supreme Beings' called by many different names in many different languages. In our people's own language of Nuwaubic/Medew Neter, we refer to them as Paut Neteru which translates as "Guardians, Watchers, and Nature" or Anunnaqi "Those Who ANU Sent to Earth". These principalities of nature became (manifested from etheric beings) into flesh and blood beings manifesting in the physical reality as the ELOHEEM "Lofty Beings" of the Scriptures. They are referred to as 'Gods' and the problem with this in today's monotheistic world, is that many see our ancient ancestors as polytheist, pagans, animists like we never had any sense before foreign concepts were enforced upon us by Arabs and Europeans, but this is far from the case as will be explained later.

The Neteru came from the high galaxy called Illyuwn 'Place on High'. It is a Tri-Solar System consisting of 3 suns and 19 planets of high energy. These supreme beings with melanin and woolly-hair travelled through the constellations of Orion and Sirius into galaxies such as, Andromeda, Dracos, Pleiades, Arcturus, and Mazzoroth among others. When they arrived here in our Milky Way, our small solar system with its 10 (not 9) planets, they chose to settle on Mars first, which still had its own atmosphere at that time. When Mars eventually lost is atmosphere, the Neteru relocated here onto Earth. For various reasons that I won't go into in this scroll, projects were started, planned to seed the planet with the progeny of the Sun God Re' (pronounced Ray) also called ANU, "The Heavenly One".

The 8 Rashunaat "Ogdoads", 4 pairs of male and female ancestors of Man, who were called Nommos, 'Lawgivers', crashed down in the Nile River 2,250,000 years ago. These Sacred Eight, Ogdoads were akin to what are called 'Greys' or Rumardians in the 'Unidentified Flying Object' (UFO) community today but were personify as more human looking, Twa people (dwarf looking) traits. Four ages of Homo Sapien man resulted from the primordial Ogdoad called Rashunaat in Nuwaubic. The pairs were:

1) Nun & Nunet
2) Kek & Keket
3) Heh & Hehet
4) Amun & Amunet (also called Niu & Niut).

Meteor showers destroyed two ages of these primitive ancestors, and the Great Deluge destroyed the third age. We are now in the 4th age of Amun & Amunet. In West Africa today, these Rashunaat are referred to as Orisha, and many other names worldwide.

The Neteru travel in an inter-dimensional mother-craft which is 3 times the size of our planet earth and capable of interstellar travel. It appears as an artificial, well camouflaged planet which has been recently uncovered by Western astronomers and referred to as Wormwood, Rylo 7, and Planet X and called the 12th Planet in the brilliant Earth Chronicles Series written by the late Zecharia Sitchin. The Ancient people in Khemet "The Black Land" (Egypt) referred to it as 'The Sacred Solar Barque', while in Nuwaubic it is said "Nibiru - Planet of the Crossing". Originally on an orbit from Illyuwn spanning 25,920 years, it is currently on a much shortened orbit of 3,600 years since the Neteru became the caretakers of our solar system. This Nibiru is mentioned upon the sacred tablets of Khemet as RE's Manjet, it is mentioned on Sumerian Tablets as Planet Marduk and its symbol, mistaken with a symbol of the sun, the winged-disk was universally recognized throughout the Ancient world civilization.

Every 3,600 years referred to as one Shar, the Nibiru returns to the solar system. The Ancient civilizations revered and commemorated this sacred event and became adept at studying the Kosmos, planets and life of the stars. They knew that everything here on earth below, was governed by that which was above and knew how to read the language of the heavens as 'Solar Biologists'. This is where Europeans get their pseudo-science of Lunar Astrology, but the Ancients, we were true astronomers without the need of today's technology. We were able to see using the Spiritual Eye with uncanny precision. Among the first Earth Anunnaqi, was the divine family, not wasn't Adam and Eve, but rather father Geb, mother Nut't and their children, Asar (Osiris), Aset (Isis), Sutukh (Set) and Nebthet (Nebtys). Ptah (Enki) and Djehuti (Marduk) gave civilization to the 'First Messiah' ASARU or OSIRIS, and his consort ASET or ISIS, and the Kushite people in Nubia (the entire Nile Valley). This civilizing knowledge came from the Abzu, "South Africa", up through Uganda, Tanzania and into the Nile Valley. It did not come from Asia or Europe as so called scholars would want you to believe. The culture which birthed the convent of civilization was African. Meluha and Magan (Ethiopia and Egypt), Africa was assigned to Enkites as opposed to Enlilites, Enki and Enlil being the two sons of the Most High ANU ALYUN ALYUN, AL or RE and Enki (EA) held the keys. The sacred city of the sun, called Heliopolis by the Greeks was where real theology was perfected. This is the place with the sacred mound where Pa Netcher RE' descended in His sacred Ben Ben which was commemorated forever within the Sacred Temple of RE' and the Ben Ben stone, in the Mansion of the Phoenix. The Sacred City of On/Anu (Heliopolis) was where the sacred cult of the Ben Ben and Phoenix Bird began. Even when the old capital of Anu/On was moved due to the threat of invasions by foreigners much later, the sacred city of the sun always maintained its sacred significance and its priesthood remained still, the most religiously sacred throughout the later dynasties of Pharaohs. The people would make pilgrimage to look upon and stare at the Ancient craft of Re' and the religious relics that were housed there as a type of Smithsonian Institute. It was a tangible reality.

Memphis (Men-Nefer) the white walled city became and remained the administrative centre of Khemet – "The Black Land" (Egypt). The location of the city had always been important as the unifying city between the North (lower) Egypt and the South (Upper) Egypt and Nubia. Because of the topography (the shape of the surface of the land), the South being more mountainous and the northern delta being flat Marshlands, the South is known as 'Upper' and the North is known as 'Lower' Egypt. Memphis was also better situated to defend against the threat of invasions.

Together with the sacred city of Anu and Men-Nefer, the 3rd great city, the final piece of the sacred Triad of cities was Waset, also called Thebes, the city of 100 gates. Thebes housed the monumental temple of Karnak and the splendid temple of Luxor. Thebes had the added advantage of being close to its Nubian roots and was undisputedly the domain of the Neter Amun; seen as the King of the Gods. These 3 sacred cities created the spine of Egyptian civilization during the time of the Pharaonic dynasties. Each district was assigned to a patron deity, Memphis to Ptah and Anu/On to Atum-Re. There were many other 8important cities such as Hermopolis assigned to Djehuti and the holy city of Abydos, another region used for pilgrimage since the most Ancient days and assigned to Asar (Osiris). It is in Abydos that Osiris's remains were buried in the Osirion - Abydos being the first holy city on earth, before

Mecca and before Jerusalem. Most of the most Ancient major cities around the globe were intentionally situated on and around the 30th parallel. The 30th parallel was along the line of the Neteru's Landing Corridor which was so brilliantly proven in Zecharia Sitchin's Earth Chronicles. Cities such as On, Sippar in Ancient Sumer, Harappa in the Indus Valley, etc. This landing corridor was anchored on Mount Ararat in Turkey before the deluge area 10,500 B.C. and then had to be re-rooted including places like the Giza Metropolis, Baalbek in Lebanon and Mount St. Katherine in Dilmun – 'Land of the Missiles' in the Sinai region.

Along with Jerusalem, which replaced the Ancient city of Sippar as the Neteru's Mission Control Centre, all of these Ancient sites and cities were geodetically linked to one another, as if the sky had been measured with a chord. A geodesic is the equivalent of a straight-line on a curved surface, such as the earth's surface. These cities and sites were also equidistant apart from one another connecting North East Africa and Mesopotamia by way of the Neteru's landing corridor.

Ancient Sumer, called Abi Shinar in the language of the Old Testament and the Jewish Tanakh (Torah), was chosen as the ideal landing sites by the Neteru because of its vast expanses of flat lands before the mountains surrounding them. These mountains such as Mount Ararat and the Cedar Forest Mountains of Lebanon, Mount Hebron in Jerusalem and Mount St. Katherine in the Sinai peninsula could be used as anchors and landing beacons for incoming crafts. This region between the white and blue Nile Rivers and the Tigris – Euphrates Rivers became known as the E.Din – 'Land of the Rocketships' and became called affectionately, 'The Window of Heaven', before any Torah or Bible. This is the vast multinational region in which the Kushite culture blossomed into the first and greatest civilizations on earth, such as (Ethiopia), the Sudan Meluha (Nubia), Egypt Magan (Khemet Ta), Sumer, Elam, The Indus Valley Aratta (India), among others around the globe. The cradle of man, again was South Africa which was referred to as the Abzu in Sumerian texts. The Abzu translates as 'The Underworld', being that the Sumerians saw their land as upwards and the West downwards. It was in the Abzu that the first genetically modified humans (Homo-sapien sapiens) were put to work by the Neteru and thus populated Mother Africa.

The Sumerians referred to the Neteru by the name Anunnaqi – 'Those who ANU sent from Heaven to Qi (Earth)'. In Aramic/Aramaic (Hebrew), the language of the biblical Israelites they were called Elohim – 'Lofty Beings', while in the Ashuric (Arabic) of the original Qur'aan, it is Malaaikat – 'rulers'. All of these languages and names are referring to the same Supreme Beings from the 19th Galaxy of Illyuwn - 'Place on High', with its 3 suns and

19 planets. Those Supreme Beings who Inhabited the 8th planet called Rizq; called Rizqiyans are known as Elohim – Dinneer – 'Righteous Ones' or Dingir in Sumerian meaning 'Of the Rocketships'. From the E.Din – 'Land of the Rocketships', the Ancient people witnessed their comings and goings to and from the Earth. The proof of this can be found in the numerous records of the many nations in this region, both Kushite nations and non-Kushite nations such as the Hittites of Hatti and the Canaanites (of Canaan).

These Ancient stories would eventually be written into the scriptures of the 3 major religions; the Abrahamic (Monotheistic) faiths in one form or another. Albeit, in a much diluted and watered-down version. All of the stories of Gods and men in contemporary religions have borrowed their themes and ideas from the multinational Kushite cultures with no exceptions. Numerous Ancient artefacts, relics and stories are proof.

When the Tamahu 'European Race' began to inherit the civilizations through constant invasions from the mountainous lands of the colder climates, they swiftly began to re-write the history books and began to spin up blatant lies about Kushite and Hamitic people due to the pent up jealousy and racism towards the melaninite children of the sun, the sons and daughters of the Anunnaqi – Neteru. Coming from the cold, harsher climates of the steppes where survival against the elements was an everyday struggle, it is safe to say that they had always coveted our beautiful, good-blessed kingdoms of easy living. Because of the harsh climate of Europe and the scarcity of food, clothing, shelter and other natural resources, the Tamahu were forced to adapt to pretty much nomadic existence which was rough competitive living at the best of times; for they lived in a spiritually-dead and barbaric, dog-eat-dog world. Having such a hellish environment they never imagined beautiful, benevolent and beneficial Gods tangibly involved in their lives and passing them the secrets of civilization creating ease and an abundance of natural resources and industries. As a nomadic cave man (Neanderthal) he was a barbarian like Conan, void of the spiritual principles of the Tamarean Africans of the Southern tropical hemisphere. This is where the racism stems from. Covetousness.

When the Tamahu finally came down from the Russian Steppes of the Caucasus Mountains, being drawn to our prosperous civilizations such as Greece, Crete, Elam, China, Khemet and Sumer, among others, what he witnessed was ease of living through agriculture and industry, spirituality – happiness and the philosophy of divinity and abundance. This is what drew the barbarians from the mountains into the various civilizations throughout the sands of time like magnets on metal.

The Kushites thus had a civilizing, gentler nature as opposed to the Tamahu. Through civilization and industry, together with the tropical nurturing climate, we found that there was always enough resources to go around. There was always enough time on our hands in our societies to ponder on the mysteries of creation, philosophy, art, literature, religion, architecture and develop a spiritual consciousness that brought us 'face to face' with God/s (Neteru – Anunnaqi). Indeed, Kingship descended from the heavens by way of the Neteru-Anunnaqi and given to man to be a go between, between the larger population of humans and these 'Lofty Beings' (Elohim). The very first Pharaohs and Rulers were both Kings and Priests who communicated the will of the Gods to the wider people and ensured the smooth running of the Kingdom, creating literally heaven on earth. For this to be effective, a strong code of justice had to reign supreme in the land, 'Bread and Beer, Justice for All, Rich or Poor – Big or Small'.

This justice was propagated by and through the system and way of life of Ma'at. Ma'at herself being the Netert - 'Goddess' of justice and consort of Tehuti, the Neter – 'God' of knowledge, writing, communication. Ma'atian principles were founded on 'Truth, Justice and Reciprocity' which brought 'balance' and respect for the natural order of things in the Universe(s). It was Ma'at herself that brought order out of chaos within the Universe. The principles of Ma'at became known as 'the Rule' by the Ancient sages and people and governed Kushite civilization and Khemet from its Pharaonic beginnings unto the end of the Kingdom. Ma'atian principles are the lifeblood of Kushites multinationally, even today after becoming so westernized, arabicized and negropean, we are witnessing the re-emergence of the rule in many quarters of the African diaspora. The re-surfacing of the Ancient wisdom will have and is having a ripple effect on the entire world, slowly but surely. We must all seriously now ask ourselves, 'what sort of world do we want ourselves and our children to live in?' Because it was this question that was at the forefront of the Kushite culture and it's glorious, spiritual civilization.

"The Scribes, full of wisdom, since the time
That followed that of the Gods,
And whose prophecies came about:
Their names shall endure throughout eternity.
They planned as heirs.
Not children born of their flesh who would preserve their name:
Their legacy is
In the books and in the teachings they wrote.
They made books their priests,
And their beloved sons were the scribe's tablet
Their teachings are their pyramids.

The scribe's reed was their son,
Their spouse was their tablet...
Their pyramids are their teachings.
Was their ever a man equal to Ptah-Hotep?
The wise men who predicted the future,
Whatever they uttered came true.
We discover that a certain things is a proverb.
And it can be found in their writings.....
Even though they are no longer alive,
Their magic power reaches out to all those who read their writings.

> Translation from the French of the text in A.H. Gardiner, Hieratic Papyri
> In the British Museum, 38 FF; translation in S. Schott & P. Krieger, Les
> Chants d'amour de l'Egypte ancienne, Paris, 1956, pp. 160-1

Ptah-Hotep was a sage and philosopher, a leading statesman in the Khemet of c.2400 B.C. At the great age of 110 years old he decided to write down and pass on the benefit of his wisdom by setting down a collection of maxims or 'wisdoms'. Miraculously preserved, his work offers not only rare ancient wisdom but additionally, a one-off inside look into the life and spiritual philosophy of Khemet during one of its golden ages. His work under Pharaoh Djedkare Isesi of the 5th Dynasty is crucial to our overstanding of the golden age of the Old Kingdom (2640 – 2040 B.C.). Through his illustrious writing we take a glimpse into the mind of a great ancestor sage and share his most passionate thoughts, intimacies and reflections. His words offer us counsel on timeless topics such as the art of governing, the nature of true knowledge and how to enjoy a harmonious, beneficial and prosperous existence. The book of Ptah-Hotep was a favourite of the Pharaohs and people. It was held as a jewel, one of the pillars of Khemetian wisdom. It is now largely considered the oldest book in the world.

The Greek poet Homer considered the Kushites 'blameless Ethiopians most favoured of the Gods' and said that the Gods would come down off of Mount Olympus to dine 'face to face' with the Ethiopians while everyone else had to go to the temple to commune with Divinity. Herodotus stated "the Ethiopians are most long lived and just of men". Indeed, far from being under the 'Curse of Ham' and the spawn of Satan as was implied by later racist European writers, the evidence indicates that the Kushites were godly people who possessed traditions that could develop you into becoming one ('face to face') with Paut Neteru or God if you like. One only has to look at the iconography inscribed upon the temples of Khemet, the near and Middle East. There are numerous depictions of Pharaohs and others 'face to face' with various deities (Neteru, Anunnaqi) or God, just as the scripture suggests Nimrod was, attaining a form of spiritual mastery that led to true civilization through 'God-Consciousness'. Pharaohs, Negast, Nimrods, Lugals, Rishis, etc. all had this in common. And not just men but Ura – 'Female Rulers' and women in general too. The Nimrod they speak about who had alluded scholars time and again is none other than Sharru-Kin – 'Righteous Ruler', called by historians – 'Sargon of Akkad', 2360 B.C.E. – anointed priest of ANU.

Genesis 10:8 – "And Kush begat Nimrod: he began to be a mighty one (Gibboreem) in the earth."

Genesis 10:9 – "He was a mighty hunter before the Lord": wherefore it is said, "Even as Nimrod the mighty hunter before the Lord."

Genesis goes on to the say:

The first centres of his Kingdom was Babylon, Uruk, and Akkad & Calneh, in Shinar. From that land he went to Syria (Assyria), where he built Nineveh, Rehoboth Ir, Calah and Resen, which is between Nineveh and Calah – which is the great city.

Of course there have been numerous lies made up about the Ancient rulers, Pharaohs, Nimrods, Lugals, Negast, etc., out of outright racism from the Europeans, Jews and even Arabs. These races took the ancient records of the glorious Kushite civilizations and corrupted the characters of many of its major players through they fabricated religious institutions, while their historians titled our Egyptian and Sumerian realities as 'Myths'. Of course, none of these Kushite records were myths but provable realities backed up by tangible evidence. All of the ancient cities, save a few in Mesopotamia have been unearthed. Tens of thousands of tablets and papyrus have been found to confirm the stories of Sargon, Menes, Gilgamesh, Etana, Naram-Sin, Nebuchadnezzar, etc. People like Utnapishtim (Ziusudra), who is the Sumerian Noah, have proven to be real folks who were neither Jewish, Christian nor Muslim. Most of the people said to be prophets of the Old Testament, (as depicted in the bible – pseudo characters) have never been found, proven or confirmed. No Moses, no Jesus, no Abraham, no Isaac, no Job, no Elijah or anyone else. It seems the only myths are the Holy Scriptures as depicted, and not the Kushite original tablets and oral traditions, and sacred texts. They literally wrote us into the bible/Koran to authenticate it and make the myth–made book appear the real word of God.

"...The authors of this chapter in Genesis were thus well informed regarding the origins and key innovations of the Sumerian civilization. They also realized the significance of the 'Tower of Babel' incident. As in the tales of the creation of Adam & Eve and of the deluge (flood), they melded the various Sumerian deities into the plural Elohim or into the All-Encompassing and Supreme Yahweh, but they left in the tale the fact that it took a 'group of deities' to say, "let us go down" and put an end to this rouge effort (Genesis 11:7) – The End of Days: Zecharia Sitchin.

"Kingship was brought from Heaven" – Sumerian King List.

".... Indeed, some anthropologists are now even open to the possibility that he legendary founder of Dynastic Egypt, King Narmer (Menes), could have himself been a Nubian from this ancestral stock". In a similar vein, American Egyptologist W.A. Fairservis Jnr, a member of the Hierakonpolist Project wrote:

"It should be noted that the Nubian origins of leaders such as Narmer is entirely possible. Indeed, there is no reason why critical motifs in the Narmer palette's iconography could not have been of Nubian origins...."

Imhotep the African, Pg 161 (In Part) by Robert Bauval and Thomas Brophy PhD.

So even the liars called Egyptologist who were sanctioned to 'try' to separate Khemet (Egypt) from the rest of Black Africa are forced by the evidence to reluctantly, indirectly admit that Khemet – Egypt was a colony of Ethiopia proper, i.e. 'The Sudan' and Nubian in origin. I take my hat off to those independent researchers, such as Robert Bauval and john Anthony West and those like the great E.A. Wallis Budge, who other Egyptologist try to discredit because they tell the truth about the African origins of Khemetian civilization, people, the linguistic and cultural connections.

"... In support of the 'Aten is the Sun' explanation, various depictions of Akhenaten are offered; they show him and his wife blessed by, or praying to a rayed star; it is the Sun most Egyptologists say. The hymns do refer to the Aten as a manifestation of RE (Ra), which to Egyptologists who have deemed Ra to be the Sun means that Aten, too, represented the Sun; but if Ra was Marduk and the celestial Marduk was Nibiru, then Aten, too, represented Nibiru and no the Sun ...." – End of Days, Pg 159 (In Part).

Kingship was lowered in Old Man Kush. When I say 'Old Man Kush', I am referring to the Kush in terms of the country of most Ancient times, as opposed to Kush the Son of Ham, Son of Noah (or rather Utnapishtim). The son of Ham was named after the country and not the other way around. The Ancient country of Kush (Upper and Lower Nubia), Ethiopia proper was not named after the son of Ham, it already existed long before him. Thus, even the Ptah Daneg (Ptahites) also known as the ANU people, who are today referred to as Pygmies – the little people (dwarves) are Kushites from Old Man Kush.

The Ancient timeline of Old Man Kush goes so far back into the Zep Tepi – 'The First, Beginning Times' of the planet it would be hard to convince most readers with words alone. The Hominid skeletal remains called Dakenesh – 'Little Lady', in the local Ethiopic language and 'Lucy' by English speaking scholars is claimed to be 3.5 million years old. She was not an ape or a missing link to humans, she was a Ptahites (Homo-Erectus) and so was the skeleton found in Kenya referred to as Kenyapithecus which is claimed to be 17.5 million years old due to C^{14} (carbon) dating. This proves what I stated in my book '2mrw Iz 2day Iz Yesterday (Vol II)', that African hominids have been upon the planet 17 million, two hundred and fifty thousand years plus. Our blood, the DNA within you Kushites body, has been on earth for a very long time. For we originate from a land before time and the Khemetians recorded this timeline as far back as they possibly could and they were proud protectors of these Ancient records of their ancestors from Mount Meru in Uganda and/or Tanzania.

Paut Neteru/Anunnaqi

The cradle of life, and of man is inside of the Great Rift Valley in Africa, Uganda. Experts claim that the earliest homo sapien sapiens appeared in Mother Africa approximately 200,000 years ago in this region. We know from Sumerian Tablets of Creation and the Lost Book of Enki, that Kadmon and Nekaybaw (The Sumerian Adam & Eve) took 49,000 years to breed and genetically hybrid from the Ptahites, and Atumite Watusi tribe also called Cuthites (as opposed to Kushites). The Cuthite, Watusi tribe called Atumites are those that mixed blood with the Black Hindu, Singh who came from Nirvana in the Sirius constellation when their dying star collapsed. Their rulers were Queen Lillith and King Atum (named after the Neter: Atum-Re). They are the parents of Kadmon 'Eastener', who was also called Zakar – 'Forgetful' and this Kadmon is the biblical Adam, a Cuthite, and Watusi. Bred from the Ptah Daneg, Pygmies was Nekaybaw – 'Tribal Leader' also called Hawwah – 'Mother (Eve) of the Living'. They were not the first hominid – humans on earth but rather, they were the first hybrids (able to procreate by themselves in the image of the Anunnaqi). This breeding and genetic manipulation, over 49,000 years, took 7 stages of trial and error and these Kadmonites better known as 'Adamites', Adamah in Sumerian 'Earthlings', were produced in groups rather than as single individuals. Cro Magnon, Homo Habilis and Australopithecus were early forms of Homo sapiens – 'Thinking Man' (Modern Hominids). The infamous Neanderthal (a region in Germany), evoluted along completely different lines, the caveman, trapped within the cold climate of the Eurasian continents. Experts recently admitted that this caveman did not die out as suggested but mixed in with other Hominids, got absorbed and most Europeans today have Neanderthal ancestry. We, Kushites, were never 'cavemen', barbarians. We were genetically engineered, by the Gods (Neteru, Anunnaqi), in the image of the Gods by way of cloning techniques in which the DNA of the Anunnaqi was mixed with the DNA of the early Homo-Erectus. This wasn't done through copulation but was carried out in the laboratory in the form of the second Adamah Project known as the 'Lulu Amelu Project' - Lulu – 'Primitive', Amelu – 'Workers'. Indeed we were created as Abd – 'Servants' of the Anunnaqi Gods. The first Adamah Project was carried out in Tamare – 'Land of the Sun', Nubia – Africa by the Neteru Anunnaqi, wherefore the Genus-Homo was grown from out of the waters to become an upright being, the Home-Erectus, a bipedal – upright being walking on two limbs (feet) rather than four. Hawwah (Nekaybaw), Eve's seed was from Havilah in Khemet meaning 'Of the Circle', a region in Kush, Kadmion, Zakai – Adams seed, the Cuthites were from the Tigris – Euphrates area, East of E.Din, where Gan – 'The Enclosed Garden' was located. Adam and Eve is a Sumerian story.

Now when you re-read Barashiyth – 'The Reconstruction' (Replenishing) which is the Aramic name for the book of Genesis, it should make a lot more sense. In order for something to be reconstructed, something would first have to be there in the first place. Henceforth Kush is mentioned before the New-Beings are taken and placed in the enclosed garden which was located in the Sumerian E.Din – 'Land of the Rocketships', to be celebrated by and serve the Anunnaqi. These hybrid people are Nubian, Havilahite – Kushites. Genesis does not begin at the beginning of the story of early hominids such as Home-Erectus (Ptahites) but much later, late in the story of the Home Sapiens, Adamah who were Kushite – Nubians.

Genesis 2: 10-15

10. There was a river flowing from Eden to water the garden and when it 11. left the garden it branched into four streams. The name of the first is Pishon; that is the river that encircles all the land of Havilah, where 12. the gold Is. The gold of that land is good; bdellium and cornelians are also 13. To be found there. The name of the second river is Gihon; this is the one 14. Which encircles all the land of Cush. The name of the third is Tigris this is the river which runs east of Asshur. The fourth river is Euphrates. 15. The Lord God took the man and put him in the garden of Eden to till it and 16. Care for it.

– The New English Bible: with Apocrypha.

Another interesting pint to note is that Nekaybaw 'Tribal Leader' was so called because she was the leader of the family and not Kadmon 'Easterner'. This matriarchal aspect is picked up by the bible in Genesis, Chapter 3, where the Anunnaqi, in punishing Nekaybaw, Kadmon and Nakash – 'Serpent Being' (The Reptilian), says that he will put enmity between Nekaybaw's seed (Kushites) and Naskash's seed (for the Satan also has a seed). Kadmon's seed is not stated because the leader of the seed of the Anunnaqi is Nekaybaw and not Kadmon.

Genesis 3:15

15. I will put enmity between you and the woman, between your brood and hers. They shall strike at your head and you shall strike at their heels.

Being bred from the Agreeable Ptah Daneg (Kushites) and the more Disagreeable Watusi (Cuthites), in disobeying the one single command of the Anunnaqi of the enclosed garden, they discovered the capacity to do Disagreeableness in the eyes of the Anunnaqi. The Tree of Knowledge of Good and Bad was metaphor for a certain type of knowledge, with different branches, for different purposes. This knowledge included the Sapphire Scrolls and the Emerald Tablet. The Sapphire Scrolls contained knowledge of seduction, lust and carnal sex, which being only 18 and 21 years old (spiritually immature), they were unprepared to control. When they indulged in these sexual acts and perversions, it ruined everything. For them, it was the death of immortality and the birth of mortality. This was the beginning of their carnal imprisonment and the sins of the flesh. Overtime we would lose our metaphysical – light being selves and from Kadmonites (Adamites) we became Enoshites – 'Maimed Moral Beings', who were now cut-off from being 'face to face(s)' with the Anunnaqi. The gland responsible for our higher perception (4 higher senses) was removed and Enosh, son of Seth, son of Kadmon, was the first human born without his Barathary Gland and higher senses. Divinity now had to be earned. God – consciousness had to be acquired by tests.

From Adamah to Enoshites:

It was then that man lost his divinity and higher perception of God – consciousness and began to worship God outside and separate from himself. Man largely lost the link to divinity within and began to call upon the name of a God (Yahweh), in order to be found worthy of God – consciousness.

Genesis 4:26

26. Seth too had a son, whom he named Enosh. At that time men began to invoke the Lord by name.

- The New English Bible with Apocrypha

Or in more common translations, 'It was then that man began to call upon the name of the Lord'. In Sumerian, this Lord was Tammuz according to Ancient Sumerian Tablets. Tammuz was the son of Dammuzi and Ishtar. They are the Sumerian equivalents of the Khemetian Triad of Horus, Osiris and Isis. But the Jewish liars may like to disagree and claim that the God called upon was YHWH or Yahweh mistranslated as Jehovah and sometimes Adonai – 'Lord'. Anyway, the identity of which God it was is not relevant to our point. The point is, the region was in habited by the multinational and globally indigenous Kushites whether; Ptahites, Havilahites, Khemetians, Nabateans, ANU, Sabeans, Elamites, Sumerians, Assyrians, Chaldeans, Kadmonites, Enoshites, Cainites, Phoenicians, Cuthites, Harrapans – Dravidians, etc., etc.

They migrated into the world by coming from the Abzu, bringing the Kushite culture up the Fallopian Tube of the World known as the Nine (Nile) River and congregating in the Nile Valley of the Nubian region of Africa. For it was here that the first civilization of Kush was cradled. This culture goes back to 100,000 B.C. Indeed Khemetian mathematics were found in the Congo dated back to 23,000 B.C., as proven by the Ishango Bones. The pyramids prove themselves to date back to 10,500 B.C., which is when their apexes aligned with Orion's Belt and the Sphinx is even older.

The Entomological meaning of Genesis is 'Genes of Isis' and the true meaning of Barashiyth is the 'Replenishing by way of Shiyth (Seth)'. Seth was born unto Kadmon (Adam) and Hawwah (Eve) after the tragedy of the Cain and Abel incident. Cain lived in the land of Nod – 'Wandering' spawning his own seed of Black Devils, through whom the recessive-genes of the Black Hindus (Anakites) were inherited. The wife of Utnapishtim (Ziusudra) called Naama, the biblical Noakh (Noah) was of this cursed seed. Through her these genes passed through Ham 'Black' into his fourth son called Canaan. This Canaan was the first Leper, the first human albino born upon this planet. He was born in 4004 B.C. and it's funny how this is the date that scholars used to claim was the birth date of the human race, making humans only 6000 years old, according to them scholars.

This Canaan – 'Lowlander' was born with the name Libana – 'Milky White'. He fathered 11 sons in the Caucasus Mountains from which we get the word Caucasian. These white or pale Canaanites weren't the only albino cavemen on the planet though. Two thousand, eight hundred years earlier the recessive gene was planted upon the earth by way of the beings from the Pleiades constellation. Through the efforts of Mad Scientist, Yaaqub, who was half Dunaakiyl and half Tero, bodes were grafted using this albino gene in which these Pleiadian Spirit Children could incarnate as flesh and blood beings on earth. This resulted in mankind – 'a kind of man', known by the names Flugelrod, Huluub and/or Halaabean. Originating from the cold climates of Europe, the Caucasus – the Steppes in Russia, they called Libana – 'Milky White', the nickname 'lowlander' because of the fact he came from flat lands. These Huluub are your original caveman. They lived inside caves in and around Mount Elbrus in the Caucasus Mountains. Like the albino Canaan, they were sensitive to direct and indirect sunlight.

When Canaan fled with his Nubian sister, Salha to these mountains, he found the Huluub occupying the caves and was accepted to live amongst them. The real Conan the Barbarian was one of their members. It's not just a movie made in Hollywood. Though this may all sound crazy, much of what Hollywood call fantasy and science-fiction is actually 'Science-Fact'. It's all a part of their plan to discredit people who know that facts and tell the truth. To speak this truth in today's false-reality takes bravery.

Make note that Canaan had Nubian features. His only difference was he was an albino, melanin-deficient. He still had woolly-hair (Afro) and African facial features as a Hamite. His sister, Salha, was normal, without the genetic mutation. Canaan took wives from amongst the Flugelrods and had 11 sons. One of these sons appropriately called Hamath was also without the deficiency and he (Hamathites) eventually mixed in with the Phoeniadians (Kadmonites). These 11 tribes of Canaan would eventually come down from the mountains when their condition stabilized. They became nomads throughout Eurasia as barbarians, uncivilized. These are your Neanderthals, the Halaabean part of them were grafted into being by Yaaqub who was telepathically controlled, mind-controlled by the Pleiadians.

The grafted race were blond haired and blue eyed and were known as the Ashkenazim and Khazars after mixing with the Canaanites. These grafting experiments also took place in other places, at others times in an effort to breed this disagreeable, albino gene out of the contaminated Kushites. One such experiment took place in Ireland and the British Isles and produced the Firbold Men. On the other side of the Atlantic, in Central America it resulted in the Aztecs, which means 'Whiteness'. These people are your grafted Devil's seed and they are currently in control of the planet. They control Hollywood, the Music Industry, the Motor Industry, the Computer Industry and everything else. Adolf Hitler carried on the work of Yaaqub in these modern times, requested to breed a superior race of blonde haired, blue eyed so called Aryan (Noble) people under the Nazi regime of the Third Reich. The Pleiadians gave him the technological know-how and the means to achieve their alien agenda. He was contacted by Madame Helen Blavatsky.

This modern witch and her associates founded the new popular 'Theosophical Society'. The reversed Swastika was a symbol first used by Yaaqub. Yaaqub died before he could witness the success of his experiments in which he sailed around the coast of Africa, kidnapping people. He began by grafting the brown man into the red man, the red man into the yellow man and the yellow man into the pale man (Caucasian), 'Caucus – Asian' which implies 'Deteriorating Asiatic'. Their very nature was barbaric and toxic. They were bred to be void of love for others. This is why around the coast of Africa you'll find paler people who often don't look black African (Negroid) but more favour Asiatic (Mongoloids) than Africans. This is not about racism because there are both Black and White devils and the worst of the devils is the Black Devils. 'Nobody wins the – Race in Racism'. I am simply stating the facts unbiasedly.

Conflicts of the Gods

Now what is of the utmost importance to overstand is that the Anunnaqi themselves have both Agreeable and Disagreeable among them. All of the emotions that humans have, they inherited from the Anunnaqi/Neteru Gods themselves: Love, Jealousy, Greed, Hate, Covetousness, Patience, Frustrations, Grievances, Happiness and Laughter, Anger, etc.

Wars were fought in the high heavens between themselves and between them and the sons of the shadows such as the Reptilians and Pleiadian Beings. These wars were fought in the high galaxy of Illyuwn, the Orion Skies, Sirius and other star systems and these conflicts followed them into this galaxy, our galaxy, the Milky Way. Two major wars were fought in the heavens which are recorded upon Ancient tablets in Khemet, Sumer and other nations around the world, such as India (The Upanishads and Bhagavad Gita) and the wars are even recorded in the Bible's book of Revelation.

When man was created by the Gods, they were used in these wars and rivalries when the Anunnaqi and other beings brought their wars from the high heavens unto the planet earth. Many times a God would be at the head of his or her army of men marching against another army and God to do battle. This was a regular occurrence in the Ancient world. There are many tables and texts in which kings have stated that they were commanded by this or that God to go to war here or there, as in the case of the Goddess Ishtar or Horus and Seth during their war. King Sargon of Akkad claimed he was chosen by Ishtar to rule in her favour along with countless others. Different Gods governed different nation states within the Kingdom of Ancient Sumer, just as is the case with Khemet and many times territory went to war against territory, like Assyria and her Gods versus Babylon and her Gods, or Horus and the North versus Sutukh (Set) and the South. Often times this resulted in volatile situations jeopardizing the prosperity of the planet Earth and it's new inhabitants both Gods and humans alike. No more so than the rivalry between the God, Enki – 'Lord Earth' and Enlil – 'Lord Sky' in Ancient Sumer both sons of ANU, ALYNN AL – 'The Most High'. This rivalry threatened to destroy the entire planet and the Gods had to take council and intervene which resulted in the catastrophe of 2024 B.C.E. in the Sinai Peninsula involving nuclear weapons. The story of this is related to the watered-down story of Sodom and Gomorrah in the Old Testament in which it is claimed 'God' rained 'Fire and Brimstone' on the site from heaven.

2024 B.C.E. was the end and destruction of the glorious Sumerian civilization by way of the radioactive 'Evil Wind' that followed the dropping of the nuclear weapons upon the spaceport of Dilmun in the Sinai region. When the radioactive cloud was pushed eastward by the wind, the genocide caused the Gods to have to flee and men, women and children died leaving the cities abandoned. The lamentation texts of Ur bare witness to this reality and its consequences. The action had to be taken to end the rivalry between Enlilite and Enkite Anunnaqi.

Genesis 9:25

25. 'Cursed by Canaan, slave of slaves shall he be to his brothers .....'

The curse of the Anunnaqi did not fall on Ham and all Hamites at all but fell onto his 4th son Canaan. The curse being the Ancient deficiency called Leprosy and Albinism, the curse of Ham with racists saying that the curse was the blackness and African traits which was a clever diversion by the Jewish scholars and the church fathers. Being born with the Ancient pigment called Melatonin or Melanin is not at all a deficiency but being born with such low levels as Europeans are, definitely is according to their own myth-made book. Melanin is a divine gift given to Nubians by our parents, the Anunnaqi-Neteru. It allows us to exist in various different natural and tropical climates with a sun-screen factor of something like 500. The Caucasian is the only being without any natural sun factor screening and cannot comfortably exist in natural tropical climates without the dreaded consequence of skin cancer developing. The worst form being Melanoma. Seven out of 10 Caucasians will develop skin cancer at some stage of their life. For the sons of Canaan read Genesis 10: 15-20.

Job 9:9

9. Who made Aldebaran and Orion, the Pleiades and the circle of the Southern Stars;

Psalms 82:1

1. God takes his stand in the court of heaven to deliver judgement among the Gods themselves.

Also read 2 Kings 5: 1-27 for another example of the Ancient curse.

Psalms 82:6 (also see John 10:34)

6. This is my sentence: 'Ye are Gods, all of you sons of the Most High ....'

Song of Solomon 1:5-6

5. I am dark but comely, daughters of Jerusalem, like the tents of Kedar or the tent curtains of Shalmah.

6. Do not look down on me; a little dark I may be because I am scorched by the sun.

Revelation 12:7-10

7. 'Then war broke out in heaven. Michael and his angels waged war upon 8. The Dragon. The Dragon and his angels fought, but they had not the 9. Strength to win, and no foothold was left them in heaven. So the great dragon was thrown down, that serpent of old that led the whole world astray, whose name is Satan, or the Devil – thrown down to the earth and his angels with him...'

- The New English Bible – with Apocrypha

These fallen angels or Anunnaqi are the 'Evil Ones' referred to as Nephileem – 'Those Who Fell Down', not to be confused with the Anunnaqi – 'Those Who ANU Sent From Heaven to Qi (Earth)'. These two groups are opposed to each other. The Nephileem abducted and raped earth women and so it was sanctioned for the benevolent, good Anunnaqi to also father children by human women in order to subdue the shady off-spring of the Nephileem. These off-spring were/are known as Giboreem – 'Mighty Ones', as were certain pharaohs and rulers such as Nimrod – Sargon of Akkad, Gilgamesh, etc. They were men of Renown and hunters, not of animals, but of Demons, Meshkem – children of the Nephileem who were adverse to civilization. Men like Nimrod and the Pharaohs hunted these Meshkem. They were mighty hunters with God-Consciousness – 'face to face' with the Anunnaqi. These were the real classical heroes – Demi Gods. (Genesis 6:1-7).

So therefore, it is virtually impossible to separate the story and Legacy of Kushite people from that of the Neteru/Anunnaqi – Gods and that of the birth of civilisation itself. Scholars have always and continue to treat the story of these Ancient astronauts as myths, fables made up by the civilizations of the Ancient world at the same time as teaching that these Ancient civilizations, especially those separated by oceans, had no contact with one and the other. This is to say that certain civilizations had no knowledge of other civilizations and therefore no trade network. Because they teach that Ancient man wasn't seafaring, they refused to admit that there was any contact made between people of the Old World (Eastern) and New World (Western) civilisations, which flies in the face of all evidence.

The so called 'New World' (the Americas) was only considered new to the Europeans who after the Greek and Roman periods, regressed and forgot that the shape of the world was spherical. All throughout the Middle Ages, the pretender called 'The Pop' taught Europeans that the world was flat and that in sailing to the ends of the seas, one would drop off the face of the planet. This was the belief that the Vatican preached all the way up to the time of Christopher Columbus and his discovery of the West Indies (Caribbean) after 1493 A.D.

Most, if not all of the peoples who inhabited the West Indies and the Americas already knew that the earth was not flat but spherical. These nations were descended from Kushite (Negroid) and Asian (Mongoloid) mixes and retained the knowledge of their Ancient Gods of the sky and ancestors who came via the sea from the East. It is remembered in their records and oral traditions, committed to memory. Thus, the Kushite nations all knew of the Americas and had contact and trade with them way before Europeans crept out of their caves to set sail on the seas in the name of King Ferdinand and Queen Isabella of the newly formed Spain and King Henry, the Navigator of Portugal. The Kushites and most certainly those who occupied these newly discovered lands of the West never considered their lands to be new but had lived there for thousands of years. Don't be fooled by historians of 'His story'.

Since the dawn of civilization, which was given by the Gods, they taught the homo-sapiens sapiens (man) by way of astronomer-priests to observe the heavens for guidance upon earth. From the pyramids of Kush, to the Ziggurats of Sumer, Akkad and Babylon, the Step Pyramids of the Yucatán and the Andes, the Valley of the Indus River and its cities – even to the stone circles of Stonehenge. The magnificent, colossal structures were precisely aligned with special apertures and features that allowed Ancient man to track the complex motions of the heavenly bodies – planets and stars. These very sophisticated plans and alignments were handed down by the Gods themselves and their orientations allowed the light of the sun and other stars to enter as a beam with laser like accuracy into the required section of the structure such as the holy of holies in say, the Temple of Karnak in the city of Thebes (Waset) or the Temple of Abu Simbel (Nubia), Aswan – at the time of an Equinox or Solstice.

That these structures were divinely inspired and planned can be confirmed by inscriptions o left by the Sumerian King Gudea (2200 B.C.) and the statue found of him containing the observable plans. In these inscriptions the King says that he saw a 'shining One' descend to the earth in his bird (aircraft) along with another who was a female. They turned out to be the God – Ningursu and Ishtar (Inanna) who were accompanied by another unidentified Anunnaqi. The Goddess Ishtar left the King with a sacred table ton which the plan for a sacred temple was drawn. The statue of King Gudea can be seen depicting him sitting with this tablet and its detailed drawing upon his lap.

Whenever scholars chance upon one of these glorious superstructures, they attribute its astronomical aspects to the needs of an agricultural society which is bogus and makes no sense to the critical thinkers of our time and age. It is a known fact that farmers do not need precise astronomical data to know when to sow and when to reap harvest, or herd sheep.

There are much easier terrestrial means, almanacs, or reading the weather (seasons) to know when, without tracking the stars with all the painstaking time and effort that this entails. Man was taught to track the movements of the heavens for spiritually religious reasons, in order to venerate the Gods themselves in the ways that they taught man and thus wished to be acknowledged and praised. The conspiracy of orthodox scholars is to divert us away from the realization of this, of this and its obvious implications, as to the reality of Paut Neteru, the Anunnaqi – Gods and the god given genius of the multi-national Kushite civilizations in the four corners of the planet earth. What these orthodox institutions and their song sheet scholars teach is deliberate disinformation and absolute hogwash. The glory of the Gods and their Ancient civilizations is indeed self-evidence, research them for yourselves.

"... The Anunnaqi, the Sumerians wrote upon numerous clay tablets, had come to earth long before the deluge. In the 12th Planet we determined that it happened 432,000 years before the deluge – a period equivalent to 120 orbits of Nibiru, orbits that though to the Anunnaqi, represent but a single year of theirs are equivalent to 3,600 earth years. They came and went between Nibiru and earth each time their planet came closer to the sun (and earth) as it passed between Jupiter and Mars; and there is no doubt whatsoever that the Sumerians began to observe the heavens not to know when to sow, but in order to see and celebrate the return of the Celestial Lord ....".

- The Lost Realms, Zecharia Sitchin, Pg 157 (In Part)

This great event was commemorated and re-enacted by the Kushite population of Mesopotamia at the beginning of the New Year with ceremonies, rituals and festivals. Other great events were also celebrated and re-enacted throughout Kushite cultures in regards to the Gods of Ancient Kush and Sumer. Evidence of the divine, astronomical knowledge given to man by the Gods was not limited to the building of temples. It was given concerning law, agriculture, science, spirituality and religion, marriage and many other aspects governing civilization.

"... All this (and more) was possessed by the Sumerian civilization that blossomed at circa 3,800 B.C. and by the Egyptian civilization that followed circa 3100 B.C. Another off-shoot of the Sumerian civilization, that of the Indus Valley, came about 2900 B.C.

Why was it not possible for such trifold developments to occur a fourth time, in the Andres? Impossible – if there had been no contacts between the Old and New Worlds. Possible, if the same grantors of all knowledge, the Gods, were the same and were present all over the earth. As incredible as our conclusion must sound, happily it can be proven ..."

- The Lost Realms, Zacharia Sitchin, Pg. 138 (In Part)

Even though I may disagree with the late Zecharia Sitchin on which civilization is the oldest and was the first to blossom, the evidence is irrefutable and undisputed, the facts are self-evident. The Nubian, Sudanese Pharaohs of the Kushites predated the Khemetian, so called Egyptian Pharaonic state restarted by Pharaoh Menes/Narmer. The evidence for this was destroyed when the Egyptian authorities of today (Turks, Syrians) decided to flood the region in order to build the Aswan Dam. The temple of Abu Simbel was re-located in order to preserve it, after being taken apart and re-erected in another location, along with the temple of Nefertari. All of the other invaluable evidence that could have shed light on the Kushite origins of Ancient Khemet and Sumer was buried underneath millions of tons of water. These Ethiopic Nubian Pharaohs go back to 4125 B.C. at least.

'... Indeed, all of the Old World civilizations had recollections of past ages, of ears when the Gods reigned alone, followed by demi-Gods and heroes and then just mortals. Sumerian texts called King Lists recorded a line of divine Lords followed by demi-Gods who reigned a total of 432,000 years before the deluge, then listed the Kings that reigned thereafter, through times that are by now historical and whose dates have been verified and found accurate. The Egyptian King Lists, as composed by the Priest Historian Manetho, listed a dynasty of twelve Gods that began some 10,000 years before the deluge; it was followed by Gods and demi-Gods until circa 3,100 B.C., the Pharaohs ascended the throne of Egypt. Again where this data could be verified against historical records, it was found to be accurate....'

- The Lost Realms, Zecharia Sitchin, Pg. 138 (In Part)

After the deluge which has been geologically proven to have happened 13,000 – 12,000 years ago, as a result of the ending of the last glacial period (Ice Age), the Gods imported (Kushite) Khemetian and Sumerian culture across the Atlantic and Pacific Oceans into America through Tehuti and the Olmecs. This Tehuti is none other than the son of the Anunnaqi, Enki (Ea, Nudimmud) God of Knowledge, Communication and Time, who gave man the gifts of civilization in the first place.

It is now taken by brave independent researchers that this took place in 3000 B.C., but it is my conviction that this happened long before the 3rd Millennium B.C., when the Sun reversed its magnetic fields and in the process flipped the planet Venus upside down making it rotate in the opposite direction to all the other planets of our solar system.

The Olmecs, named after the region their relics were found in, a region of plentiful rubber plants were Kushite, negroids as is evidenced by their colossal sculptured heads of rock, weighting up to 25 tons. As much as 18 of them were found at various sites throughout this Yucatán Peninsula of Mesoamerica in Mexico. The Olmecs, 'Rubber People' were miners who were mining gold for the Anunnaqi/Neteru and their sites were mineral refineries, where gold and other resources were mined out of the mountains and caves with technically advanced tools that the American Indians never possessed. The American Indians confirm the Olmecs being their teachers and progenitors through records and oral traditions. Those such as the Nahuatl speaking tribes (Maya, Aztecs, Toltecs and others) and even the people of the Andean regions of South America attest to the authenticity of the Gods and Kushites being the true Native Americans, as opposed to American Indians. Quetzalcoatl – 'The Plumed/Feather Serpent' was none other than Enki along with Itzamna (Tehuti), Viracocha (Menes) and others. The Olmecs are undisputedly the mother culture of Mesoamerica who all others including the Phoenician – 'Bearded Ones' borrowed from. The East Indians mixed in with them to produce Mayans, Aztecs and others. These Olmecs travelled West through Mesopotamia into China to become the first two Chinese dynasties of Xiu and Sheng and were even recorded in the glories of Memnon of the battle of Troy, 14th Century B.C. - The Xi (Shi) people.

"... Of all the lost civilizations of Mesoamerica, that of the Olmecs is the oldest and most mystifying. It was by all counts the mother civilization copied and adopted by all others. It dawned along the Mexican Gulf Coast at the beginning of the second millennium B.C. (or, some hold by 1500 B.C.). Spreading in all directions, but mainly southward, it made its mark across Mesoamerica by 800 B.C.

The first Mesoamerican glyphic writing appears in the Olmec realm; so does the Mesoamerican system of numeration of dots and bars. The first long count calendar inscriptions, with the enigmatic starting date of 3113 B.C.; the first works of magnificent and monumental sculpted art; the first use of Jade, the first depictions of hand held weapons or tools; the first ceremonial centres; the first celestial orientation – all were achievements of the Olmecs. No wonder with so many 'firsts', some (as J. Soustelle, The Olmecs) have compared the Olmec civilization of Mesoamerica to that of the Sumerians in Mesopotamia, which accounted for all the 'firsts' in the Ancient near East. And like the Sumerian civilization, the Olmecs too appeared suddenly, without a precedent or a prior period of gradual advancement ...."

- The Lost Realms, Zecharia Sitchin, Pg. 96-97

".... that these were individuals, all of the same African Negroid stock but with their own personalities and divine headgear, can be readily seen from a portrait gallery of some of these heads ..."

- The Lost Realms, Pg. 100

".... We always see the same black African faces, as on jades from the sacred cenote of Chichen Itza or in golden effigies found there; on numerous terra-cottas ...."

- The Lost Realms, Pg. 101

Kushite cultures are the legacy of the true and living Gods and until the so called scholars accept the facts, the enigma of the sudden cultures of Khemet and Sumer will never be solved but all is about to change.

Contrary to what scholars and others, even such as Zecharia Sitchin teach, we Kushites predate and are the parents of all religions, sciences and spirituality on the planet. Going back at least 40,000 years but more like 100,000 years – since the primeval collision of Nibiru caused its seed of intelligent life to be planted upon the planet then called Tamtu/Tiamat. We birth the people of Atlantis and those of Mu. Our Ancient Kushite ancestors were the first to record religious doctrine, the first to use magic, which became the root of religious miracles. In fact, we were the first to write and record, and the first to pray, of which system we call Ashutat. We were the first to set up ritual ceremonies, initiations, temples, chapels, lodges that later became Churches, Synagogues and Mosques. We, Kushites were the first to respect nature as a whole creating a symbolism for the recognition of each living thing. We have been duplicated, perpetrated, imitated but never replicated. Many have borrowed from us and set up great institutions pretending to the world that they don't know or remember that the sources and font of all knowledge is Tamare (Kush).

Abrahamic – Monotheism, Hindus, Buddhist and all others, are committing a fraud and are guilty of misrepresentation for the simple fact that they refused to give due recognition to the source of their teachings; Egypt (Kush). Not the Egypt you see today in North East Africa and certainly not the perpetrators who reside there today, but Pre-Dynastic Khemet, which birthed the 46 Dynasties, of which Egyptology only recognizes 31. Present day religious establishments have stolen prayers, rituals and practices from our people, rituals and ceremonies stolen from ancient Egypt. Their languages have even borrowed words form ancient Kushite languages, such as Egyptian and Sumerian.

New discoveries are confirming the grandeur and majesty of the ancient Kushite Kingdoms every day and the pictures on the walls do not lie. Who the ancient Egyptians and Sumerians are and what race these ancients belonged to island apparent, though the pretenders have occupied Egypt and have begun to repaint the faces and fabricate false evidence to deceive the descendants, us and the people of the wider world.

Of the 3 original (Hominid) races, the Negroid - the first race, the Mongoloid, the second race and the Caucasoid – the cursed diseased race, archaeologists have proven beyond a shadow of a doubt that the oldest inhabitants of this planet are the Negroids. And what renders one a pure Negroid (Negro) is the hair which is nappy or woolly, not the colour of the skin. Their royal crown is the sign of the first race, The God Race, the one race, the only race of humans on earth with nappy hair. We are the mothers and fathers of all others.

The world 'Negroid' is from the Latin word 'Negro' from Negrito meaning 'black'. The same as the world Moor from Maurenos, simply describing the Nuwbuns who after being mixed with invaders, became the Nubians, the mixed seed as you see today with many different shades of skin colours and hair textures. Still, all are from the original black seed of Sudan.

As you can see, names were grafted and changed and even later, the descendants of the Nuwbuns (Ptahites, ANU) inherited new titles such as, negro, nigger, Black British, African American, African, Caribbean, Jamaican, Nigerian, Ghanaian and many other national titles; when it all comes down to the Nuwbuns, the original Egyptians, Negroid are the mothers and fathers of civilization; the root seed of incarnated divinity. Simply, the Gods that all others worship yet refuse to respect today.

Our mystery language of tones, vibrates with the body so that you may find your place in The Grand Plan. Prayer is an exercise just for that purpose and language is the key to prayer. You speak first in the prayer system of Ashutat 'Meditative Peaceship', then you learn the true art of listening.

The earliest known writing, discovered in 1988 A.D., by archaeologists was found in Egypt (Khemet), not Sumer in Iraq, as previously mistaken. Sumerian culture is Egyptian culture. In 1988 A.D., they found on this stelae, a relief of a tree and the symbols of the name of a Pharaoh who name reads as Agrub 'Scorpion', discussing taxes and other important governmental and national policies. So, it was our Ancient black ancestors who gave the world its first and one of its greatest achievements and civilizations, recording all of these great things, they did and saw. Not to mention all the sports, governmental laws, astronomy, solar biology, sciences, trade and the list goes on. So move on from false – contemporary false religion with pride. Know and be proud of the fact that every Kushite – black person is a true Egyptian – Kushite.

This means that we, the Tamareyaat (Egyptians) were writing long before the Sumerians. As mentioned before, we the Tamareans were the first to do all things and different cultures grafted their lifestyles from the Ancient Egyptians, such as the way we prayed. Even though our prayer may look like the Muslims' prayer or Salaat; the Muslims stole their prayer system from the Christians and the Christians stole their prayer system from the Jews' - Selah (Taful) and the Jews stole theirs from the Persians' - Gahs, and both the Persians and the Jews stole theirs from the Tamareyaat (Egyptians), Ashutat which is us, (Tama – re) meaning Ta – 'Earth', Ma – 'Water' and Re – 'Sun'.

All critical thinkers know that the Commandments of the Old Testament are the same negative confessions of Egypt from 'The Book of the Coming Forth by Day (into the Light)', mistakenly called 'The Book of the Dead' by European so called scholars, Egyptologists. This sacred book was recorded by the Waab – Egyptian Priest, Ani.

It is no coincidence when proof says that in the Judaic religion, they too stole ideas from Egyptian culture. The Ten Commandments of Leviticus 20: 1-19 of the Bible was taken directly out of the Book of the Coming Forth by Day, from the 'Declaration of Innocence' before the Neteru of the Tribunal, such as 'Thou Shalt Not Kill' (Old Testament 20:13) is the exact same thought as 'I have not lain people'. Only, the Bible, they take the 'Declaration' and turn them into 'Commandments' from a so called all powerful God who has create laws.

Take a look at a comparison with some of the thoughts within the Book of the Coming Forth, which existed from long before the Old Testament of the myth made Bible.

Egyptian Declaration of Innocence	Monotheism Ten Commandments
1. O wide-strider who came forth from ANU (Heliopolis), I have not done wrong.	1. You will not prostrate yourself to them: for I, a Yahuwa Elohim am a jealous El, the one visiting the iniquity of the fathers upon the children of the third and fourth generation of them that hate me.
2. O fire-embracer who came from Khemennu (Hermopolis) – Ancient religious city of Middle Al Kham associated with Tehuti (Thoth) – I have not robbed.	2. You will not steal.
3. O swallower of shades who came forth from Kernet, I have not slain people.	3. You are not to fight to kill.
4. O terrible of face who came forth from Rasta (Rosetjau – name of the Necropolis of Giza or Memphis, also passages in the leading to the other world). I have not destroyed the food offering.	4. Remember the Sabbath day to keep it Holy.
5. O doubly evil one who came forth from Busiris, I have not had intercourse with a married woman.	5. You are not to commit abominations.

The Jews acquired their lifestyle from Egypt, when they came in along with their masters, the Hyksos as Hyksos, which is a Greek word meaning 'Rulers of Foreign Lands' and 'Sheppard Kings'. In the Ancient Egyptian language of Nuwaubic, it is said 'Heka-Khasut'. The Hyksos lived under the Canaanites in the land of Canaan, the cursed seed of the Torah, Old Testament in Genesis 9:25, Leviticus chapters 13-15. The seed was cursed with leprosy or albinism and they fathered the Hyksos. The Hyksos conquered a small area called Gebelein in the Delta (Northern Egypt) along the trade route to southern Palestine with Avaris at its centre and reigned there for a period of roughly 100 years.

Seqenenre-Taa, the ruling Pharaoh of that time initiated conflict with the Hyksos vassals but was killed in battle. His wife, Queen Ahhotep then took over the Kingdom and inspired the Kingdom, through her two sons to liberation. It was the son Pharaoh Kamose who commanded the first wave of attacks against these Hyksos invaders. Pharaoh Kamose, the elder son, made the greatest impression of the Kingdom. Records of his reign are recorded upon wooden tablets. The Pharaoh summoned his council and explained the situation to them. It was far from hopeful:

"I know what my courage is for. There is a Pharaoh at Avaris and there is another at Kush. I am sitting like a hyphen between an Arab and a Nubian. Those who dwell in the black land (Khemet) share their possessions with me. I cannot make him cross at Memphis the water of Egypt; now he is in possession of Khmunu (Hermopolis). There is no one left who is not overwhelmed by the taxes of the Asiatics. I am going to meet him to cleave his belly. It is in my heart to deliver Egypt and to strike the Arabs".

The councillors didn't believe that the Pharaoh should take action as they didn't think that there was a lack of anything. However, Pharaoh Kamose acclaimed himself as liberator of Egypt and so he went with his army with no resistance until it reached Middle Egypt. The Hyksos King now tried in vain to establish contact with the ruler of the Nubian Kingdom of Kerma in order to engage Thebes on two fronts', however, his messenger was captured. At this time the southern Nubian Kingdom took the instability in Egypt as an opportunity to show defiance against Egypt. Needless to say, the Hyksos were conquered and expelled, which is the true and factual story of the biblical Exodus for which there is no concrete evidence or confirmation other than the expulsion of the Hyksos.

Pharaoh Kamose commemorated the victory with two stelae. They are written in the same way and they may have been set up besides each other in the sacred 'Temple of Karnak'. The second stelae is still intact. Pharaoh Kamose saw himself as the master of Avaris, though the final expulsion was achieved by Queen Ahhotep and her younger son Pharaoh Ahmose. Pharaoh Kamose spent the last years of his life preparing his tomb, like his ancestors of the 17th Dynasty but unfortunately, he did not live to see the entirety of his accomplishments. Pharaoh Kamose's brother, Pharaoh Ahmose was the next in line to keep control of the Theban Kingdom where he continued to struggle. He and Queen Ahhotep conquered and pushed the Hyksos pretenders out of Egypt back into Canaan.

Pharaoh Ahmose led the second attack on the Hyksos, which was even more successful than his brother's. The city of Memphis was recaptured and the Theban fleet led by Ahmose, marched on to the city of Avaris which was the Hyksos capital. Finally, the city surrendered. Ahmose took over the capital which he then extended, fortified and re-decorated.

This was the end of the Hyksos and the 2nd Intermediate Period, which is reference to the 2nd time pretenders invaded to rule Egypt and cause confusion throughout the Kingdom with fake Monarchs and/or Nomarchs ruling in their local occupations and districts. The first of these periods happened after the 6th Dynasty and lasted onto the 11th Dynasty in which Pharaoh Montuhotep II came up from Thebes (Waset) to restore the rule (c.2040 B.C.). The 2nd period took place after the 12th Dynasties – 'Golden Age' and lasted up to the 17th Dynasty, up to Pharaoh Seqenenre-Taa and Queen Ahhotep and their sons Pharaoh Kamose and Pharaoh Ahmose. The original rulers were back in power and the foreign invaders had been defeated. The boundaries of Egypt had been redefined and the southern border was situated deep in what is now Sudan near Abu Hamid, while the northern border extended as far as the Euphrates to a country called Naharin. Egypt rose to a 'World Power'.

Between this period of circa 1400 – 1200 B.C., the Hyksos took with them Egyptian culture and spreading it throughout the Middle East; it along with Sumerian ideas, became the foundation of the three monotheistic religions: Moseism (Judaism), Christism (Christianity) and Muhammadism (Islam), that plague the world today.

Now as for the 46 dynasties, there is no coincidence that the 46 dynasties relate to the 46 chromosomes and is referring to the mixing of the races. Mixing our seed with the cursed seed of Canaan is why we are no longer pure, but are now Nubians. This mixing opened the gate and invasions of Europeans such as the Armenians, who became Gypsies, which is one of the reasons why the land was renamed Egypt. Egypt and Egyptian is not one of our words. It is not what we called ourselves Ayguptos – 'Burnt Faces', but a name our ancestors saw as the invaders, Europeans. Black people's faces don't burn. It's all a trick on words, a Spell of Ignorance (of Spiritual and Racial Blindness). The key is within language and how we 'spell' words. {Ayguptos originally came from the Ashuric (Arabic) word Al Qubt "The Axis", as in Kush/Khemet being 'The Axis', around which ALL other nations were inspired}.

Other invaders included the Turks, the French, the Greeks, the British along with other Europeans and Arabs from the 11 sons/tribes of the cursed seed of Canaan who were either allowed to settle in Egypt or ended up conquering it.

As these different tribes invaded Egypt, such as the Armenians, Ashurians (called Chaldeans) who crossed over from the Tigris – Euphrates, who were called Ibree, Habiru 'Hebrews' or 'Jews' in the Bible, they plagiarized documents from the Sumerians and Phoenicians with names and stories lightly altered to give a nomadic wondering cursed seed race, an identity even to the point of referring to themselves as 'God's chosen'. Also, the God of the Babylonians was Baal, who was none other than Menes (Narmer), Enoch, Adafa, and Idris – the 1st Dynasty's 1st Pharaoh, whom they worshipped. On the other side of the Atlantic, among the people of the Andes civilization of Tiahuanaco (Tianaku) he was immortalized as Viracocha. The Babylonians called him Baal Hadad, Adad – 'He of the far away mountains', the Sumerians called him Ishkur, while the Hittites called him Teshub – 'God of Storms, Thunder' – his symbol being the lightning bolt. So the myth made Bible referred to these invading tribes as the Chaldeans, Misrayimites, Kishites, Syrians, Phoenicians and eventually the Greeks (Idonians) and the Roman creating your Hyksos, the 46 dynasties, for 46 chromosomes referring to the mixed races. Dynastic Egypt is not Egypt at its peak, but Egypt going through its death and mixing down into mixed seeds contrary to what you may have believed. By then (Menes), it was already thousands of years old and trying to prolong its glory against invaders and usurpers. Because we are not racists by nature, we allowed many to live among us as equal citizens while keeping and defending our purity and identity in general. We remained and still remain negroids from beginning to end.

Different names were given to our original Tama-reyaat (Egyptian) ancestors to suit their cultures like Khemet, Khamites from Kham aka Ham of their Bible in Genesis 6:10, the Father of Canaan. Ham was the son of Noah, Genesis 6:9. But Noah again, was really Utnafishtim of the Gilgamesh Epics. Again, another history or stolen story that was taught to you as a fairytale. Many things were picked up from the original Tama-reyaat (Egyptians) and incorporated into their different cultures, festivities and religions in Judaism, Christianity and Islam. But it all came from Egypt, even the secret societies such as Freemasons, Shriners, Magi, Rosicrucians, Knights of Columbus, Astara and others. They all got their teachings and ideas from Kushites. All of the Masonic rituals, stances and symbols come from the Ancient Egyptians but the Euro-Masons perverted the sacred principles and turned it into Satanism by way of their Black Devil brothers (Cainites). Everything leads back to Egypt through Sumer and there is no denying it. We predate the birth of Moses, Jesus, Muhammad and even Abraham and Adam.

"You may say I'm a dreamer, but I'm not the only one. I hope someday you'll join us. And the world will live as one".

- John Lennon

"As I Walk In the Dark Hand In Hand

Beside This Masonic Enlightened Man

As He Guides Me On My Way

I earn What It Is I Must Say

As I Am Given My Tools

I Understand That A Wise Man

Avoid The Fools

As I Perform My Masonic Rights

I Know What Was Meant By "Let There Be Light"

By: Dr Malachi Z. York-El 33/720

– 2000 A.D

Chapter 2: Identity Crisis

".... If you should die doing the work of the Most High, ANU/RE, (God's) may your Ka inspire another heart. The only effective weapon in the face of misfortune is unity. The only payment in life is the service we do unto others. Look for the opportunities. The Most High always puts them in front of us. The older we get, the further away we get from who we thought we were ...."

- Ali Shahiyd Ashshuaara

" .... Everybody fears time, but time fears the pyramids"

- Unknown

Without having to go into the endless evidence which is direct proof concerning how contemporary religions have all took their ideas and mythologies from Egyptian and Sumerian realities, let us move on. Since the point of this book is to successfully show that the need for the ancient wisdom of Egypt and the spirituality of the Pharaohs, is the only way of thinking that can relieve the apocalyptic ailments of our first Mother (Earth) today.

I feel that there is enough writings and media work that has already exposed the Egyptian origin of religion, largely focusing on different proverbs, quotes, ideas and actions. But I don't think enough has been written about what the real spiritual teachings of Maatian Principles, meant for Kushites and what this spirituality did for the vibrations of this planet and even universe(s). The ages of prosperity that these spiritual teachings brought to the ancients. Something we are so far away from now in today's world of materialism, corporate greed, deception and sexual perversions. I feel I have written enough about the religious aspects in '2mrw Iz 2day Iz Yesterday (Vol I)', and enough about the scientific and philosophical aspect in '2mrw Iz 2day Iz Yesterday (Vol II)'. In this writing I am appealing to spiritual and emotional elements of yourselves, to awaken in the world of men the ability to 'feel' our connection to everyone and everything again; to do more for others than we would do for ourselves. For this is, I believe, is the only way to usher in the 'Age of Aquarius', in the correct way; the only thing that can result in this potential Nu-Utopia, a new spiritual Golden Age. The only thing which can turn Armageddon, the end of the world (as you know it) into a better 'Here-After', because existence and life will guaranteed be here, after.

The extra-terrestrial theme has always been fundamental to the truth and the 'Realization of the Oneness of All'. I desperately tried to find a way to not have to get too deep into this topic, in this book, but I don't feel that I would've done justice to the Legacy of our ancestors if the theme of the Gods/Neteru – 'Guardian, Watchers', (the Messengers of the One True Creator of all, the Mother/Father Universe) wasn't spoken of in an extra-terrestrial context. I have tried my best to put the bulk of the tabooed theme, in the first chapter. All in all, the 'Ancient Astronaut Hypothesis' is covered in great detail in my other writings and books and the magnificent works of others. My wish is for this writing to penetrate into areas, it otherwise would not have and help to change the perception in the world today about our ancient forebears.

The fact that I know the sceptics and the critics will come for me, all guns blazing, makes me weary. My attitude has always been to live a peaceful existence with wife and children and show gratitude to the Neteru. Sometimes, I wish I never had to spend countless time and energy writing these books for the sake of others, but I have to. It's my response – ability as a spiritual being; my life path as an 'Awakener' and an 'Awaken One'. When we turn on our lights on the inside of us, we begin to live by and for one another rather than against each other and the path reveals itself when we take our steps.

These books are the works that I leave for my family and children; for Kushite people and spiritual people worldwide. Something for them or others to be inspired from and add on to the works. For this is how I myself was inspired. Inspired by our own modern equivalents of what the classic Greek writers are to the Europeans. Great men such as, Cheikh Anta Diop, Dr Ben Jochannon, Dr Henrik Clarke, Ivan Van Sertima, Ashra Kwesi and Noble Rev. Dr Malachi Z York, among others. They are to Kushites today, what Socrates, Plato, Aristotle, Pythagorus, Homer, etc., are to the white world.

So, we know that our Kushite ancestors came up from South Africa up through Central Africa following the river. At this time we need to remember that in those days the climate was different to what it is in many regions today. Especially after the last Glacier Period which ended the ice sheets on the northern and southern hemispheres. This altered the climate and ecology globally. Vast areas which used to have summer monsoons, in Central Africa, were perfect places to live and prosper and some of our ancestors lived in areas as such, having an abundance of resources.

When the climate began to change and the Central African monsoons dried up, the people were forced to find water sources elsewhere (the Nile especially) and continued their northward trek up the river forming more subsistence farming communities, even tens of thousands of years ago. Indeed in 1973, the site of Nabta Playa was discovered in the Egyptian Sahara also called the Western Desert. It is a vast rectangular region and is considered one of the most remote arid and inhospitable locations upon the planet. This desolate place has remained largely unexplored until recently. Egyptologists believed that because of the remoteness of the unwatered region that the Pharaohs of Egypt never ever ventured there. They said that it was impossible for the ancients to travel that far without periodic waterholes and none have been found. Because of this belief, the Egyptologists have been disinterested in looking into it.

But as stated in 1973, Nabta Playa was discovered. The site is like a miniature Stonehenge, a pre-historic astronomical star clock in the sand. In the 60's when the Egyptian government began the construction of the Aswan Dam, just south of Aswan, the resulting artificial Lake Nasser (named after the then President Nasser) threatened to flood many of the surrounding Nubian Temples and several pre-historic UNESCO World Heritage sites. The archaeological world was in uproar. Temples such as the famous Abu Simbel which Pharaoh Rameses the Great, erected in Nubia and the temple of Isis on the island of Philae, threatened to be ruined and lost forever. Quickly the funds were raised for a rescue of these two temples and sites, such as Nabta Playa, but many more sites and invaluable temples and silent witnesses to the Sudanese, Nubian origins were lost. If it wasn't for the efforts of those like, Fred Wendorf, much more of our Legacy would have been lost for all times.

Other sites in the Western Desert, the Egyptian Sahara, such as Gilf Kebir, Jebel Uwainat and Jebel Ramlah yielded evidence of its early inhabitants. These inhabitants were the ancestors who drew the 'rock art' in the area, the descendants of the Tebu, Goran, Bidiat and others who live in and around that region today. C^{14} – dating puts these areas in the timeframe of 7000 – 3400 B.C.E. The evidence suggests that the residents travelled back and forth to these sites, eventually settling there. They were following the summer monsoon rains and when they finally dug large deep wells to catch the waters of the monsoons for the year, they made these Oasis's their permanent homes. Sites such as Nabta Playa had a lake that was filled by the monsoons. Evidence points towards the ancestors settling their by 6500B.C.E. and that the people abandoned the area circa 3300 B.C.E. around the time when Pharaonic Egypt is said to have emerged out of nowhere.

A ceremonial complex was left by the people when they abandoned Nabta Playa. In the surrounding area many skeletons and cattle bones were unearthed which the scholars say is evidence of a cattle cult similar to the cattle cults of Netert Het-Heru (the Goddess Hathor), Aset (Isis) and Nut, all of whom were regularly depicted with the headdress of cow – horns. This can also be linked to the Apis Bull Cult in Memphis. As the experts stress how Egypt rose up fully formed as a Legacy with no development stages, they were right. The development was done outside of Egypt, way before the time of the first Egyptian Dynastic Kings. All institutions of Law, Science, Astronomy, Metallurgy, Religion, were already fully formed by the time of Menes (Narmer). Egypt is the Legacy of the Black Gods and the Black people, negroids in race, in Nubia.

When astronomers were brought in to study the site of Nabta Playa they were shocked to see that the site had been tampered with, moved and finally relocated to the Aswan, Museum. The famous Cow Stone had also disappeared from the site and nobody seemed to know where it was. When they finally got to study the Tumuli, stones and alignments which had a precise East – West, North – South orientation, those such as Dr Kim Malville, an astronomer of the University of Colorado, discovered through the science of archaeastronomy that the site was connected to yet other sacred sites such as Dendera and Saqqara in Egypt. And according to the overwhelming evidence the site of Dendera dates back to as far as 12,000 B.C., which is way before Sumer and all other Ancient sites.

Archaeastronomy is a new field of science that has developed over the last few decades with growing interest among scholars. The science can be summed up as the study of the astronomy, astrology and cosmologies in relation to the alignments of monuments and buildings of ancient cultures. It has emerged as a vital tool for the field of archaeology, because in recent years it has become clear that the cyclic motions of the stars, sun, moon and planets were indeed a fundamental and integral part of the religious ideologies of the ancient peoples, pioneered by Kushites. The ancestors applied this sacred science to the alignments and designs of their monuments. It is paramount that this nomad eye science of observation is used to fully appreciate and overstand fully the purpose and meaning of the designs, alignments and sometimes the choice of location of ancient temples and other monuments, sometimes even whole cities.

".... (Charles) Dupuis had located the birthplace of the zodiac in an Egypt older by far than any chronology based on textual arguments and especially on the Books of Moses could possibly allow. (Standard biblical chronology placed the origin of all things at about 4,000 B.C. ....). According to Dupuis, the zodiac and astronomy itself, was born near the Nile over

14,000 years ago. The Greeks, he insisted, were scientific children compared to the Egyptians, whose knowledge and wisdom underlay all of western science and mathematics ...."

- Jed Z. Buchaid, Technology Historian

".... The cosmos itself is what mattered to our ancestors. Their lives, their (confirmed) beliefs, their destinies – all were part of this bigger pageant. Just as the environment of their temples was made sacred by metaphors of cosmic order, entire cities and great ritual centres were also astronomically aligned and organized. Each sacred capital restated the theme of cosmic order in terms of its builders' own perception of the universe(s). Principles, which the society considered its own – which ordered its life and gave it its character – were borrowed from the sky and built into the plans of the cities ...."

- E.C. Krupp

The ancestors were masters of 'Applied Sciences' built atop a deep, meaningful, underlying spirituality. Pyramids and temples were aligned to the heliacal rising of the stars like Sirius, the Polestar, Orion's Belt, Pleiades and many other stars. Observatories were situated in order to witness the return of the celestial Lord, the mothership, Nibiru (RE's Manjet) also referred to as the Sacred Solar Barque. Many cities today in Europe and America have stolen these principles and incorporated them into the layout of cities like Paris and Washington D.C. The cities are awash with the stolen Masonic symbolism of the ancient Kushites.

Today a few universities have added the field of archaeastronomy to their subjects and the attention it has garnered has caused a major breach in the firewall of Egyptology. Archaeastronomy has now come parallel to archaeology as the best tools to study the Ancient architect's pyramids, temples, texts and tomb reliefs of the Pharaohs.

The discovery of Pharaoh Djedefre's water mountain located in the Dakhla Oasis was more proof of ancient Egyptian travel through the remotest parts of the Egyptian (Western Sahara) desert and beyond. The area which resembles the Nabatean Petra rock palaces and tombs in the trans-Jordan contains beautifully carved hieroglyphs of Pharaoh Khufu and his son and successor Pharaoh Djedefre, of short notes from stone masons, figures and enigmatic signs (water mountain symbol) placed on the rock deliberately ordered. The notes also mention an expedition sent to the land of Yam by Pharaoh Khufu three times.

The people of Egypt (Khemet) saw the people of Yam as their ancestors. Scholars have long argued about exactly who these people were and where the land of Yam was located. According to Harkuf and his father, Iry, who served under Pharaohs, Pepi I, Merenre I and Pepi II of the Sixth (6th) Dynasty and the inscriptions that they left on the island of Elephantine, near Aswan; they undertook a desert expedition and mounted several more during their life time. They travelled to the 'land of Yam' bringing back many luxuries from the faraway land. Iry had been chief lector priest to the Pharaoh Pepi I and retained the post after Pepi's untimely death then serving Pharaoh Merenre I (6th Dynasty 2323 – 2150 B.C.E.). After Iry passed away, his son Harkuf took up the post under Pharaoh Merenre 1st and also to this pharaoh's successor, the young Pharaoh Pepi II. Harkfuf was also appointed governor of Aswan and Elephantine and it was under the orders of Pharaoh Merenre I and later Pepi II that the several expeditions into the desert were carried out. For more on this thread read the brilliantly written: 'Black Genesis' by the author Robert Bauval and his co-writer Thomas Brophy, Ph.D.

"..... [The] isolated but identical presentation of the water ideograms [near Dongola] more than 700 kilometres south of the Dakhla area..... bares implications for the question of early Egyptian relations with Sudanese Nubia. It suggests a line or a network of communication across the Eastern Sahara as late as the 3rd millennium B.C..... The new evidence supports the scenario that even after 3,000 B.C. the Libyan Desert was not completely void of human activity. In its southern part, cattle keepers could survive as late as the second millennium B.C..... Apparently, the Egyptian Nile Valley and the Oasis were connected with these regions and farther African destinations beyond by a network of donkey caravan routes crossing southern Egypt...."

- Rudolph Kuper

Other Pharaohs such as Mentuhotep also left inscriptions about expeditions to Yam. His inscriptions were found in Jebel Uwainat. The exact location is disputed but most agree that the region of Yam is probably Sudan, South of Jebel Uwainat or the Tibesti highlands of North Eastern Chad.

Shortly after the great deluge, approximately 13,000 years ago due to the end of the last Glacial Period, the region currently covered by the Sahara Desert was considered 'Aqualithic'. The climate of the area was much wetter than it is today being regularly watered by monsoon rains which created a fertile living area for both man and animals. The Kushite culture that flourished in this region was known as Tamana, including Jebel Uwainat (Western Sudan), then known as Yam.

After having come from 'The Mountain of the Moon' (Mount Meru) today's Uganda, the Kushite culture settled in this vast fertile region covering thousands of miles. It was when the monsoons failed to come to these habitations within the Sahara region that the people abandoned their settlements in favour of the Nile Valley and Delta and also spread further out into the fertile plains of the Levant and Mesopotamia. This resulted in Khemet Ta - 'The Black Land', Elam in Iran and Sumer in Southern Iraq. After other nations such as the Indus Valley settlements, Petra in the Tans-Jordan, Hatti in Turkey and even Minoa (Crete), Greece and China also sprouted in no particular order.

All of these Kingdoms were established by Kushites. Some of these regions were already inhabited by the ANU people, the Ptah Daneg called Pygmies in today's language. As stated, the Ptahites (Twa) were/are the ancestors of the Homo – sapien, Kushites, the Twa being Homo – Erectus species of earlier hominids. The Ptah Daneg were used to genetically manipulate modern humans (sapiens) into existence as the new beings (Nubians). These ANU people were mixed with Anunnaqi blood.

The tribe of Kushites who were the first to leave Tamana, which is the Sahara region, after the monsoons failed, were the Xi/Xiu (pronounced Shi) people who moved into Iran founding Elam and Sumer, mixing in with the ANU/Twa culture which was already inhabiting these regions. Xi people then moved into the Indus Valley region of India and then on into China establishing the first two Chinese dynasties of Xi and Sheng before being conquered by the Zhou nomads. The Xi people crossed the Pacific and settled also in the Yucatan Peninsula of Mexico becoming the so called enigmatic 'Olmecs' who also called themselves Xi/Xiu people of the Manding strain. Their American settlement was called Atlan.

Atlan in Ancient Nuwaubian means 'Home Away From Home'. This Kushite civilization in the western hemisphere in the Americas produced the legendary tales of Atlantis. North America and Central America was referred to as Atlan, while South America was referred to as Amexem. The colonies of the Americas were founded by Enki and his sons circa 3113 B.C. In the region Enki, the Sumerian Anunnaqi – God, became known by the name Quetzalcoatl 'Feathered Serpent', and also Itzamna 'He Whose Home Is Water', identical to his Sumerian epithet Ea – 'He Whose Home is Water'. In South America Tehuti was known by the name Viracocha. These tremendous Kushite people left the Sahara region of Africa before it dried up, due to desertification. They settled in the Americas, Europe and Asia. The classical Greek testified to the Fact that all civilization originated from these proto-Sahara people and this is backed up by both Khemetian records and the ancient writings of places like the Indus Valley and Yucatan. These all confirm that the Kushite culture ruled the world for thousands of years. Though many of the things claimed are legends. Most of the information which has come down through the ages is unarguably anthropological and archaeological facts backed up by Kushite civilizations is irrefutable, undisputed and beyond the shadow of a doubt.

Asiatic Black Man: The Asian Gene-Isis

Approximately 12,000 years ago in the highlands of the Sahara the Xi people developed a unique and awe-inspiring culture, which included astronomy, solar biology, writing, pottery and boat technology. At this time the Sahara region was aqualithic so many waterways criss-crossed the highlands. Numerous waterways spilled out into the Indian Ocean and the Mediterranean basin.

As stated, the many branches of these most ancient Kushite cultures encompassed an area spanning from the Sahara (Tamana) and Nubia (Tamare) in the South to Persia (Iran) in the North. These Kushites were the first people to civilize Arabia before Muhammad (570 – 632 A.D.), in the form of Nabateans and Himyarite people. It was them who built the beautiful settlement of Petra in Northern Arabia (the Trans-Jordan). These spiritual and peace loving Kushite are called the Thamud and the Ad in the Qur'aan and have been lied upon and misrepresented by its authors along with the Sabeans. Those of you who call yourselves true Muslims need to real-eyes the character assassination being done to your ancestors by these so-called Muslims (Mohammadans). Though you may not like to hear it, the pale Arabs of today's Arabia and Egypt are actually Turks (Hittites) and Syrians who have always made themselves the sworn enemies of us Kushites and in these more recent times, these barbarians were the first to enslave us Africans by way of Zanzibar. They enslaved Africa long before the Europeans and they are still some of the most racist and prejudice people on the face of the planet, like it or not. From the inhuman slave trade of Zanzibar, the word Zinji was coined. Zinji is Arabic equivalent of 'Nigger' and still the Turkish/Syrian Semitic (Shashu) Arab will claim that there is no racism within the folds of the Brotherhood of Al Islam, which is a blatant lie. The prophet Mustafa Muhammad Al Amin (p.b.u.h 570 – 632 A.D.) himself was a Himyarite (Kushite) Arab fighting against the Northern invasion of his time. This is why he, himself, retreated to Abyssinia (Ethiopia/Kush) to seek sanctuary with the Negus – 'King', even visiting back to his grandmother's house while there. For we know that Ishmael, son of Abraham (Ibrahim) – p.b.u.t – was mothered by Hagar, who was the daughter of Imhotep and we know for certain just who this great father was and how he looked. So cease from believing in these racist lies and defend the honour of your ancient mothers and fathers, your Kushite family tree. Give them back their fabricated religious 'isms and schisms. Read what is said about the so called Arab, Bedouins in Qur'aan 9:97.

Anyway, we Kushites were also the first to civilize Canaan before the Canaanites as Kadmonites (Genesis) we were there before the Khazars and Ashkenazim Jews or Habiru (Hebrews); Mesopotamia before Assyrians and Elam and India before the Indo-European speaking Aryans who descended from the Caucasus Mountains and were called 'The Steppes People', from the Russian Steppes of the Trancaucasia.

In Ancient times the Sudan was known as Ethiopia proper and was affectionately referred to as Kush – 'Black' and today's Ethiopia and Somalia was known as Punt, while much of Mesopotamia and the Indus Valley was known as Puntya and Kushiya. We therefore had two Kush', one in Africa and one in Asia known today as the Hindu Kush region. Greco-Roman writers such as the fabled poet Homer clearly mentioned two different Kushite states in Africa and Asia. He wrote:

"A race divided, whom the sloping rays; the rising and the setting sun surveys".

There are various different groups of Kushites. Archaeologists call the first group the 'A-Group' and this group originally came from Qes. Qushana. The Khamites (Egyptians) rendered them K'sh and K'shi, while the Hebrews called them Kush. These Sudanese Kushites were called Kushiya in cuneiform inscriptions. In the Abyssinian (Ethiopic) inscriptions of King Aezana, the Kushites were called Kashi or Kasu.

Now one of the major ethnic groups among the Kushites was/is the Manding and Dravidian – speaking people. The Manding refer to themselves as Si people. As stated earlier, it was this group which founded the Xia civilization of China, where they were called Xi (Shi) and the Olmec civilization of Mexico and the Yucatan Peninsula, who also referred to themselves as Xi (Shi).

In cuneiform Sumerian inscriptions the Kushites were called Meluha which would mean Kasi (Kush). This was referring to the Africans and Nubia and North-East Africa. The ancestors of the Kushites dwelled in the Sahara and are therefore referred to as proto-Saharans. These proto-Saharans originated in the Uganda area at the Mountain of the Moon (Mount Meru). They then migrated through Nubia and the Sudan settling in the highland areas and through into Khemet. Again this period of history is referred to as Aqualithic.

The world historians like to misinform the masses about the ingenuity of the Kushites and their contributions to the civilisation of the planet. We mentioned earlier how historians like to teach that there was no connection between ancient civilizations, especially those separated by vast expanses of water. They falsely claim that the Old and New World civilizations had no contact whatsoever with one another, when all the evidence and fact based records say otherwise.

The ancient Kushites were known to be great seamen. They settled North Africa, West Africa, Europe, Asia and even the Americas in their sewn boats of great workmanship. Those found buried on the Giza plateau bare-witness to their technological know-how and the ability of Kushite craftsmen. Far from being mythological, the boats depicted upon the walls of monuments throughout Nubia and Khemet were real. The French linguist, Lacouperie stated: *"Their activity in trade, their boldness in seafaring expeditions and the extensive spread of civilization, which followed their efforts, have won them a lasting fame"*. It was recorded in the Indian book called 'Matsya' the world belonged to the Kushites for 7,000 years.

The Greek historian Herodotus said the Ethiopians were 'the tallest most beautiful and long lived of the human races', and again, the Greek poet Homer described these Kushites as *"the most just of men; the favourites of the Gods"* long before the Jews began to consider themselves as God's chosen (the Children of Israel). Many sources such as, the Roman author, Diodorus claimed that the Khemetians (Egyptians) and their civilization came from Nubia, which is the modern name for Kush. The ancient Khemetians themselves recognized their origins in the interior of Kush, by erecting alters to Kush in Men-Nefer (Memphis), Waset (Thebes) and Meroe under the name of 'Khons' also said 'Khonsu', the son of the Neter (God) Amun-Re and the Netert (Goddess) Mut.

The Meroitic Sudan influenced the bulk of Khemet's history. It was from this region that the Khemetians (Egyptians) learned the 12 hieroglyphs that were used to form their Nuwaubic alphabet called the 'Medew Neter' – 'Sacred Carvings of the Gods'. It is in the Meroitic Sudan that you can find the same plants and animals that are represented in the Medew Neter.

Contrary to what most Egyptologists will preach, the first empire of Nubia was Nwh (Nuwh) which sprouted up before 4,000 B.C. Some say 3,800 B.C., while those that don't know argue between the dates of 3300 B.C. – 3100 B.C. This is done in order to claim that the civilization of Sumer is older than that of Nubia and Egypt. The fact remains that the Nubian – Kushites founded the first Monarch in world history. Artefacts recovered within the area inside the Qustul tombs near the Egyptian – Sudanese border bearing various symbols of Nubian royalty later used by the Khemetian (Egyptians) attest to this undisputed fact. It is now well known that the Shekem/Aaferti – 'Ruler' (Pharaoh) Menes/Narmer was of this same Meroitic (Sudanese) Nubian stock.

One of the names of this ancient Nubian civilization was Ta-Seti – 'Land of the Bow' and the people were known as 'Steu' Bowmen. This name Ta-Seti can be found on the engraved plaque of the Shekem Hor Aha, from Abydos in Egypt and the Gebel Sheikh Suleiman inscriptions and sealing from Nubia. This is all very significant because it shows that over 6,000 years ago, 700 years before the rise of Khemet (Egypt), that the world's first monarchy in the world was established in Nubia, just as the Egyptians themselves, the Greeks and the Romans had recorded. Ta-Seti and Egypt had the same funeral customs, music, musical instruments, pottery, agriculture and related artefacts. The major pottery was the beautiful red and black ware, which these Kushites later took with them into Asia.

The Kushite A–Group culture founded civilization in Nubia and we know about them by way of their pottery styles. The Qustul incense burner indicates kingship and royalty, wealth and government in Nubia. The A-Group cemetery L had tombs that rivalled or even exceeded the Egyptian tombs of the 1st Dynasty of Egypt. The A-Group cemeteries extend from Kubaniyya in North, to Malik en-Nasir in the 2nd cataract to the South. The connections between the A-Group civilization and the Khemtian dynasty I include:

1) The Shekem (Pharaoh) figure, 2) Haru (Horus – the Falcon God), 3) the palace facade and 4) The sacred barque (boat).

Three ancient relics of the A-Group hierarchy which are 1) the Faras seal, 2) the sarras seal and 3) the siali seal indicate royalty. The Faras Seal shows a depiction of the palace facade and sacrifice. The Sarras West seal shows a barque (boat), a man holding a staff or harpoon near the stern of the vessel and a stepped throne. The siali seal has an archaic falcon perched atop a place facade, same as Horus, the falcon seated atop a 'Serekh', while a man sitting on a throne, has his hand upraised over an archaic bow with rectangular figure below it and a bovine (cattle) behind the man which equal the name Ta-Seti (i.e., the bovine and bow standard).

The Asian proto-Saharans were also called Kushites or Ethiopians. Ethiopian is a Greek term: Ethios – 'burnt' and ops – 'face', as a result the term means the 'burnt faces'. The writings of the classical Greek writers made it clear that the whole region from Egypt to India was called by the name Ethiopia. Thus, the Elamites of Ancient Iran called themselves Khatam and their capital Susa; Kussi. In addition the Kassites, who occupied the central part of the Zagros Mountains were named Kashshu. The Kushana, who helped to form the Meroitic (Sudanese) civilization, formerly inhabited Chinese Turkistan (Xinjiang) and the Gansu province of China. These Kushites in Asia, as in Africa were renowned for their skill as bowmen, indicating their connection to the Steu – the Kushites of Ta-Seti (Nubia)

Rawlinson, who is famed for deciphering the Ancient cuneiform inscriptions of Mesopotamia, said Puntites and Kushites were well established in Asia as he found both mentioned in the inscriptions of Darius. He also clarified that the name Kush was similarly applied to Southern Persia, India, Elam, Arabia and Colchis (a part of Southern Russia/Turkistan) in Ancient times. Some even state that Colchis was fathered by the Shekem Sesostris' army and that the early Colchians were akin to Khemetians in appearance and customs. They were reported to be tawny (brown) skinned with Woolley hair.

The Europeans called Armenians, who became the Gypsies through their travels, also clearly stated that the ancients called Persia, Media, Elam, Aria and the entire area between the Tigris and Indus Rivers – Kush. Writing in his 'Book of the Laws of Countries', in the 2nd century AD, claimed that the 'Bactrians who we called Qushani (or Kushuans)". The Armenians called them Parthian – Kushuan and acknowledged their connection with them. Homer, Herodotus and the Roman Chronicler Strabo called Southern Persia – 'Aethiopia'. The Greeks and Romans called the country east of Kerma (Nubia) – Kusan.

From Iran the Kushites used the natural entry point to go into China, from the Zagros Mountains to the Altai Mountains and the Dzunganian Gate. There is archaeological evidence indicating farming settlements were erected along this path dating back to 3500 B.C. The evidence indicates that these early settlements spread from West to East.

The fact remains that the cultures and civilizations of Western Asia cannot be the oldest cultures because, geologically speaking, Mesopotamia is a very young formation.

The first group to split from the proto-Saharans were the Ancient Khemetians who settled in the Nile Valley, moving up to the Nile Delta. They are Kushitic speakers while the Puntites are the so called Semitic speakers. The Egyptians settled in Nubia with some Kushites and

Semites migrating into the eastern desert regions bordering on the Red Sea. Other Kushitic elements migrated into Arabia and down into East Africa.

The Kushitic speakers, now located mainly in East Africa formerly lived in Arabia and Mesopotamia and were both herders and farmers. They are believed to have cultivated the area since, at least, 6,000 B.C. The Kushitic and Puntite (Semitic) speaking folks were very close. The Puntites main homeland was the horn of Africa, which was referred to as Punt in Ancient times and still is called Puntland by some like the Somalians of today. It was here that Ura – 'Female Ruler', Hatshepsut, sailed South during her illustrious reign. The people of Punt were great seafarers. They were referred to as Meluhhaitos (Meluhaites) upon Sumerian Tablets. The merchants of Punt traded cattle, lapis lazuli, carnelian, two types of wood and reeds. It was a resourcefully rich area. The majority of the Puntites (Meluhhaites) remained nomadic herders like the Martu tribes.

The Puntites dwelt in the Eastern Desert of Egypt for many years and also upon the horn of Africa. The earliest representatives of this group are depicted on the ivory label of the A'aferti/Shekem Den (Udimu) of the first dynasty of Khemet (Egypt). During the Neolithic 'New Stone Age' sub-pluvial the Red Sea area also was wetter, having more rainfall. The area was thus blanketed with vegetation and the people grew barley, ensete and dates and grazed sheep, cattle and goats. The Puntites inhabited East Africa and Arabia and many modern day Africans such as Djiboutians, Ethiopians, Kenyans and Somalians are their descendent.

Puntites colonized Arabia and Yemen during the Neolithic Age and at this time Arabia and Yemen was a vast Savannah of lakes and marshes. What is now known as the Rub al-Khali or Empty Quarter today, an arid mountainous area was then well watered. In Arabia Puntite and Kushite tribes settled, hunted and fished. Approximately 3,500 and 2,500 B.C., a group of people entered Mesopotamia from Africa that spoke African (Kushitic) and Semitic languages. These people called themselves 'The Black Headed' people, from around 3,000 B.C. to the very end of Sumerian history. The African speaking group – Kushites – founded Sumerian civilization.

Both the Sumerians and Elamites came to Mesopotamia by way of boats. These boats were first used in the Eastern Sahara and upon the Red Sea. The Sumerians birthed what is referred to as the 'Mother Culture' of Mesopotamia and remained in control for many years. They were usurped by a group referred to as Akkadians who inherited their culture and cuneiform script from the Sumerians. Babylonians usurped Akkadians and Assyrians usurped Babylonians before the rise of the Persian Empire, all borrowing from the Ancient Kushite, Sumerians also said Shumerians.

Around 2,334 B.C., a group of Puntite speakers again called Akkadians under the Sharru-Kin (Sargon of Akkad) – 'Righteous Ruler' took over Mesopotamia. This unity of Akkadian and Ethiopian languages is supported by both Sumerians and Akkadians who both state that they originated from the Egypto-Nubia and Punt (Kush/Ethiopia) to West Asia. It is also supported by the Myth made Bible in Geneses 10:9, as referred to earlier mentioning Sargon of Akkad, who is none other than Nimrod.

Most modern scholars such as, Joan Oates, suggest that Magan (Egypto-Nubia) and Meluhha (Punt) were South Eastern Arabia and the Makian Coast to as far as the Indus Valley (India/Pakistan). But according to those such as, Samuel Noah Krammer, the leading expert on the Sumerians and Akkadians, from the time of Sargon the Great (2,334 B.C.) down to the first millennium B.C., 'Magan' and 'Meluhha' was Egypto-Nubia and Punt (Ethiopia) respectively. According to these writings ships from Meluhha and Magan brought trade goods to Mesopotamia.

It was the French Orientalist, Julius Oppert, who named them Sumerians in an attempt to separate them from the Black African, Kushites. So I say to David Icke of conspiracy fame; 'no they are not 'some Aryans' (Sum-arians) as was suggested by him in 'Tales from the Time Loop'. Sir Henry Rawlinson, who deciphered cuneiform and traced the writings traced the Sumerians and Akkadians back to Nubia and Punt and called them Kushites. According to W.J. Perry, in 'The Growth of Civilization', the myths, legends and traditions of the Sumerians pointed back to Nubia as their origin. Sir Henry Rawlinson again, in the 'Journal of the Royal Asiatic', was correct in calling them Kushites. The title of 'King of Kish', was a highly prized title/status by subsequent Rulers of Sumer as a claim of supremacy over the whole country.

The Kushite Sumerians established themselves upon the left bank of the Tigris. Towards approximately 2,300 B.C., the plains of the Tigris and Susinka were ruled by a dynasty of Kushite Kings. The features of its people were dark skin and woolly hair, which was mentioned by Herodotus during his visit to the area in the 5th century B.C. He referred to them as Ethiopians. Sir Harry Johnston noted that the Elamites 'appear to have been Negroid people with kinky hair and to have transmitted this race's type of Jews and Syrians'.

The Sumerians learned all of their knowledge from the ANU. They extended dykes to hold back the regular floods of the Tigris and Euphrates Rivers and dug canals and reservoirs to store water and carry to the plains. This led to grand harvests yielding 200 to 800 grains per plant, in an area today where the Turks live a miserable existence.

Sumerians built their cities from unbaked bricks. Many, if not most, of these ancient sites and cities such as Ur, Eridu, Uruk (Erech), Nippur and Akkad have been unearthed and excavated. These discoveries support the Biblical accounts and skeletal remains of the ancient inhabitants of Chaldea (the birth place of the mythical Abraham/Ibrahim), verifies that they were Black Africans. These Blacks-Kushites were short with thin lips and noses.

The Anunnaqi God, Enki, also called Ea – 'He Whose Home Is Water' and also Nudimmud – 'He Who Fashions', was known as Ptah in Magan and Meluhha (Egypto-Nubia), one of the creator Neteru (Gods). He is said to have come to His City of Eridu – 'Home Away From Home', situated at the head of the Persian Gulf by the sea. The Sumerians spoke two different languages, one was Kushitic (African) which was Sumerian and the other was Akkadian which can be considered the Mother and Father of all Semitic languages, including Aramic/Aramaic (Hebrews) and Ashuric (Syriac), Arabic. Magan and Meluhha are mentioned as early as the writings of Sargon the Great and Gudea. Both countries are frequently named in the Sumerian and Akkadian records. Sharru-Kin – 'Righteous Ruler' (Sargon the Great) of Akkad (2,334 B.C.) recorded the boats of Magan, Meluhha and Dilmun were anchored in his capital of Agade. Gudea wrote that he received Diorite Stone for his statues from Magan and wood for the building of temples from Magan and Meluhha. The Meluhhaites were referred to as 'The Men of the Black Land'. They traded in Carnelian, lapis lazuli, Gold and other metals, stones and minerals among other goods.

Dilmun, sometimes said Dilmun – 'Land of the Missiles' is sometimes said to be in the Indus Valley but recent evidence indicates that Dilmun was actually in the Sinai Peninsula. It was considered the 'Abode of the Anunnaqi' by the Sumerians. It was here that the Demi-God and King Gilgamesh of Sumeria travelled to, to seek out Utnapishtim (Noah) in search of the 'plant of eternal youth' and the secret of eternal life which was granted to Utnapishtim according to Sumerian tablet records. After travelling to the Cedar Mountains and being denied a 'Shem' – 'Sky Vehicle' in Lebanon, at the site of Baalbek which was the Anunnaqi landing site and launch pad, he decided to travel to Dilmun to seek at his relative Utnapishtim who is also called Ziusudra and Atra-Hasis and is the true biblical Noah, to continue his quest for eternal life. He travelled with his friend, the wild man called Enkidu.

The story is recorded as 'The Epic of Gilgamesh' and also 'The Tablet of Atra-Hasis' records the independent story of Utnapishtim/Ziusudra/Atra-Hasis. These Egypto-Sumerian realities became the mythologies of the so called Holy Scriptures.

According to Sumerian tradition, Enki – 'Lord Earth' (Ptah), had come from Dilmun. Dilmun became the spaceport of the Anunnaqi after the Great Deluge approximately 10,860 B.C., left the Sumerian E.Din – 'Land of the Rocketships' waterlogged and buried under mud. The Sumerian E.Din is called Abi Shinar within the Bible, which means 'Flatlands'. Both the E.Din and Dilmun was considered the 'Abode of the Gods' and therefore paradise on earth to the ancient Sumerians and Kushites. From this Sumerian E.Din – 'Land of the Rocketships' is where the Jewish authors of the Tanakh (Torah) and the church fathers derived their watered down 'Garden of Eden' story in the Bible. It is also interesting to note that the Sumerian language was also closely related to Dravidian, the language which was spoken in the Indus Valley in ancient times. The Indus Valley script is still said to be un-deciphered up to now.

The most important Kushite colony in Iran was Ancient Elam. The Elamites called their country, Khatam or Khaltam (Ka-taam). The capital of Khaltam which is referred to as Susa today, was call Khuz (Ka – u - uz) by the invading Aryans from the Caucasus Mountains, Nime (Ni – may) by the people of Sumer and Kushshi (Cush – she) by the Elamites themselves. In the Akkadian inscriptions the Elamites were referred to as Giz-Bam – 'The Land of the Bow'. The ancient Chinese or Bak tribesmen who dominate China today called the Elamites Kashti. Moreover, in the 'Bible', Book of Jeremiah (X1XX, 35), we read 'bow of Elam'. Both Khaltam-ti and Kashti as the name for Elam, is the same as Ta-Seti, the ancient name for Nubia/the Meroitic Sudan.

Again, there were already ANU/Ptahites (Homo-Erectus), Pygmy people occupying the area of Iran and Arabia etc., by the time the proto-Saharan Kushites infiltrated into the area of Western Asia. Approximately, 3,200 B.C., the Kushites began to settle into the area. They were able to dominate these lands because the former rulers of the land, the ANU/Ptahites had suffered a decline in their influence after the Great Flood which seems to have wiped out much of their civilization globally by at least 4,000 B.C. They may have also been dominated because of their more benevolent, peaceful and passive nature compared to the more aggressive Kushites.

The Kushites in Elam settled the Susiana plains of South Western Iraq (Uruk) in Mesopotamia. They arrived with their own writing in their own boats. Because a trading network was already well established in this region, the early Elamite settlers abandoned the proto-Saharan script and began to use the cuneiform script, which like the hieroglyphics scripts, was invented by the Anunnaqi and given to the Ptah Daneg or Twa (ANU) people.

It was logical for the early Elamites to use cuneiform because the script was already in use by the merchants of West Asia, therefore in using this established script they were able to monopolize the trade network in the region without any unnecessary complications that an unused script would cause.

It was beyond the shadow of a doubt that the Kushites established Elamite civilization. It was recorded by Strabo, the Roman geographer that the colony of Susa, was founded by Tithonus, a King of Kush and father of Memnon of heroic legend. Strabo in book 15, chapter 3,728 wrote, 'In fact, it is claimed that Susa was founded by Tithonus Memnon's pa and that his citadel bore the name Memnonium. The Susians are also called Cissians and Aeschylus, calls Memnon's mother Cissia. Some scholars believe that the Sekhem (Pharaoh) Amunhotep III, maybe Memnon.

Although this is a reoccurring opinion held by some scholars and researchers, the fact that the ancient writers made it clear that Memnon came not from Egypt, but from Kush, suggest that he was not Khemetian (Egyptian). It is more likely that Memnon's ancestors had lived in the proto-Sahara.

A tomb related to Memnon is said to have been formerly established in Troad, an area near Troy in North West Anatolia, according to Martin Bernal, in volume II of Black Athena. This tomb was associated with Memnoides or Black Birds. This identification of Memnon with Black Birds suggests that he was a member of the Bird Clan, which also founded the Shang dynasty. It should also be remembered that it was from Elam that the Manding and Dravidian explorers of Central Asia and China first made their way into East Asia. This fact is supported by the Elamite language, which is evidently related to Dravidian and Manding. The Elamites established a vast and extensive trade network linking them to the Sumerians to the West of them and the proto Dravidian and Mande speaking people of Central Asia and the Indus Valley. They also had trade relations with Africa.

Archaeologists use ceramics to identify cultures. The ceramic style from Susa and Godin, parallel the ceramic inventory at Warka IV and Nippur XV in Mesopotamia. Moreover, a distinctive style of chlorite (steatite) bowl manufactured at Yahya, with identically carved motifs have been discovered at excavated sites of the Sumerian Early Dynasty II/III city.

The French historian Lenormant, observed that when the archaeologist Dieulafoy excavated Susa, he found that 'the Master of the Citadel, is black; it is thus very possible that Elam was the prerogative of a black dynasty and if one refers to the characteristics of the figures already found, of an Ethiopian dynasty'.

The Elamites later conquered Sumer. They called this line of Kings the 'Kings of Kish'. As said, this term bears affinity to the term Kush, which was given to the Nubian Kerma dynasty, founded by the group C tribes of Kush. It is also interesting to note the close relations between African languages to the Elamite, Egyptian and Dravidian languages.

Before Europa: Europe Revisited

Black modern scholars such as Ivan Van Sertima and others have brought to light, the fact that Europe too, was first settled by Blacks. As a result, we find that Troy was a great centre of African civilization in the region of Turkey. The Caucasian Aryan speaking Greeks were called Ionians and Donans.

The founding pioneers of Grecian civilizations were the Blacks who came to Europe from proto-Saharan Africa. They were referred to as Eteocretans (real Minoans), Pelasgians, Achaeans, Gadmeans, Lelges and Carians/Garamantes. The Eteocretans early settled Europe. They originated in the highlands of Libya called the Fezzan. The Eteocretans allegedly founded Troy, Mycenae, Tiryns, Thebes and Orchomenos.

The Greeks often referred to the ancient Black Greeks as Achaeans and Pelasgians. The Pelasgians founded the city of Athens, the greatest of the Greek cities and also Thrace and Attica. The Achaeans founded the cities of Argolis, Pylos and Messenia. The fact that Kushite Blacks founded all these cities and Athens explains why many sources claim that Socrates was Black. It also explains why the ancient Greeks always depicted their Gods as Blacks too and their pantheons similarity to Egypto-Nubian Neteru/Anunnaqi Gods. The evidence can be found not only in the classical literature of Greece, but also in the art pieces which depict these Blacks, such as the 'Lion and Spearmen Hunt', the 'Stag Hunt' and the 'Siege Scene' on the Silver Rhyton Cup.

Black China and the Far East: By Dr: Clyde Winters and Ra Un Nefer Amen

For this small section I am going to turn to Dr: Clyde Ahmed Winters and Ra Un Nefer Amen. I will be relying on their writings heavily, in regards to "Black China". So by now, it should not surprise you in hearing that these same Kushite elements occupied the Far East from the earliest of times. This also includes the ANU/Ptahites group. In fact Peking, the old name of today's Beijing, was claimed to indicate the (Pygmy) Ptahites origin. Among the Black elements were also Africoid, Negrito and Austroloid types.

Febre d'Olivet stated that, *"The Black Race was dominant upon the earth and held the sceptre of science and power; it possessed all Africa and the greater part of Asia..... The Black Race existed in all the pomp of social state. It covered Africa entirely with powerful nations sprung from it; it possessed Arabia and had planted its colonies all over the Meridional Coasts of Asia and very far into the interior".*

Harry Johnson observed that, *"The Asiatic Negro speed – we can hardly explain how, unless the land connections of those days were more extended through Eastern Australi to Tasmania and from the Solomon Islands to New Caledonia and even to New Zealand to Fiji and Hawaii. The Negroid element in Burma and Annam is therefore easily to be explained by supposing that in Ancient times Southern Asia had a Negro population ranging from the Persian Gulf to Indo-China and the Malay Archipelago".*

The Xia and Shang civilizations of ancient China were founded by the Li Min – 'Black Headed People' by the Zhou dynasty. It is clear to spot the connection to the Sumero-Akkadian term – 'Sag-gig-ga' – 'The Black Headed People', a term that the Sumerians and Akkadians applied to themselves. These Li Min are associated with the Chinese cultural hero, Yao. The exploits of Yao and Shun who succeeded him with the Li Min people can be found mentioned in the 'Annals of the Bamboo Books'.

Very little is known about the ancient Chinese other than their language's sounds were very much different to middle and modern Chinese dialects. This is because China was established by very diverse ethnic groups eg. Xia and Shang dynasties: Dravidian and Manding speakers founded Li (ie, Black Shang). Classical Mongoloids and Zhou founded Shang Yin, contemporary China. This explains the different in pronunciation for ancient China spoken by the Xia and Shang peoples and old and middle Chinese or a variant there of, which was probably spoken by the Zhou people.

The clan emblem for the ancient Manding was the lizard/dragon. The same dragon motif was also found in Elamite/Iran and Babylonian Assyrian civilization and the Anau civilization in Russia, which had similar painted pottery to the pottery styles of Henan (Xia). The Li Min settled near the rivers, lakes and streams of China and they are mentioned in the oracle bone writing. The tree most sacred to the Xia was the pine tree which is often used to symbolize the Pineal Gland in Buddhist tradition. The Xia naming system was identical to the Shang.

The founder of the Xia Dynasty was Yu who was fathered by Gun Yu's son, founded the Pa culture, which was a Megalithic culture. Great Yu was the regulator of the waters and builder of canals and it was him who invented Wetfield agriculture. The decline of the Xia Empire and civilization led to the rise of Shang Li (Black Shang) as the leading state in the confederation. The clan totem of the Shang Li was the bird. In the 'Yen Ben Zhi', it is stated that a Black of Xia impregnated the mother of Xieh, the founder of Shang Li.

There were two Shang empires. The first we will refer to as Shang Li (Black Shang) and it was ruled by the Li Qiang (Black Qiang). For the last 273 years of the Shang Empire, the capital was located at Angyang. This empire founded at Angyang was established by the Yin nationality. We call this empire 'Shang Yin'. Thus, we have Shang Li and also Shang Yin. The Yin were classical Mongoloid people related to the Thai and other small Mongoloid Austronesian speaking peoples of South Eastern Asia.

The use of the 'black bird', as the Pa of Xieh, relates to the 'black bird' as a popular totem of black ethnic groups in China. The founders of Shang were of mixed origin. The eastern coast was a major area of black habitation and the fact that the black bird myths are concentrated on the east costs, since this area was the heartland of Ancient China, adds more weight to the 'Black Origin Theme'.

Archaeologists including K.C. Chang suggest that the Neolithic Mongoloid population of North China resembled the Oceanic Mongoloid type, but not the modern Mongoloid group we find living in China and much of the South East of Asia today.

According to the Shang poem 'Xuan Niao' – *'Heaven bade the dark bird to come down and bear Shang'*. The black bird who founded Shang was Di Ku or Emperor Ku/Ju. In the 'Oracle Bone Inscriptions' Jian's husband was styled Emperor Ku/Jun. Ku is also considered the Pa of the 'ten black bird's in the Mulberry Tree Tradition'. The references of 'black birds' in the Chinese literature relate to the African origin of the Shang rulers. Many of the Shang spoke a Dravidian (dialect) language.

The founders of Shang are often called Yi. Yi means 'Great Bowman'. The symbol of Yi in Chinese is translated dagung. This character has two parts DA – 'Great' and Jung - 'A Bow'. The name Yi and its similarity in the name Kuishang (Kushana) and Kushshu highlight the archaeological evidence pointing to a western origin for many elements of Chinese civilization. The bird totem of Shang suggests that the Shang were predominantly Dravidian speakers and we have already shown the evidence to indicate that the Dravidian speakers originally came from Nubia. They were related to the C group, Kushite people, corresponding to the Steu – the name of the founders of the Ta-Seti culture, the first Monarchy in history. The Yueh, as opposed to the Yi, were speakers of Manding. The Yueh are usually the Xia Dynasty founders of Ancient China.

The first Shang King was Xuan Wang, 'Black King' (Xuan means black). He was also called the Xuan Di, 'Black Emperor'. The founder of the Shang Dynasty was called Xuan Niao – 'Black Bird'; another Shang King was called Xuan Mu – 'Black Oxen'. The Shang Kingdom flourished in the Yellow River basin in the Henan province after 1766 B.C. They cultivated rice, millet and wheat. They used many metals including copper and tin.

Each Shang town had its own king. These Kings recognized the ruler of Shang (Shang Di) – the Emperor of Shang as the head of the confederation because his rule and power were considered to be ordained by the Heavens. Like the Egypto-Nubian and Elamite/Sumerian rulers, the Emperor of Shang was seen as both a spiritual and military leader of the people; both a ruler and a high priest. As a high priest the Shang Di made sacrifice and paid homage to the Gods for the entire nation of people. This was the custom of all Ancient Kushite Kingdoms.

Written history begins in China with the Shang Dynasty (c. 1500 – 1027 B.C.). The sources of the Shang history are references to them in ancient Chinese books, archaeology and the Oracle Bone Inscriptions. After heating the bones of animals, the Shang priests would interpret the cracks and answer questions on various subjects relating to every day Shang life. Other Shang records were kept on tablets of wood and bamboo.

The Shang Li capital was founded at Zhengzhou. Out of 30 Shang rulers, 16 were of the Shang Li, the other 14 were Classical Mongoloid, but not Yueh people. During the Shang period, the Li Min recorded loads of information on bones and turtle shells. This is referred to as Oracle Bones Writing. This writing is analogous to the Manding, Harappan, proto-Elamite and proto-Sumerian syllabic scripts. The sun signs refer to the ten clans that formed the basis of the Shang people. The so called Myth of the Mulberry Tree from which 10 suns rose may relate to the rise of the 10 founding Shang clans by ten suns (sons) which are identified as 'black birds' (Allan 1981, P.294).

Both the Ancient Chinese and Africans had the same naming systems. As in Africa the Shang children were named with both a day name and a night name, regular name. The child was named according to the days of the Zun, on which he/she was born. There were 10 days in each Zun. These 10 days were known as the 10 celestial signs.

Shang society was based on totemic clans called Zu, which were based on animal signs. The clan signs can be seen in clan emblems in bronze and oracle bone inscriptions. The symbol of the Shang was the bird.

The Zhou Dynasty conquered the Shang in 1027 B.C. The Zhou founded the first dynasty in China are related to the contemporary (Edomite) Chinese people who were originally nomads. The Chinese people of today are the 'Children of Esau', brother of Jacob. The Li Min of Shang (Kushites) were uncooperative when the Zhou Kings took power. The Tai clan, which entered Shanxi and adopted the Shang culture, led the Zhou people. The 'Annals of Bamboo Books' record that one of the Zhou Emperors – 'Tai Kang' was on the throne as a sham sovereign. By idleness and dissipation he obtained his virtue until the black headed people all began to waver in allegiance'.

In summary the Li Min – 'Black Headed People' of China originally came from ancient Iran and the Fertile African Crescent. They entered China both by land, from Iran and by sea.

They dominated both North and South until the coming of the Nomadic – Edomite – Zhou people. These Li Min spoke related Dravidian and Manding languages, which are a substratum language of Chinese. They remained disorganized in independent city states until the members of the (Na) Kunte clan led by Hu Nak Kunte entered China from Elam in the late 3rd millennium B.C. It was these Li Min who established Xia, the first monarchy in China. It was from the Xia and later Shang Dynasty that China inherited its political system and government.

Atlantis - Awakenng: Atlan and Amexem;

Contrary to popular belief the Maya were not the mother culture of the Yucatan and Mesoamerica. In the Gulf regions of Mexico, it is clear from artefacts recovered from ancient sites and Mayan traditions and records that a different race occupied this area before the Nahuatl speakers settled in the region.

Friar Diego de Landa, in 'Yucatan Before and After the Conquest', wrote that: *"some old men of Yucatan say that they have heard from their ancestors that this country was peopled by a certain race who came from the East, whom God delivered by opening for them twelve roads through the sea"*. Other traditions also record the settlement of Mexico by a different race. They landed in Panotha, on the Mexican Gulf and remained there until they began to move South in search of mountains. This tradition is indicative of the 12 Xi (Olmec) migrations. This is supported by stone reliefs from Izapa, Chiapas Mexico published by the New World Foundation. In Stela 5, from Izapa we see a group of men on a boat riding the waves.

The Xi (Shi) or Olmec Empire was spread from Yucatan in the East, to Guerreo and the Pacific Coast on the West, through Guatemala, Salvador and Costa Rica on the Southwest. Here the Xi (Olmecs) continued to use the proto-Saharan script, which was later adopted by the Mayan civilization.

Most scholars claim that the Olmec civilization lasted from 1500 – 100 B.C., but some say that the Olmec came over to the area as early as 3113 B.C. and lasted up until 600 A.D.

Both men and women lived on the habitation sites, which were used to mine gold for the Anunnaqi along with other resources and minerals. If the Olmecs had only been a group of merchants, as many scholars have suggested, we would not find so many sculptures of African (Xi) women in addition to men at Olmec sites.

The deciphering of the Xi (Shi) writing and Manding speaking language of the Olmec indicates that the people spoke one of the Mande languages closely related to the Manding group. As the Ancient Mande of Tichitt and along the Niger River (West Africa) the Xi (Shi) were 'Mound Builders'. Ancient Mexican traditions say that some of their ancestors came from a country across the sea, led by Amoxaque or Bookmen. The Mexican term Amoxaque, agrees with the Mandinke-Bambara term – 'A-Ma-Nkye' – 'He is a Teacher'. The Olmec's writing system was a syllabic system and the most famous inscriptions are the La Venta celts. In addition to writing inscriptions on celts and stelas, the Olmecs invented paper around 1000 B.C.

The Olmecs were accomplished in arts, sciences and engineering. As evidenced by the function of their ancient sites which were various metal and mineral refineries, the Xi (Shi) Olmecs were Alchemists of the highest order. Thus, their civilization was highly developed and it influenced all later cultures and civilizations in Mesoamerica. The Olmecs constructed complex earthen pyramids and mounds and large sculpted monuments weighing tons, such as the gigantic sculpted heads found at various sites. What is also interesting is that under the pre-classic Maya pyramids we find dirt and rubble which suggests that the Olmecs had already built pyramids and other monuments at these sacred sites that the Maya built their newer sites over. The earthen mounds over the Olmec tombs were covered with stone pyramids in pre-classic Maya times.

The African features, somatic traits of the colossal Olmec heads astonish most song sheet archaeologists. The so called epicanthic fold is associated with the Negroid (African) Kushite type. Large stone characterizes the fine art of the Olmec monuments, especially the heads of the Kushite rulers found at the site of La Venta and San Lorenzo. In addition to this monumental art, Olmec personal art includes human figurines, ceramics, masks, axes and small stone sculptures. Some of the colossal heads weigh up to a staggering 28 tons, carved out of one single piece of gigantic rock. The traditions remember them as giants and it is not hard to overstand why.

Some racist archaeologists and others tried in vain to dismiss the Africaness of the Xi (Shi), so called Olmec sculptures. They tried to claim that they were just ordinary American Indians with strong features exposing their own subtle, institutional racism but the fact that, at several sites children's toys were found representing elephants, African elephants at that, indicates that these Olmec people came from a place with (African) elephants. The Americas have had no elephants since the Woolley Mammoth, so in order for the Olmecs to remember elephants, is proof that they came from somewhere else that had them, and that place was none other than Tamana – Proto-Saharan, Africa.

".... But there are elements in the Nahuatl versions that point to a very early source, rather than to relatively recent pre-conquest centuries. One is the fact that the Nauatl tales of creation of man follow a very Ancient Mesopotamian version that did not even find its way into the book of Genesis!

The Bible, in fact, has not but two versions of the creation of man; both draw on earlier Mesopotamian versions. But both ignore a third version and probably the oldest one, in which mankind was fashioned not out of clay but out of the blood of a God. In the Sumerian text on which this version is based, the God (Ea), collaborating with the Goddess, Ninti, 'prepared a purifying bath' – 'Let one God be bled into it', he ordered; from his flesh and blood, let Ninti mix the clay'. From this mixture men and women were created ...."

- The Lost Realms; Pg 35 (In Part), Zecharia Sitchin

Many researchers have identified the link between the Olmec and Ancient Chinese civilizations. Both the Olmecs and Xia and Shang Dynasties of the Sahara originated in the proto-Saharan, Tamana civilization. Some of the founding mothers and fathers of Xia and Shang China spoke the same Manding group of languages spoken by the Ancient Xi (Shi) – Olmecs. Another affinity between the Ancient Olmecs and Chinese, is the 'Bird' symbolism. Moverover, the fact that Xi, was the first civilization of China by name, may go back to the fact that the Manding or Xi people founded both the Xia civilization of China and the Xi (Olmec) civilization of Mexico and Mesoamerica.

The unity of these Ancient Kushite civilizations makes it clear why the legend of Memnon was not isolated in Africa and why the legends of Atlan – 'Atlantis' were so far reaching. As we know, Memnon was at Troy to help his relatives. This should not be a surprise, for in ancient times the relatives of Memnon – the Kushite – were established throughout the world; a world given vivid detail in 'Shades of Memnon', by the prolific Brother Gee.

All of these Ancient Kushite civilizations were interlinked and connected back to Tamare/ Tamana which spawned the civilizations of Khemet (Egypt) – Magan, Meluhha – Nubia, Abyssinia, Elam (Iran), Sumer (Iraq), Nabataea and Sheba, which was Yemen and Arabia, Petra (Northern Arabia), , Minoa (Crete), Greece, Kadmon (Canaan), Phoenicia, Assyria, China, Mexico, Colchis, West Africa – etc., etc. As is long proven, the Ancient Kushite and Puntites were great seafarers and travelled the 7 seas and continents before records began. Thus the Ancient ANU and Kushites are in fact indigenous to the entire planet and not just Africa, the mother continent alone. The fairytales of Atlantis made famous by Plato and others, is based on the reality of Atlan and the Xi (Shi) people of the Yucatan Peninsula and North and South America.

It is time for you modern Kushites of the diaspora to reclaim your 'stolen legacy', refute the racist lies and disinformation spread by the white world agenda and cease from associating your story with the history of slavery alone. It is time to become an 'Awaken One', to raise the consciousness level of the entire planet along with your own. You all must become the change that you wish to see in the world. Now is the time to empower the children with this liberating 'Outformation'. This is the true knowledge of self and kind and the entire planet in its correct and right perspective. The 'whole lies and half-truths' which were cast upon us 6000 years ago as the Spell of Sleep (of Ignorance) – spiritual and racial blindness have long began to wane in power. As the sun grows hotter in this Nu Solar Cycle, it is a symbol of the time of the 'Children of the sun' to re-engage in the spiritual sciences and technologies that made them gods and brought harmony and righteousness to the earth. Only in the rediscovery and re-engagement of our own superior culture can we truly 'Know Ourselves', as our ancestors said, turn ourselves inside out and revolute into 'Homo-Spiritus', manifesting the 'Philosopher's Stone' of the sacred Emerald Tablet. We must turn the 'lead of self' into the 'Gold of Self!!!' now.

Until you Kushites 'real-eyes' your own contribution to humanity and the civilization of this planet earth, then nobody else can acknowledge you for the Gods that you are (Genesis 6:1-7, Psalms 82:6, John 10:34). Give the Steppes people (Caucasians/Neanderthals) back their 'Isms and Schisms' of religion and left brain thinking and realign yourselves with the spirit of your ancestors. For us Kushites are the living riddle of the Sphinx and hold the key to unlocking all religions, all religious and spiritual truth. But you cannot know and unlock these universal truths until you research, transform and know thyselves. Only then will you pick up the Ankh 'Cosmic Key of Eternal Life' again.

The modern Kushite can have any contemporary religion or none at all. Because all of the spirituality incorporated into these various religions and cultures including Islam, traces back to us. Indeed, today, most of these religions don't have a shred of righteousness, correctness or spirituality loft. They have all become empty shells, remnants of a higher culture that was lost; out of touch with nature, and the true nature of the Universe(s). Since 1200 B.C's – Great War, we have lost ourselves.

The future of the Kushite – Nubian – Blackman is in jeopardy globally because our people are suffering from an Identity Crisis. Our youth are killing each other while engaging in profanities and celebrity culture – drugs, sex and rock and roll – the wise man is an endangered species, just as the prophecy suggested of the last days of the world (as you know it). Most people will overlook the words written within the scroll because the subject is not at all interesting to them. Most of them have long lost their minds in the chaos of entertainment and pleasure seeking of the world today – The Pursuit of Happiness.

Our families are still ignorant to their own culture of African spirituality of reverence to the creator and the many expressions of the mother/father source and are in the mental chains of unproven belief systems (religions) with no facts or working spiritual principles. Your ancestors are labelled as sun worshipping Pagans and you swallow that disrespect 'hook, line and sinker'. Have you ever given time to researching the validity of that racist and prejudice statement? Or have you stopped thinking for yourselves and allowed your Pastors and Imams and Guru's to do your critical thinking for you? There is nothing wrong with the word Pagan. All powerful God of All. Let's now go a little deeper into this.

"The more man meditates upon good thoughts, the better will be his world and the world at large"

- *Confucius*

Chapter Three (3): Endarkenment

Eye Am He. The One to help expose the White Light Illusion. The Light of Chaos; which is not the 'True Light', the True Light being the Supreme Blackness, The Omnipotent, The Blackprint, The Hidden (AMUN). Let me be a beacon for the True-Seeker of the Facts, a vessel for the Universe. In the Light of the Sun (RA), the light of truth, I endeavour to destroy The Matrix. Do not run away from yourselves fellow Kushites or you will be lost to yourselves forever. For wisdom 'Hikmah' is the only worthy mistress. The true seeker of the facts will follow her to the ends of the earth, wherever she may lead, to savour her presence, taste her mysteries and share her divine thoughts.

Never confuse the Supreme Blackness, the Black Light with 'Darkness or Shadow'. The sun rising triumphantly every morning can be seen as symbolic of the victory of light over shadow, life over death. For humans are all slaves, created in bondage to their vices and flaws, unaware of how heavy their chains are. But; they can free themselves and each other from these mental and spiritual chains, as long as they no longer look outward, without turning their attention inward into the shadow of self, to expel the shadow within The Self, as an Alkhemist . One must be ready to stare truth in the face.

At least once in a life time, every Kosmosan finds themselves at the crossroads of Endarkenment, shedding the ignorance of dogma, and unconfirmed beliefs for the embracing of Maat, The True Universal Religious Rites of our illustrious ancestors. For you dear reader, that time is now at hand and the decision is yours and yours alone. We neglect the wisdom of our ancestors and fill ourselves with useless anecdotes and fairytales of religion. All this does is rot the mind, distort the potential and bring humanity back to infantilism, such is the way of contemporary religion. Neglecting this sacred wisdom is the same as choosing the blind alley of ignorance, the Spell of Sleep (of spiritual and racial blindness), worshipping in idle, blind-faith, sterile knowledge. All this leads to the Spiritual Death of Maat, the Black People, Humanity itself.

The revelation of Sacred Truth must be accompanied by a commitment on the part of the Receiver to make a pact with preserving and protecting that which is best kept sacred. You must commit to doing your own research and study, in order to real-eyez the true power of 'Right Knowledge, Right Wisdom and Right Overstanding – Sound Right Reasoning'. Only then will the full potential of the mind, by way of mental liberation be achievable, breaking the mental chains of unconfirmed and biased beliefs. But do not commit yourselves lightly.

Don't believe me or anybody else. Check it out for yourselves, within your very own courtroom where you are the judge (The Mind). Don't let others, no matter what title they have or what letters they have behind their name, do your thinking for you. Think for yourselves and be critical and with every step you take, the path to Endarkenment will reveal itself unto you. For every journey one may take, is also a journey within.

You modern Kushites 'Blacks' are your ancestors' spiritual heirs. Both western Kushites and eastern (Puntite) Kushites. Only you can succeed in altering the world's course of destiny. You have already travelled a part of the journey, now you must choose to continue to the very end, the destination. But know that your existence will be entirely altered as a result and you will never perceive history, religion, science, spirituality – the world of physical persons, places, and things – in the same way again.

If you give in to the fear that the world programmes into you through the media, religion and society in general and you fail to choose, you will remain in limbo between two worlds and this will cause you great anguish and unfulfilment. The dissatisfaction and uncertainty, the feeling of this missed opportunity to stare the ultimate truth in the face, will haunt you for the rest of your time in this incarnation on earth. You will never be able to forget it soon, so do not run from yourselves.

There still exists one small chance in our corrupted unrighteous, modern – materialistic world, for the True Light to triumph over the shadow and it is you spiritually balanced individuals of all races, who embody this chance. You modern Kushites must once again be the pioneers and take the lead becoming the beacons of the Gods – Paut Neteru/Anunnaqi, the repositories of the ancient spiritual technology of consciousness (Alkhemists) you were born to be. Be the examples of the higher consciousness and wisdom, the unified expression of the Oneness of all things (ALLness). It is indeed an immense response-ability, a heavy job that you may refuse to shoulder. No one will blame you for refusing. It is a job only for those who work to perfect their being - The Alkhemists, or Salihiyn "Those Who Work to Perfect Their Being", in Arabic.

It is an obstacle far, far greater than anything you may have encountered before. For when we confront the forces of destruction (6 Ether), fear is the first hurdle we must rise above and conquer. Without succeeding in this, we remain unconscious and ignorant to our true and higher selves. We will be unable to develop the 'Astral Body'.

Unlike the missionary religions of today's world, Maat does not does not wish to dominate others by any means. It does not compel anybody against their own will unlike the self-righteous, missionary religions of today, such as Christianity and Islam which are prepared to use force if necessary. It has nothing in common with the materialistic ambitions of the current isms and schisms of the world we now inhabit. Maat's only mission is to restore and maintain the balance and natural order of the Universe(s) through a harmonious and reciprocal relationship with all of creation, animate and inanimate.

Know that the Wisdom of the ancients is not meaningless paganism as the (Mistranslated) books of the Bible and Koran falsely teach, and I stress the word mistranslated. The ancient Maatian Culture is NOT the dwelling of the devil (Satan) or the place of ignorance, but the celestial place which houses the Kosmic Key (the Ankh) to unlocking all truths; past, present and future. The Master's Key to unlocking all doors to 'Eternal Life'. Tamana/Tamare "Ancient Africa" (Alkebulan) founded the Spiritual temple of the whole world which has been the light of the world for the past 100,000 years. Indeed, the wisdom 'Hikmah' and knowledge 'Ilm' of our ancestors, Al Awwaliyna 'The First time Ones' (The Ancients) is from beyond this world, solar system and galaxy.

You must commit to reinstating and preserving this treasure, without which the world will continue its descent into the light of chaos and humanity will lose its head and regress into insignificance. Sometimes, one person is enough to change the future and a group of like-minded individuals can achieve what was seen as impossible, so do not underestimate yourselves. You can achieve more as a part of a Brotherhood/Sisterhood, than you can by yourselves. Humans are social creatures.

Your word must again become your bond. Sincerity (especially in regards to self) must once again rule hand in hand with honesty. Once you are true, to and with yourselves, you can begin to 'Live in Truth' like those who walked the earth millennia ago. In this way one can align and commune with the immortal souls of our ancestors once again. And this is not ancestor worship, but the spiritual science of ancient Kush, the High Culture of Endarkenment resurfacing.

Because of the materialism and injustice in the world today, tragic upheavals which are both political and spiritual are inevitable. Unless you Kushites of the diaspora (and others) lead a revival in the ancient 'Rites of Maat' and restore the natural equilibrium of the Mother Earth, which is out-of-sync with the rest of the surrounding solar system, the world will enter into a perilous apocalypse (WWII), Armageddon which it may not survive as you know it. The earth will always be here in one form or another, but the survival of humanity is not guaranteed. Only in turning yourselves inside out do you have a chance of transcending the reality of death – the great illusion. Because 'The Hour-Glass Is Empty', WWIII is coming on swift wings, to a city near you!

You humans on the planet earth (Tamtu/Tiamat) must cease from thinking that you are the only intelligent beings in the galaxy and wider universe(s). You must stop considering yourselves to be the sole concern of the God(s) in creation and dissolve the ego-self. Until this is achieved, you will not be able to perceive the ultimate reality and transcend this lowly realm of Naasuwt (The Physical World) of gross matter. Not until you realign with the 'One Mind' and 'The One Thing' or BA KULUWM "THE ALL", merging your own will and consciousness with the greater plan in the multi-verse, will the purpose of creation present itself to humanity individually and collectively. Know that time is fast running out and is against us. The sacred knowledge which enables humans to birth a second (spiritual) body and turn themselves inside out is encrypted within the Emerald Tablets of the Neter: Djehuti (Thoth), also known as Hermes, thrice great. The legacy is with the Al-Khemi (Khemetians) meaning 'The Blacks, The Black People' or Kushites - The pioneers of the (black) spiritual science of Khem-mistry (Chemistry), "The Sacred Mystery Science of Mind over Matter". May the Gods guide your feet.

Oh Deities of all the Deities

You all are the nature above nature,

You all are life above all life,

We are here each day and night

To pray that you will protect and

Guide us through all times.

In Ancient Egypt, our ancestors prayed and paid respect and homage to the forces of nature and all of its creatures. This is inclusive of the things you see, hear, taste, smell and feel. They were thankful for the gifts that had already been given to them. They showed their appreciation for the Ta – earth, the Ma – water and the Re – sun, as in the ancient name of Egypt, Tama-Re. Then our ancestors would be silent and let nature speak back to them. That is what real prayer was about; not always taking but giving back. And this is why we perform our Ashutat (prayer) like our ancestors, the ancient Egyptians and respect 'All's' creation and all creation. Not just grovelling on the floor asking, begging, pleading and talking. Religious prayer of today has been made into nothing more than 'What can I get from God', sessions.

When you look up the word prayer in the English language it means 'to quest, to plea'. What people do is beg God and tell God what they want and tell God about their problems. When they have no problems, most people do not pray. In Jewish, Christian and Muslim prayer everybody is asking for things and never showing any gratitude for the very sun that shines. For without it, in a matter of minutes, life as you know it would cease to exist on the planet. Through monotheistic religions, you have been taught to take and never give anything back.

Jews, Christians and Muslims are constantly talking to an unknown God who never answers because he doesn't exist. However, Jews, Christians and Muslims never think that this God just might say: *"I am not interested, because I don't like your nature"*. They don' think that God might say: *"You didn't give me anything extra, than what was passed down to you through the generations"*.

Oh deities, let me be of those who help you without question or doubt and live day and shadow hour period with you as their garment. Let me wear you in warmth and bathe myself in your beauty. Let the scent that comes from my body, be your sweet scent, so that when people see me they smell the splendour of your gardens.

MAXIM I

On humility and the quest for the perfect word

Don't be conceited about your own knowledge. Take advice from the ignorant as well as from the wise, since there is no single person who embodies perfection nor any craftsman who has reached the limits of excellence. The perfect word is as rare as an emerald yet it may be found among the maid servants working at the millstone. – The Sage Ptah-Hotep.

".... Listening is the basis of a child's upbringing. The ability to listen is a most important quality. The power of the word is stronger than the power of death. Whenever someone's

gaze alits on the names of the dead written in hieroglyphs, it brings them to life, shattering the obstacle of time.

Do not be content with what you hear but look deep into the secret depths of men's hearts. The life of a man is rarely in accordance with the law of Ma'at. Only a Godself can save man from his own baseness. Be silent and useful to others. Destiny strikes in a moment, as swiftly as an Eagle or Falcon that swoops down on its prey. The wife is the mistress of the house because only a lady can make a house into a true home, filling it with love, light and affection. Inner purity must be accompanied by impeccable physical cleanliness ...."

- Djedefre Memnon KKR 360°

The helping hand is at the end of your own arm

- Nob: Rev. Dr. Malachi Z York 720°

The Good Fight: Personal Legend

Do not confuse independence and freedom. You are only really free at the privileged moment when you no longer have a choice. And you no longer have this choice. By setting out on the path of truth, the only one which has heart and which puts our human condition in its rightful place, you have decided to participate in the only battle which is worth the effort, that of light –vs- shadow. It is not our choice but our responsibility, as Warriors of the Light (Lightworkers) - As humanity. I do not expect any less from the heirs of our ancestors. They never gave up against all odds.

The Ankh 'Kosmic Key of Eternal Life', gives us the key to gaining access to the secret of creative light and eternal life. You must 'Real-Eyes' what is at stake here follow Kushites, the importance of the 'Great Work' and the task ahead of us (all). It is a sacred quest we must all take by the route that leads within our sole pre-occupation must be the welfare of others, of humanity as a whole.

According to the Ancient Kushites, when a man and woman live under the same roof, they are married. These words should not be taken lightly. Beyond the union of the bodies and the celebration of desire, an eternal, unchangeable bond must be created. This love will make both beings invincible. 'The difference between the men who make it and the men that don't make it, is their women'. Every day the Universe(s) present the miracle of creation, in a myriad of different expressions. Not least in the union of man and woman, male and female. So savour the miracle, which has the power to make you forget everything that is not born of the sacred and divine love, of the oneness of all things. These intense moments of happiness and pleasure, are most expressive of the infinite now. Let your spouse(s) be your best friend(s). Friendship is the best foundation for love.

Every truth seeker should compose a veritable library of books and educational media (DVDs, pdf's, eBooks, etc.). For these will be not objects, but rather watchful guardians, with the mission of protecting the sacred wisdom of the ancient spirituality now set to resurface among humanity. Be wary of the magic power of the sacred wisdom and spirituality of the Great Gods. He/she who violates it will be a being hated by the light and cannot receive water upon the Alter of Asaru (Osiris). They will die of thirst in the other world and cannot pass on their wealth to their children.

You must remember that certain knowledge is sacred and not for second rate people. Even though you may have the urge to shout out the truth from the roof tops to any and all, some people will despise you for destroying their equilibrium and sense of certainty. The diffusing of the vital truth and ultimate reality must be done in sequence, to the right people and with caution. In a world of backwardness, the truth can often seem stranger than fiction and many people who are aware of its explosive power have spent money, time and effort to keep it repressed from the masses. These servants of the Serpent know that it has the power to destroy the false institutions of religion and unconfirmed beliefs, science, racism and re-write the entire history of the planet earth - indeed, many archaeologists, etc., have concealed their finds due to this, especially those finds concerning the Ancient Kushites, Egypt and the Pharaohs. They fear the rude-awakening of humanity to the spiritual truths too long forgotten.

By committing to the great work and legacy of the ancient spirituality, you will inevitably come into conflict with many enemies, both visible and invisible. You must keep your intentions pure and your thoughts positive and not give into fear. By revering the Gods (Neteru/Anunnaqi) – the Elohim of the Bible and wearing talismans and amulets, you will place yourself under their protection. And their protection will sufficeth for us. Being without the protection of Paut Neteru, is like being on a modern battlefield without armour or weaponry - nothing less than suicide. Don't lose sight of the essential goal - spiritual liberation and upliftment for the planet as a whole – Utopia.

The mind – control programmes that you call religion do not wish for the liberating truth about the divinity and spiritual nature of humans to see the light of day. Control of the earth and its resources will slip away from them with the revelation of the divine reality. Their power structure would disappear in an instant. The meek and spiritually natured would then, rightfully, inherit the earth bringing on a spiritual Utopia; a new golden age similar to days long gone. First you must fight 'The Good Fight'.

But most people have been ruined by materialism and vanity, the celebrity culture that has become the new religion of these modern times. They say that money is the route of all evil. But is also the cause of all suffering today in the evil hands of these unnecessary institutions. Everything is about money, Power and the need to possess. The accumulation of wealth, the possession of things, luxuries, even people – The true cause of death being desire, which we torture ourselves with, when we already have everything that we may ever 'need' to prosper. You must Real-eyez that 'want' and 'need' have become confused they are not the same thing. The lines have been blurred; you must distinguish between the two.

So, what is the true purpose of creation, humanity and love? Why are we here? Where are we headed collectively? Do you ever ask yourself these questions? Do you really want to discover the answer? Because I do, so let us stick to the facts, and I guarantee you that it won't be easy for most. Only for those who work to perfect themselves, those who refuse to be unconscious slaves and 'Silent Devils'. Are you dear reader one of the 'Awaken Ones', the Enlightened/Endarkened?

For the past 6,000 years, the world has fallen deeper and deeper under the spell; The 'Spell of Sleep', Ignorance, Leviathan, Kingu, Amaam, Apepi – a spell of spiritual and racial blindness - a mental and spiritual amnesia which was cast by the 'Evil Ones' upon the original inhabitants and order of the earth. Unfortunately, most, if not all of us, are still under the spell, in one way or another and as far fetched as it might sound, it is realer than the breaths you take to stay physically alive.

These books have been written to assist those who wish to stop being mentally lazy. Those who wish to take back their thoughts and stop them being manipulated by others, such as the Media, Education Institutions and contemporary religions which do not have a shred of spirituality left. The same spirituality they stole from the ancient ancestors, while accusing the ancestors of being superstitious pagans and idol worshippers. It is high time for the

Kushites to reclaim their stolen legacy and reintroduce it to the world. We now need Ma'at more than ever. Not for ours but for the glory of the Gods – Paut Neteru. In order to real-eyez this we first need to re-identify its universal principles. Then we can demolish these fabricated religions, philosophies and song sheet science. So let us examine this Kushite spiritual science in more depth and detail. Let us have a closer look at what made us men of renown.

Ancient Spirito-Science:

The spiritual sciences of the ancients were well developed and advanced by the time of the pharaonic founding of Ancient Khem/Kham and Sumer. These spiritual sciences and philosophies were given by the Neteru (Anunnaqi) to the first race of men, the ANU people and they gave the legacy to the homo sapien Kushites better known as Nubians (New Beings). Both the ANU people and the Kushites transported these spiritual sciences around the planet as they migrated into different areas when the Sahara region (Tamana/Tamare) began to dry up into desertification (between 7500 – 3800 B.C.E).

As said, the first region to be concentrated was the Nile Valley, Meroitic Sudan, especially and from there, they migrated from Nubia into southern (Upper) Egypt and northern (Lower) Egypt into the Nile Delta. Egyptologists speculate that the resettling and reunifying of Khemet (Egypt) happened c.3100 B.C. We the Black People know that the movement of Kushite/Nubians from Meroitic Sudan, which already had kingship established within different groups, happened more like c.4125 B.C, at the very latest. Under the proto-Dynastic Kings, a group which includes the very first dynastic Suten: Menes (Narmer), the Khemetians/Egyptians only continued the Meroitic/Ethiopian/Sudanese institution of kingship and royalty. It was began in Kush and perfected in Khemet. And by that, we mean that 'the culture was spread north, perfected and sent back south'. These are cultural facts regardless of what history and religion try to assume. Archaeology will back these words. The ruler was known as Aafeerti – 'Ruler' and/or Shekem Ur Shekem – 'Great Power of Power', as in life force power. The word Suten was also used for them, and is the origin of the Persio-Arabic term Sultan. Female rulers were known as Ura – 'Female Ruler'. The word Pharaoh itself means 'Great House', and was used to describe not just the Suten, but the entire royal house.

The Meroitic (Sudanese, Ethiopian) civilization was the first nation on earth to recognize the divinity in humanity and creation in general. These Kushites were also the first nation to venerate and revere the Neteru, Anunnaqi as 'Gods' or 'Messengers, Expressions' of the One Mind which is the Source, Mother – Father creative force of will referred to as Hu, Huhi, Huwa, Hiya. This Hu – 'The Creative Force of Will' (One Mind), the Universal Intellect works within the Nun, which can be viewed as the 'One Thing', the Invisible and first Matter, to mould and manifest creation into the physical Universe(s).

It is the legacy of our Kushite ancestors that gave the Jewish religion today the adapted term for God – 'Ya-Huwa' – 'Yahuwa', which was rendered Yahweh and then mistranslated into Jehovah by the Greeks. In Islam the 'Hu' was suffixed onto Allah, as in 'Allah-hu-Akbar – 'Allah is the Greatest'. In both cases this can be translated as 'Great Divine' – 'I Am That I Am' or 'The Source'. Indeed, the Abrahamic faiths or big 3, monotheistic religions of Judaism, Christianity and Islam owe a great debt to the pioneering Kushite sons and daughters of Ancient Tama-Re, re-read John 10:34 and Psalms 82:6.

Every Kushite man and woman was seen as divine, as a God even. We were/are all sons and daughters of the Most High, AMUN-RE/ANU - children of the Neteru – Anunnaqi without exception. This rendered Kushites divine, spiritual beings having a temporary physical existence and experience in order for the spiritual growth of the Greater Unified Whole, the Universe(s). We are all, children of BA KULUWM "THE ALL". This view permeated the entire Kushite nation of the Nile Valley in every corner of the planet Tamtu/Tiamat – 'Maiden of Life', and was responsible for the great civilizations that sprang up out of our remarkable culture. For the history of history is culture.

The Five Great Kushite Nations:

The five (5) Great Kushite Nations or Groups from Tama-Ra (Tamana), the Sahara region of Africa, who propagated and stuck to the ancient teachings the most, the spiritual sciences were: The Khemetians (Egyptians), Hal-tam-tians (Elamites) – Ancient Iranians, Xiu (Ancient Chinese and Olmecs, etc.), ancient Canaanites (Kadmonites) and the Meluhans.

The Khamites (Khemetians) were responsible for the great civilization of so called Egypt (Khami, Khemet-Ta). The Haltamtians spawned the great civilizations of Elam and Sumer in the region of today's Iraq/Iran, the Xiu founded the great civilization of China and Mesoamerica (the Yucatan), the Kadmonites populated the area of Kadmon (ancient Canaan) before the birth of Canaan, Libana – son of Kham/Ham, son of Utnapishtim – the leper, albino born in 4004 B.C.E and of course, the Meluhans are the originators in Meroitic/Sudanese – Nubia (Kush) which is Ethiopia proper, a civilization that both predates and outlasted pharaonic Egypt. From Shekem Ur Shekem – Menes/Narmer, Egypt (The Pharaonic State) lasted 4000 years, while Kush (Meluhha) lasted 5000 years, facts which the scholars constantly try to refute. These scholars are more in De-Nile (Denial) than the Pharaohs themselves.

The spiritual sciences of the Kushites/Ptahites were or are spiritual technologies of consciousness, upliftment, natural resource manipulation and social ordering. These included oracle systems, spirit possession/trance, natural healing, meditative techniques, Kula Yoga, the manipulation of earthly and human energies (pyramids, acupuncture) and the coercion of the laws of nature through heightened spirituality combined with the higher mysteries of esoteric (hidden) knowledge (magic). The Kushites and ANU shared in a civilization complex/network that recent anthropology proves stretches back 100,000 years, originating near the Mountains of the Moon (Mount Meru). It was during this 100,000 year period that the spiritual sciences were developed.

One of the main spiritual sciences was the knowledge and manipulation of the life force within humans and also within the earth. The life-force in humans were known as Shekem, Kundalini, Rau, Chi, etc. This life force ether rises through the chakra system and meridian points of the human body and globe. Martial artists and Guru's today will tell you this knowledge can perform miracles, because it can certainly do so. This knowledge can be called Hudu, which was the forerunner of Tai-chi (Chi Kung). It can be used for relaxation, meditation and self-defence.

The spiritual science of self-defence was known as Pan-Kau-Rau-Shen, which would translate as – 'Defeating the Enemies with the Force of Ra'. This is an Ancient Kushite Montu (not Martial) art form. Montu is the Kushite Neter of War, whereas Martial is a Greek God of War. So I'd rather refer to the Kushite spiritual science as a Montuart form. A form of it survives today in modern day Greece referred to as Pankration and also generally in South Eastern Asian self defence systems such as Muai-Thai - Thai boxing in Thailand. Examples can be sited in the Elephant Warriors depicted in the Tony Jaa blockbusters of Ong Bak, The Warrior King and The Warrior King 2. It's interesting that the main character, Tony Jaa is named 'Kham' – 'Black' and his little elephant is named Khons, which is the name of the son of Amun and Mut and is also a name used in connection with Nubian, Meroitic (Sudan) or Kush.

Other aspects of this ancient and miraculous spiritual science included the Oracle, which was developed to provide insight into the inner workings of any given situation, decision or occurrence. True Oracles are never fortune telling devices but rather provide a means of examining the underlying spiritual structure of a situation, similar to modern computer programmes that analyse stock market trends. Card games, dice and other games of chance of today are based upon Oracles developed by Anu and Kushite people thousands of years ago. The Chinese I-Ching – 'Book of Changes' and its system is also based upon this principle. The most famous oracles in history were situated in Waset (Thebes – Egypt), Siwa (the Libyan Desert), Delphi and Dodona in Greece and the oracles of Ancient Babylon (Sumer). Crystals and other stones which pulsated were used within the oracle method.

Another spiritual science was that of the Shepsu – 'Honoured Ancestors'. This is the science of Ancestor Communication, misunderstood by modern European Monotheism as Ancestor Worship. A person who became exalted or deemed 'True of Voice' in life would be found worthy of special communication efforts by the living after their death. This sacred Kushite science was given a bad name by the Bible in the story of King Saul and Prophet Samuel. When King Saul conjured up communication with the dead prophet, he was swiftly condemned by Samuel who was angry about it. According to the myth made Bible and Monotheism, this ability is evil and forbidden. This was done to tarnish the legacy of Black Africa and label all of our traditions as heathen, pagan, sun and idol worshippers; to discredit our beloved ancestors and make us to appear as primitive people with unsound minds and no spiritual worth. But all of the evidence is irrefutable and suggests otherwise.

The Kushites were not Polytheists but actually monotheists and so is Kushite (African) spirituality in general. The group of deities called Paut Neteru were never worshipped in the modern day sense but were revered as conscious forces or principalities of nature, aspects of BA KULUWM 'THE ALL', which manifested with the creator AMUN/ANU, assigned to run the universe(s) and keep order and harmony. Statues and images were/are used as reminders of this reality, as well as focal points for meditation to control Neter forces inside creation and human beings. Today this is misunderstood as 'Idol Worship' by the simple, self-righteous minds of contemporary religions, such as Judaism, Christianity and Islam, but who are they to judge us and our ancestors when they themselves are 'Idle Worshippers'? For they do not even know who or what they are worshipping. Therefore their blind faith has them all worshipping in 'Idle'. The devil makes work for idle hands. The fact remains that the Abrahamic faiths unconsciously acknowledge the Great Black God Amun – 'The Hidden', at the closing of all of their prayers and supplications – Jews say – Amon, Christians say – Amen and Muslims say – Ameen, Amin.

All glorifying Amun – 'The Hidden', the Meroitic Black Creator and manifestor of the Atom (Atum) - The King of the Gods (Neteru). Read Psalms 82:1 and know where these monotheists stole another Kushite thought. It is all your glorious legacy. It is time for you brainwashed blacks to reclaim it. With all of the sacred spiritual sciences comes the recognition of Uachet and Nekhebet – The hot and cool electromagnetic force of the sun reacting upon the magnetic field of the earth. It is responsible for many psychic phenomena. Within the Uraeus, Uachet and Nekhebet were harnessed for psychic attack or protection, represented by the rearing snake (and vulture, in the case of Suten Tutankhatun) worn on the brows of Kushite/Khemetic deities and royalty. The Ancient Khamit texts describe the power of the Uraeus as laser-like and instantly fatal. While most Khamite rulers wore the rearing cobra on itself, the Shekem Ur Shekem – Tutankhatun (Tutankhamun) wore his Uraeus with both rearing cobra and the vulture, signifying the 'Feathered Serpent', symbolism of the suns 11.5 year radiation cycle and its 96 micro-cycles which we shall get into later.

Ra, pronounced 'Ray', is the deity that represented the 'Great Power' behind all creative life, the creative life force emanating from Amun, accompanied by Ptah, Huhi, Hika and Sia. Ra is misrepresented as the 'Sun God' because the Khemetians depicted the Sun with a black dot in the middle (•) as Ra's symbol, or the Atun (Aten). Through their spiritual sciences, the Khamites discovered that all life is sustained by interaction with the radioactive, electromagnetic energy of the sun, which is a modern day science-fact, not fiction. Along with the Neteru – 'Guardians or Watchers', the sun was revered and not worshipped in the modern, religious sense. Therefore the ancestors were not 'Sun Worshippers', neither had 'Idol Worshippers based on the facts that you have just read. The so called Atenism of Shekem Ur Shekem (Pharaoh) Ankhenatun or Akhenaten – 'Life of the Aten' was not sun worshipping either. It was a reverence of the sun as the 'Father of Fertility' and an attempt to re-establish the Old Kingdom monotheistic aspect, as the New Kingdom had fallen into Pantheism and Polytheism, largely because certain principles were lost and corrupted through time and invasion. The Alchemical Operation and sacred science of the sun was lost, overlooked and had to be passed down. Ankhenatun and Tutankhamun inherited the responsibility to pass this vital information on.

Lastly, Kula Yoga was the spiritual science which can be seen as a third great use for sex, which is called Tantra or Tantric Sex. It is the use of yoga and meditation techniques during intercourse that combine male and female Rau/Chi for use in healing, creativity, psychic phenomena, spiritual cultivation and/or magic. Today Kula Yoga is practiced primarily in African and Asian cultures, such as Ethiopia, South India and Tibet. It is the skill and ability of harnessing and storing Rau in each other, for use in other endeavours outside of sexual creation.

All of this sacred knowledge of spiritual science made us a formidable nation of people in the four corners of the planet earth. It enabled us to form spiritually rich civilizations that ran uninterrupted for many thousands of years. This is the stolen legacy of Black peoples, which all others have borrowed from in some way or another, without giving due credit to our ancestors, the pioneers that they were and their (our) priceless contribution to world civilization and technology. Here, I have only touched the tip of the iceberg. It would be impossible to put all of the greatness of our people, from then until now, between the two covers of a book, but I have tried to make this writing as comprehensive as possible, without it becoming unreadable, without losing the spirit of the message.

I'm sure that most of you open-minded readers can appreciate why such an effort had to be made to cut you off from your own glorious legacy and culture. Without this, you could never have been enslaved, neither physically or mentally. Your kind, caring nature was used against you to infiltrate, study and breakdown your social institutions and spiritual civilizations. This was done by the Sons of the Shadows, the Servants of the Serpents (Reptilian Beings), who were both black and white devils. This wasn't done overnight, but over a 4,000 year time period. Before and during this remote period, we Kushites created the greatest achievements known to humanity, seeding in the planet with our esoteric knowledge and puzzling mankind (Europeans) with spiritual sciences that have yet to be fully understood.

The ancient trading regions of Tamana, trading cities and countries located in what is now referred to as the Sahara Desert, were linked by race, languages, spirituality and technology. The fantastic engineering feats accomplished attest to the level of ingenuity and ability of our so called spiritual ascendants. Megaliths and monuments left as evidence around Africa and the wider world bare witness to the Blackman's contribution to the progress made by generations of humans under the banner of civilization. When the Sahara (which is larger in land mass than the United States) dried up, the people of Tamana migrated and established the greatest civilizations that the world has ever seen, up to this day.

If the God of monotheism is as 'All Powerful' as monotheists claim, then how is it that Allah or Yahweh or Jehovah or whatever name you want to call him, cannot replicate or better the great civilizations of the so called polytheists, sun-worshipping, idol-worshipping heathens? Neither Judaism – Israel, Christianity – Greece and Rome, or Islam – Arabia (since Islamic times 632 A.D.) can come anywhere close to Egypt, Sumer, Elam, Xia and Shang China, Nabataea, Phoenicia, the Xi Nation of Atlan, etc. None of today's self-righteous religious groups have added anything new to what the civilizations of the ancients already established under AMUN-RA (ANU AL'YUN AL'YUN, AL). No major breakthroughs have come under the banner of Judaism, Christianity or Islam, don't let Europeans/Arabs fool you. Only war, racism, bloodlust, secularism, and materialism.

They all stole ideas from Ancient Kush, after invading and inheriting its civilizations coming out of the caves of the Caucasian Steppes as 'Cavemen', contributing next to nothing to what was already established. All that they brought was destruction by way of materialism, deceit and greed. In this way they destroyed all that was good. These barbarian cavemen from Caucasia inherited China, Russia, India, Arabia, Elam, Sumeria, Canaan, Minoa, Greece, Rome, Sicily, Mesoamerica and eventually Egypt and Ethiopia. Anyway, let us get back to the spirituality being discussed.

The Universal Principles

The code of spirituality along with the spiritual sciences just discussed, the ethnics that our Kushite ancestors propagated to the world inspired awe among the Greeks, who referred to them as 'blameless Ethiopians' and called them 'the most favoured of the Gods'. Here is the pattern of behaviour, a list compiled from the ancient tradition of the Kushite ancestors of times long gone which we recorded among ourselves and what witnesses such as the Greeks recorded within their classical writings:

1. Covet no land or riches that the Supreme Being does not naturally grant you.
2. Respect the opposite sex as your equal and your compliment.
3. Give unto the world what you would have the world give unto you.
4. Always seek balance in all things, for only in harmony can there be growth.
5. Honour your ancestors, especially those who sought justice and balance in their time upon the earth.
6. Seek not simply to do good, but encourage others to do good as well.
7. Always seek higher wisdom in all of life's endeavours.
8. Honour and safeguard the children, who have come to forge the future of the world.

9. Seek to be a part of a brotherhood, sisterhood or group, for we accomplish more together than apart.

10. Have no tolerance for evil and injustice, so that you will forever be known as blameless.

Now ask yourselves whether that sounds like the principles of unsound minds who are lost worshipping idols and the sun, or the writings of a people who have the deepest spirituality and respect for all life. The history of the Caucasian and the biased views of contemporary religion kept this legacy from you for obvious reasons. The racist views propagated by White people – Tamahu, from the 15th century through to the modern now, were designed to lock you into the 'Slave Mentality', making you think automatically that the only history we have is the history of modern slavery. Hollywood is just as guilty, as another tool of the education institutions. They switch your black identity of characters such as, Yashu'a in the 'Passion of Christ' – by Mel Gibson, Exodus' Moses played by Christian Bale, Noah starring Russell Crowe and Gods of Egypt with Gerard Butler as Horus to mis-educate the masses and perpetuate the blatant lies and racism. The Discovery Channel and National Geographic and the likes also do the exact same thing deliberately. They cannot afford to caste you in your true divine light as Gods.

The 42 Negative Confessions of the Neteru of the Tribunal:

1. I have not committed sin.
2. I have not committed robbery with violence.
3. I have not stolen.
4. I have not slain men or women.
5. I have not stolen food.
6. I have not swindled offerings.
7. I have not stolen from God/Goddess.
8. I have not told lies.
9. I have not carried away food.
10. I have not cursed.
11. I have not closed my ears to truth.
12. I have not committed adultery.

13. I have not made anyone cry.
14. I have not felt sorrow without reason.
15. I have not assaulted anyone.
16. I am not deceitful.
17. I have not stolen anyone's land.
18. I have not been an eavesdropper.
19. I have not falsely accused anyone.
20. I have not been angry without reason.
21. I have not seduced anyone's wife.
22. I have not polluted myself.
23. I have not terrorized anyone.
24. I have not disobeyed the Law.
25. I have not been exclusively angry.
26. I have not cursed God/Goddess.
27. I have not behaved with violence.
28. I have not caused disruption of peace.
29. I have not acted hastily or without thought
30. I have not overstepped my boundaries of concern.
31. I have not exaggerated my words when speaking.
32. I have not worked evil.
33. I have not used evil thoughts, words or deeds.
34. I have not polluted the water.
35. I have not spoken angrily or arrogantly.
36. I have not have not cursed anyone in thought, word or deed.
37. I have not placed myself on a pedestal.
38. I have not stolen what belongs to God/Goddess.

39. I have not stolen from or disrespected the deceased.

40. I have not taken food from a child

41. I have not acted with insolence.

42. I have not destroyed property belonging to God/Goddess.

The precept of an 'Afterlife' has always been fundamental to Kushite, African thought and the 42 confessions embody this idea; Upon standing before the Neteru of the Tribunal, overseen by Pa Neter Asaru (Osiris) who sat on the square, acting as Judge, one had/has to confess these negative confessions to him and the jury of 12 Neters. If you were found worthy and 'True of Voice' you would be admitted into the realm of the Gods, as a 'Light (Etheric) Being', to dwell in their humble abode. If you were found guilty, then your soul would/will be devoured by the 'Soul Devourer' called Ammit, a monster consisting of the various parts of different creatures.

Upon your appearance before Paut Neteru of the Tribunal, your heart is weighed upon the 'Scales of Justice' and the whole trial is recorded by Pa Neter (Tehuti) Thoth, God of Writing, Time, Measurement, Communication, and Wisdom. Your heart is weighed against the feather of an ostrich, which is also the feather of Ma'at, symbolic of all things good; Truth, order, justice, balance, harmony, reciprocity, etc. If your heart weighs heavier than the plume of the ostrich, then you are judged guilty of a sinful life and justly condemned. If your heart weighs lighter than the ostrich plume, then you are found 'True of Voice' and deemed worthy to dwell in the abode and company of the Gods.

The Netert – 'Goddess', Ma'at wears the ostrich plume upon her head. It is said in Khamit tradition that mother Ma'at is the one who brought order from out of chaos at the beginning of our physical universe(s). The Goddess Ma'at is one of the wives of the great God of Learning called Tehuti (Thoth), who the Greeks identified with their own God, Hermes. The 'Rites of Ma'at' is not a religion in the modern day sense of the word. It is a chosen way of life which is not institutionalized in the same way as contemporary religions. At the end of each life, the person had/has to confess and account for the type of life they chose to live upon the planet.

The Rites of Ma'at was affectionately referred to as 'The Rule'. This ancient and original way of spirituality deals with the relationship that we have for all things in creation – animate and inanimate, and seeks to establish balance in all things and a fond respect for all of creation from rocks, to trees, food, animals, Neteru, one another, men and women, work ethic and leisure, nations, etc. The Rites of Ma'at established the natural order of creation, giving everything its deserved place and importance. This peaceful way of life is many thousands of years older than any Islam – 'Way of Peace' or any other religion for that matter including Hinduism.

All religions today worthy of the name have borrowed from the principles of Maat, which are universal in scope. The justice system of the world today uses the 'Scales of Justice' as their emblem to promote the secular laws of man. Again, they take all of their concepts from our ancient Kushite precepts.

Kushite civilizations were 'Theocracies' rather than 'Democracies' because the role of the Gods, their given laws and spirituality was superimposed over all else with no exception or favouritism. Our societies were never secular and materialistic like the societies of the world we live in today with all the malevolence today's societies produce. With the 'divine right to rule' – our Rites, rituals and ceremonies never failed us. Rather than being backward, the things are what made us glorious and great and run prosperous Kingdoms, beacons of light shining even through a world of growing darkness; a miracle of planning, a magnificent achievement, unmatched by any.

Metaphysical: adjective 1. Relating to metaphysics, 2. Beyond physical matter: the metaphysical battle between Good and Evil. 3. Referring to a group of 17th century English poets (in particular John Donne, George Herbert, Andrew Marvell and Henry Vaughan) – known for their complex imagery.

Metaphysics: plural noun (usu. Treated as sing) 1. Philosophy concerned with abstract ideas such as the nature of existence or of truth and knowledge, 2. Abstract theory with no basis in reality.

Origin from Greek 'ta Meta ta phusika' – 'the things after the physics', referring to the sequence of Aristotle's works.

Hierophant: hy-roh-fant/noun – a person, especially a priest who interprets sacred mysteries or other things that are very difficult to understand.

Origin from Greek 'hieros' – 'sacred' + 'phainein' – 'show'.

Esoteric – e-suh-te-rik/ adjective - intended for or understood by only a small number of people who have specialized knowledge of something.

Origin Greek 'Esoterikos'.

Alchemy – al-kuh-mi/ noun – 1. The medieval forerunner of chemistry, concerned particularly with attempts to convert common metals into gold, 2. A seemingly magical or mysterious process:

Derivatives alchemical adjective – alchemist noun.

Origin from Greek Khemia, Khemeia – 'art of transmuting metals'.

The metaphysical and esoteric aspects of Ancient Kushite, especially Khemetian (Egyptian), spirituality attracted the admiration of many people from diverse nations. The Greeks borrowed their philosophy from our Ancient Kushite ancestors which was later adapted into religious theologies, such as Judaism and Christianity which later spawned Islamic theology. As a matter of fact, all religions and philosophies borrowed ideas, philosophies and rituals from Ancient African spirituality; Hinduism, Buddhism, Taoism, Shamanism, etc.

Being taught by the Neteru/Anunnaqi (Elohim) themselves, Kushites were given a complete overstanding of the Kosmos and the universal principles that kept harmony and divine order. Various patron deities taught the new humanity how to manipulate and regulate the invisible energy for the betterment of the earth and all creation. We were taught how to visualize this energy and hear it using ESP, 'Extrasensory Perception'. Sacred texts were given to man which enabled us to master this 'alchemical Knowledge' and the sages became the alchemists whose writings influenced the writings of many others and shaped the spirito-scientific foundation of our great civilizations and kingdoms. One of the most enigmatic texts – 'The Emerald Tablet', was authored by Pa Neter Tehuti towards these ends. This God of science and learning has been immortalized under the Greek name of Hermes and his writings became known as the Hermeticus.

The first hierophants to absorb this sacred information are remembered as the Ahkus – 'Transfigured Ones, Light Beings', also called Shemsu Haru – 'Followers of Horus', the God (Neter) who reigned after Tehuti (Thoth) in the time of the Neteru, when they themselves ruled upon the earth.

For a description of the contents of the Emerald Tablets, I will turn to Dennis William Hauck, the author of 'The Emerald Tablet: alchemy for Personal Transformation'. His book is one of the best writings of the Emerald Tablet that I have come across to date in my research on its formula.

"…. In recent years, fictional accounts about the rediscovery of ancient spiritual insights have become overnight bestsellers. These stories strike a chord in people weary of a commercialized world in which endless materialistic striving seems to be the highest aspiration. As we approach the new millennium, many of us are fed up, eager to move toward a more spiritual culture on earth, but what if there really were an ancient science of soul designed for achieving spiritual perfection in very specific and comprehensible steps and whose only goal was to accelerate the evolution of mankind's spiritual nature?

Not only does such a science exist, it is based on a single document whose origin is lost in legends that go back over 10,000 years, called The Emerald Tablet because it was moulded out of a single piece of emerald or green crystal, it carries a powerful message full of hidden meaning and prophetic depth. According to some reports, the wondrous tablet was translated by Alexandrian Scholars and actually put on display in Egypt around 330 B.C.E. one of the most mysterious documents ever put before the eyes of man. The Emerald Tablet has been described as everything from a succinct summary of neoplatonic philosophy to an extra-terrestrial artefact or gift from Atlantis. The text is written in extremely generic terms and is the unaccredited inspiration for many of our spiritual and religious traditions. Its most obvious legacy is at least seventeen centuries of alchemy, a period in which some of the most creative minds in the world delved into the intertwined mysteries of matter, energy, soul and spirit …."

- Dennis William Hauck

The story of the Emerald Tablet and Alchemy (Al-Khem-I) led back across the burning sands of the Sahara Desert to Tamare/Tamana, especially to Khemet – 'The Black Land' (Egypt). Now that the Kosmos has entered into the new Age of Aquarius, the hidden reality is again being revealed to the inhabitants of the planet on many different platforms. Books of learning are being re-written in many different fields in acknowledgement of what the ancients already knew to be ultimate truth. Intelligent people all around the globe are now bearing witness to the legacy and the transitional period the earth is inevitably going through. This spiritual side of reality can no longer be ignored by the modern world psychologically or physiologically or spiritually.

".... What is the Emerald Tablet really? In simplest terms, it is a scientific document that actually works with something we perceive as metaphysical in nature, thus presenting a spiritual technology for the human race. It shows mankind how to consciously work together with the forces of evolution and gives individuals the opportunity to transform themselves outside the inherently imperfect and artificial structures of schools, church and government. The Emerald Tablet offers each one of us the chance not only to directly participate in the quantum leap in consciousness that can safely lead us into the third millennium, but also to do so as real people true to ourselves and in accord with the Soul of the Universe ...."

The many layers within the enigmatic Emerald Tablet regarding its meaning and interpretation make it near impossible for the uninitiated and closed minded to comprehend. Rather than the transmutation of lead into gold, the main focus of the text is the transmutation of the physical (lead) body of individuals, into the spiritual (gold) of the second multi-dimensional body. This is what Pa Neter Tehuti (Thoth, Hermes) intended to transmit to humanity; To enable us to initiate into 'Light Beings', once again revoluting our consciousness and upgrading into homo-spiritus, which is the next step for humanity and the planet earth.

Over the last two millennia, Europeans – many theologians and philosophers have noted that the Tablet contains the sum of all knowledge. The few who truly perceive its revelation are forever transformed by its truth. This Emerald Tablet is a part of a family of writings which we Kushites referred to as 'The Sacred Wisdom of Tehuti', teacher of humanity by way of the quill. The living wisdom of the Neteru will find those who are worthy and would help the world to benefit from its formula. Of this you can be sure of, especially during those transitional times humanity is going through. The secrets of creation are revealed only to the initiated and true seekers of the facts, the ultimate reality; those who are able to see behind the illusion of contemporary religion. This can only be done through a commitment to study and research things yourself, using your own God given faculties, rather than the indoctrinations of religious institutions and biased opinions. Indeed, 'many are called, but few are chosen' and the work of the Gods knows no rest.

You are all capable of realizing truth and reality for yourselves, without the need of fabricated contemporary religions and their unconfirmed beliefs and dogma. The legacy of our Ancient Kushite and Anu ancestors was to live a spiritual existence whilst having a temporary physical experience we refer to as life. The ultimate purpose of this physical reality was growth and transcendence into a higher dimension of the spiritual plan. The challenges of this physical material plane was a catalyst towards this ambition and thus in coining the famous phrase, 'Know Thyself', the real underlying true self without the mask of the ego-self, they never forgot who they (we) were - Children of the Neteru (Gods), Etheric Beings.

The seven stages of alchemical transfiguration of the Being are activated by way of the seven major chakras and the nine spheres (seals) of Mother Earth. In the Nuwaupic (Medew Neter), these Chakras or Lotus Seats are referred to as Pa Sabed Arushaat – 'The Seven Seats'.

1. Jathur A'rush – Root Seat
2. Suru A'rush – Naval Seat
3. Sadrun A'rush – Solar Plexus Seat
4. Galb A'rush – Heart Seat
5. Hanjur A'rush – Throat Seat
6. Hajub A'rush – Brow Seat
7. Taj A'rush – Crown Seat

The seven degrees/stages of Alchemical transformation are thus:

1. Calcination
2. Dissolution
3. Separation
4. Conjunction
5. Putrefaction/Fermentation
6. Distillation
7. Coagulation

This Emerald Formula is elaborated on in Dennis William Hauck's brilliant book which is a must read for all true seekers of 'Enlightenment', so I will not go into the details here, but I will say that the transformation is done through the A'rushaat 'Seats', the 7 major chakra points within your being. Again both the 7 chakras and the 7 steps of spiritual transformation are linked to the 7 planes, the 7 sub-planes and the 9 spheres of the earth.

1. Gumash Yasway – Material Plane
2. Yasway Shil Shaduy – Plane of Force
3. Nafusal Yasway – Spiritual Plane
4. A'glu Yasway – Mental Plane
5. Hadus Hagug – Divine Truth
6. Hadus Haguget – Divine Reality
7. Yakhud Kar Pa Amun Re/Anu – Union with Amun/Anu

1. Sulb – Solid
2. Sa-El – Liquid
3. Ghaz – Gas
4. Kahrub Ather – Electric Ether
5. Hayuh Ather – Life Ether
6. Nawur Ather – Light Ether
7. A'gul Ista-Akaas – Mental Reflection

The Spheres and Planets: Pa Sefuraat Wa Kowkubaat

1. Joe Sefur – Atmosphere
2. Esu Sefur – Exosphere
3. Hatu Sefur – Heterosphere
4. Hum Sefur – Homosphere

5. Yabus Sefur – Lithosphere

6. Mezu Sefur – Mesosphere

7. Satur Sefur – Stratosphere

8. Tharm Sefur – Thermosphere

9. Tarub Sefur – Troposphere

* Shamul Nasfa Sefur – Northern Hemisphere

* Jenub Nasfa Sefur – Southern Hemisphere

1. Sun – Afsub (Apsu), Utu, Shamash – 'One who exists from the Beginning'

2. Mercury – Mummu – 'Very Large'

3. Moon – Sheshgi (Kingu, Lunar) – 'Moon'

4. Venus – Lahamu – 'Lady of Battles'

5. Mars – Lahmu – 'Deity of War'

6. Earth – Tiamat (Tamtu) – 'Maiden of Life'

7. Jupiter – Kishar – 'Foremost of the Firmlands'

8. Saturn – Anshar – 'Force of the Heavens'

9. Pluto – Gaga – 'Counsellor of Anshar'

10. Uranus – Anu – 'Heavenly One'

11. Neptune – Ea – 'He Whose House is Water'

12. Nibiru (Neb-Heru) – 'Planet of the Crossing'

Contrary to what is taught in institutions of learning today, the ancient people were far more advanced in the details of the quantum workings and spirituality of the Mental Universe(s). They were more advanced in the applied sciences of the Kosmos, than our song sheet scientists of our modern era. Things, breakthroughs, innovations and discoveries attributed to the Greeks, were already long known to the ancient tribes of the planet; the original man, the Kushite – Nubians and their parents, the Nuwbuns (Ptah Daneg/Twa), the Anu people.

Using the science of the circle and the square (Sacred Geometry) and the knowledge of the Fabonacci Sequence, we engineered the awe-inspiring and earth balancing ancient monuments in accordance with the eternal universe(s). These megalithic monuments were built to stand the test of time by applying sophisticated science, math including the use of the 'Pi' ratio, said to have been discovered by the Greeks, namely Pythagorus – who learnt in Egypt, under the Kushite.

The Kushites engineered these monuments inside and outside of Africa, all around the globe, such as, Stonehenge in England, Nabta Playa, Giza, Babylon, Tamana, Petra, the Shensi/Xianxi province of China , the Yucatan, North America, South America, Romania and Europe, North America, etc. Twa (Anu) and Kushite remains have been found around, and at all of these ancient sites. The same Twa/Anu and Kushite people that left Tamana and migrated into the wider world seeding all of the Homo Sapien nations into which the Neanderthals (Flugelrods) invaded after mixing with the children of Canaan (Libana). These ancient sites were built to harness and balance out earth energies and chart the precession of the Equinoxes, as miniature and giant star clocks.

The Alchemical overstanding of our people went into the four elements of earth and those of heaven which are:

1. Earth

2. Water

3. Wind

4. Fire

5. Sulphur

6. Mercury

7. Salt

These are the elements of alchemy, its tools of engagement, whether on an outer level within the world/lab, or on the inner/individual self-level. The Law of Correspondence states: *"As above, So Below"*. The wisdom of Djehuti also spelled Tehuti (Thoth), emphasized the existence of a supreme force referred to as Nun, which can be called 'The One Thing', which has no perceptible form and out of which all matter manifested, densified and formed creating the physical world. It has no perceptible form until it is 'grounded' or expressed in material reality. Some may call it 'Wave-form Energy'. The expression of its form is guided by the One Mind of AMUN RE (ANU), who operates within BA KULUWM 'The All'. This is the One Mind of the Supreme-Being and is Super consciousness (Intelligence or Outellect) responsible for the creation/generation of the universe(s). The ancestors saw the 'One Thing' as the primordial waters, plasma-energy that takes the form of the idea or thought projected by the One Mind (AMUN RE). The unseen forces (Paut Neteru) can be contacted and controlled by the worthy through 'Divine Union' – a merging with the One Mind through meditation and prayer. Lasting union can only be achieved by an inside out transfiguration of mind, body and soul, until the terrestrial man is so transformed, refined and purified that he/she becomes AMUN'S vessel for the force.

The Shekem Ur Shekems (Pharaohs), were the embodiment of this principle and force of Amun-Re and esoteric men throughout the ages realized this power, though it has many different ways of expression. Kushites taught that we are all in the Nun and the Nun is within us. The latent power of the universe(s) is mirrored within each and every one of us, including Paut Neteru, as attributes and elements 99^{+1} in number. This was the true origin of the Jewish and Islamic 99^{+1} attributes/elements or names of God (Yahweh, Allah). A Kushite precept (reality) turned into a Biblical/Qur'anic mythology once again.

The ancient people were able to see through the illusion of death. Far from being obsessed with death, our ancestors were obsessed with the higher, subtle existence where the soul shed its matter and lived on as a 'Light Being' (Etheric) in the realm of the deities. Therefore Kushites spirituality was a celebration of life and existence from this realm, through to higher ones. This is why the book was called 'The Book of the Coming Forth by Day (into the Light)', not the 'Book of the Dead' as called by White people who cannot perceive the spirituality of the original man in full depth because his pineal gland has calcified and his melanin is dysfunctionally low; he can never fully comprehend the mysteries of the 'Black Matter', even with all his scientific modern technology and computers. As hard as they try, they will fail.

".... When the body is exhausted, the soul soars to the space above full of contempt for the harsh, unhappy slavery it has suffered. But really, what are these things to you? You will know when you are no more. It is the way of everything here in the world below that when it is filled out with matter it is visible, but it is invisible, owing to its subtlety, when it is rid of matter - Then why this false notion of birth and death? Why has this false notion remained so long without being refuted? Some foolishly believe that what has happened through them

they have themselves brought about. They are ignorant that the individual is brought to birth <u>through</u> his parents, not <u>by</u> them. The real change which comes to an individual is not caused by his visible surroundings but rather is a change in the one thing which is in every man ...."

- Apollonius of Tyana (16 C.E. – 98 C.E.)

The Great God – Tehuti

Pa Neter Tehuti (Thoth) is the scribe of the Neteru (Gods) and the patron God of learning and hidden knowledge. Tehuti transcends anything we normally think about Gods and men. He is the personification of the powers of thought and logic, for it is Pa Neter Tehuti (Thoth) who was responsible for teaching humans how to interpret things, articulate their languages and speech in logical patterns and write down their thoughts. As the inventor of the hieroglyphic system, Tehuti instituted record keeping and introduced the sciences of Maatmagic (Mathematics), astronomy and medicine. The word Thoth, is the origin of the word 'Thought' as Tehuti is commonly referred to as the God of Thought of the Khemetians/Khamites. Some claim that Tehuti and other Neteraat are Gods from Atlantis which Egypt inherited, but the fact is that the Pantheon of Paut Neteru are Meroitic – Ethiopian/Sudanese – Nubian Gods, messengers of the Supreme Black God Amun-Re.

Pa Neter Tehuti (Thoth) is the ultimate archetype of the 'word of God' who uttered the 'Sacred Sound of Creation', which initiated the manifestation of the physical universe(s). Knowing the secret of the sacred 'Aum' principle, Tehuti is the 'Source of the Word', Sacred Sound – 'the Soul of Becoming', who fashioned the universe(s) along with Amun-Re, Ptah, Hika and Sia, as creator Gods. So this idea of Christianity, that Jesus is the world of God or Kalimallah 'Word of Allah', in Qur'anic (Islamic) thought, has its origins in the Kushite-Khamite mysteries. 'What emanates from the opening of His mouth', says a Khemetian (Egyptian) text, 'that comes to pass; he speaks and it is His command'. As the 'Reckoner of the physical universe', Tehuti is the source of all natural law, as the 'Shepard of Men' and 'Vehicle of Knowledge', Tehuti is the higher mind in man that provides inspiration and inner knowledge, a higher consciousness. In the Ebers Papyrus, a 68 foot long scroll on alchemy, that along with 'The Teachings of Ptah-Hotep', has been called the oldest book in the world, it states:

".... Man's guide is Tehuti (Thoth), who bestows on him the gifts of his speech, who makes the books and illumines those who are learned therein and the physicians who follow him, that they may work cures".

One of the alchemist – physicians whose fame has recorded him as histories first recorded genius, a student of Tehuti, is named Imhotep, builder of the Step Pyramid located at Saqqara, Egypt.

As the 'Revealer of the Hidden' and 'Lord of Rebirth', Tehuti is the guide to alternate states of consciousness, the initiator of human Enlightenment. It is said that one of Djehuti's books, 'The Scroll of Breathings', teaches humans how to become Gods, Thoth's animal symbols/totems are the ibis and the baboon. The God embodies both the rational powers of the sun as well as the intuitive, irrational powers of the moon. The Ibis is the Khemetian symbol for the heart and as the 'Recorder and Balancer', in the company of the other 12 Neteru of the Tribunal, Tehuti presides over the 'weighing of the heart', the ceremony which determines who is admitted into heaven. Tehuti is the judge who weighs individuals 'True Words', the innermost intents within all our thoughts and actions.

Our ancestors stated that Tehuti had authored 36,525 scrolls which contained the sum of all knowledge. The God is said to have three incarnations according to Khamite traditions.

Tehuti is called different names in different languages and has been identified with the Babylonian Murdoq (Marduk), also called As Aralim-Nuna, Asarluhi, Mariutu, Amar-Utu, Atrahasis, Malachi, Melchizedek and Al Khidr. According to ancient tradition, just before the Great Deluge, Tehuti hid and preserved the ancient 'wisdom', hidden under the heavenly vault which could only be found by the worthy, who would use such knowledge for the benefit of humanity.

The Sacred Wisdom of Tehuti, gives initiates his ability to navigate through all realms as a Karama – 'Mystic' of the higher mysteries. This Sacred Wisdom allows us to put on the 'Mask of God', turning men back into Elohim (Hebrew, Aramic) Malaaikat (Ashuric, Arabic), Anunnaqi (cuneiform), Neteru (Medew Neter) or simply Gods, Divine Beings (Light or Etheric Beings). The Greeks remember the God – Tehuti (Thoth) under the name of Hermes Trismegistus – Three Times Greatest!

"Was he one or many, merging
Name and fame in one,
Like a stream, to which, converging,

Many streamlets run?

Who shall call his dreams fallacious?
Who has searched or sought
All the unexplored and spacious
Universe of thought?

Who in his own skill confiding,
Shall with rule and line
Mark the border – land dividing
Human and divine?

Trismegistus! Three times greatest!
How they name sublime
Has descended to this latest
Progeny of time!"

- Henry Wadsworth Longfellow – 1882 (Hermes Trismegistus: Poem)

".... Like the exalted life of Hermes Trismegistus, the history of the Emerald Tablet is clouded in myths and legends. Several contemporary authors have suggested that the tablet was a gift from extra-terrestrials or originated in the lost civilization of Atlantis. Few have postulated that Thoth, either as an alien or Atlantean, wrote the tablet 36,000 years ago or was incarnated several times over the centuries to propagate its principles. According to other sources, the tablet was created in Egypt about 10,000 years ago, though some historians point to a date around 3000 B.C.E., when the Phoenicians settled on the Syrian Coast. Egyptian papyri dating as far back as 2000 B.C.E., contain many of the same phrases and principles stated in the Emerald Tablet, including references to the One Mind, One Thing and the correspondences between the Above and the Below. One papyrus known as 'an Invocation to Hermes', which dates from Hellenistic Egypt, actually mentions the tablet: "I know your names in the Egyptian tongue and your true name as it is written on the Holy Tablet in the holy place at Hermopolis, where you did have your birth.

Wherever it came from, the Emerald Tablet contains an extremely succinct summary of the Hermetic tradition, undoubtedly the oldest spiritual tradition in the West. The generic quality of its concepts allowed the tablet to permeate the foundations of human civilization and while no direct evidence links the tablet to Eastern religions it shared uncanny similarities in concepts and terminology with Taoism, Hinduism and Buddhism. In the West, the Emerald Tablet found a home not only in the pagan tradition but in all three of the Abrahamic religions (Judaism, Christianity and Islam) ...."

- Dennis William Hauck: The Emerald Tablet – Alchemy for Personal Transformation, Pg 32 (In Part)

Even the Freemasons, Rosicrucians, Golden Dawn, Theosophists, Gnostics, Sufism, Jewish Cabala, Fourth Way and many other New Age Spiritualists and Philosophers are also heavily indebted to the Emerald Tablet in principle and concepts. Most modern day Kushites have no idea that the world, civilization was founded on the backs of our ancestors, way before the advent – blood, sweat and tears – of the terrible Transatlantic Slave Trade of the 1500's.

Many modern Kushites (Black people) are even more ignorant of the enlightenment brought on by the movement of the Moors (Maurs) from Africa into Spain and Europe during the 9th – 12th century. Indeed, in both ancient and modern times, Black people were and are the 'Light of the World', the vice-regents of Pa Aluhum Shuyukh, 'The Elder Gods' who came from Illyuwn – 'Place on High' (the 19th Galaxy), through Sahu – 'Orion' and Sibtu/Septet – 'Sirius'. The Supreme Beings of the Crystal Green Light of AMUN (ANU) are the 'Ancient Astronauts' that N.A.S.A has speculated about. Those who came down here and altered the genetics of the early Hominids, causing homo sapien to appear almost overnight in genetic terms. There is no missing link other than the Gods and their activities. This is the legacy that Kushite people have been robbed of for millennia and it is now time to reclaim this Nubian reality and become blameless again.

".... Oh deities, who gives life and causes us to transcend this realm to eternal life, please make me worthy through my actions, my deeds and my practices in this life to be with you, when its time expires and its eternal abode begins. Let me be worthy to enter into it...."

" .... Oh deities, oh precious ones, I seek not to possess anything but to be in your grace. I desire for nothing, but your approval and to return unto you and bathe in your humble abode. I want nothing, because you have and are everything. Oh precious ones, my real happiness is in making others happy ....."

- Pa Ashutat "the Prayer": Nob: Rev. Dr Malachi Z. York 33°/720°

Of the power bequeathed to them by Paut Neteru, the Shekem Ur Shekems, Aafertiaat (Rulers) exercised not power over the people but a duty to uprightness and it was this responsibility and devotion to the Rule (Ma'at) which prevented the Pharaohs from acting as tyrants. His role was not to enslave his people but to liberate them from themselves.

Men are perverse and dangerous animals. They occupy themselves in defiling and destroying the earth and endangering humanity. When they are backed into a corner of destruction, which they have created themselves, no argument can sway them. They are stubbornly determined to cause their own ruin and regression; their own downfall is committed by their own hands, because over the millennia human beings have been distancing themselves further and further from spirituality and the Gods (Paut Neteru) 'Principalities of Life, Nature', when every link has been severed, only fanatics will remain, manipulated by tyrants, terrorists, dictators who will reign over an immense population of Sheeple (Robots – programmed by way of various Isms and Schisms), with a Sheep-Mentality (Mind-Controlled).

In the shadow of the monarchs, when your fundamental values are at stake, you must concede nothing, but always embrace the differences, the individuality in people. Uniformity gives birth to monsters, nations devoid of genius, sheeple with a sheep (herd) mentality. Do not conform to fear. You see, only a Pharaoh could divert men and women away from their natural flaws, stupidity, greed and laziness and guide them back to the bosom of AMUN RE. The ancients knew that when the world no longer presented the world a single Shekem Ur Shekem, it would disintegrate into spiritual and racial blindness, chaos, drowning in the blood of centuries of pointless and materialistic warfare.

".... How good it was to be able to rely on Ramses for vital decisions! Pharaoh, for his part, had no other guides than the invisible and the hereafter. Alone, face to face with the Divine, in the heart of the temple, he was also face to face with his people, whom he had served without thought for his own reputation. And for centuries, the Pharaonic institution had overcome obstacles and survived crisis because it did not belong to this world ...."

- Ramses. Under the Western Acacia: Pg 102 – Christian Jaq

Khemet became the last defender of the Rule, which had guided the fate of the world of men for over 10,000 years. The Pharaohs possessed a double nature - One celestial and one terrestrial. The original evil originated and perpetuated by the Black Devils, the Cainites (Children of Qayin/Cain), Nodites, Cuthites called also Watusi, the Black Hindu Aratara from Asia. Then in 4004 B.C.E., as prophesied by the Elohim Shuyukh on earth – a 'Kind of Man' (Mankind), The Neanderthal's descendants, 'The Tamahu' (Caucasoid) inherited the mantle.

These mountain men from the Northern Russian Steppes spread carnage all throughout the Ancient World, threatening the respect of the Rule. Egypt took the last stand against this threat which was killing the spirituality of the world replacing it with secularism, materialism, democracy and capitalism. The fall of the Rule, Ma'at and the ancient way of life was inevitable, but it could be prevented enough to preserve this sacred way, the legacy of the Ancient Kushites. We must acknowledge and pay homage to the ancestors, especially those who lived to achieve this noble feat, save lives and prevent an even greater degree of spiritual regression. This is the true legacy of the Kushites, especially of the Shekem Ur Shekems of which the last great Egyptian one was Ramesu/Ramesh III and of the Nubian (Meroitic) ones, those warriors of the glorious 25th Dynasty. Without these great ones; us, modern Kushites would have no reference, no link or knowledge of our glorious past; of when we were god-Kings on earth. The 25th Dynasty Rulers wore two rearing cobras (Ureaus), symbolic of the joint kingdom of Kush and Khemet.

"…. By extension of such rhetoric, therefore, it could be said that the function of the Giza blueprint is to provide a virtually indestructible 'holographic' apparatus for the use of 'reincarnated' or 'reborn' entities of the Horian lineage in order to induce 'remembrance' of a 'divine' genetic origin in Egypt in the time frame of 10,500 B.C. The ultimate function, however, appears to have been to perpetuate the 'immortality' of their souls into 'time' – in short, the ultimate Gnostic experience entailing the release of the spiritual part of the living entity from its material, inert, part. To put it in other terms, 'living' man is the result of a holographic union between matter and spirit. It would very much appear that the 'Followers of Horus' understood the cosmic mechanism to somehow re-separate the two …."

- Keepers of Genesis: Pg 319 (In Part): Robert Bauval and Graham Hancock

Our lives don't always conform to our wishes. The world is not created solely of what is visible. Invisible, hidden forces circulate within it and form the web of reality. The bitterest truth is better than the sweetest lie. The life of one man is sometimes very important to the fate of the precious world. The Aaferti 'Pharaoh' was the link between the visible and invisible; the Royal couple the personification of male and female universal creative force.

To compromise with evil will only lead to disaster. When a man knows the mission that he must accomplish upon this earth, he is no longer hindered by doubt. Even if you think you're alone, it only seems that way, you're never alone. The two aspects of physical reality are life and death. To overstand their message is the beginning of all knowledge and wisdom.

When the Barbarians invaded and disrespected the sacredness of the Kushite civilizations, especially the Nile Valley and Black culture, it signalled the beginning of the end of the spiritual sciences and the rule. It is the nature of chaos to want to devour order. This is the reason why the Pharaonic state was sent down to earth. It alone can consolidate the reign of Ma'at. The Pharaohs were the first servants of Ma'at, along with the Royal Wives, the Grand Viziers and the High Priests of the sacred temples. Without them, nothing but disorder and confusion has spread throughout the planet earth.

In life and love, a person must give as much as they take, because giving is receiving.

"By way of heirs, scribes who have attained knowledge leave behind books of wisdom. The writing palette is their beloved son. Their books are their pyramids; their brush is their child, the stone covered with hieroglyphs, their wives.

Monuments disappear, sand covers the stelae, tombs are forgotten, but the names of the scribes who have lived with wisdom endure because of the influence of their works. Become a scribe and engrave upon your heart this thought; a book is more use than the most solid wall. It will serve you as a temple even after your death; your name will live on in people's mouths through the book; it will be stronger than a well-built house ...."

True love far surpasses physical union and its pleasures. It is not only the person that charms/enchants, but above all their radiance. The lovers, two together, form one being and are synchronized and in communication at every moment, even when apart from each other. They share a love from beyond this world. When love shines over a people, it offers them more happiness than any amount of wealth.

The way of righteousness is to act on behalf of those in need of help, for just deeds enrich the reawakening of Ma'at and protect us from chaos. The Kushite rulers ensured the presence of Ma'at upon the earth, especially the Aafertiaat 'Pharaohs'. They ensured the presence of the Rule and the impartiality of Justice. Thus, they never interfered in judicial matters even when friends and family were involved they never used their influence to show favour. They allowed justice to prevail uninterrupted. Instinct is a direct way of overstanding beyond reason, which can lead us astray or raise false hopes. Some people are able to transform instinct into intuition and are able to use it with genius, just like a sixth sense. Too much wine clouds the minds of sages and scribes and prevents them having a steady hand. The magnificent gifts of the Gods are not to be despised.

A real friend will help you to fight against your worst self and bring your best self to the forefront. A true friend will tell you what you may not want to hear. To flatter a friend is an unforgivable fault. These days, a true friend is as rare as precious stones, as valuable as precious metals. True friendship is sacred and divine. There can be no peace for men with blood on their heads until justice has been served 'Bread and Beer, Justice for All, Big or Small'.

Luck is the favour of the Gods misunderstood. In this way, we make our own luck. Only the Gods 'Paut Neteru' can grant it, for no man could acquire it without their favour. Only second rate authors gaze at themselves in the mirror of their words. Words of power have the power to manipulate matter.

What is a Pharaoh? - He who makes his people happy. How is that achieved? By actions which are beneficial to the principle, to the Rule and to the Gods, so that they are reflected on to humanity.

No man can escape his destiny, but by living in awareness of it, one can parry the blows of fate. If you know how to turn everyday life into magic, you'll possess a power which will enable you to learn the secrets of heaven and earth, day and night, mountains and rivers and you'll overstand the language of the trees, seas, birds and the fish; you'll be reborn with the sun at dawn and you'll see the divine powers over the waters. To realize and achieve this, you must overcome vanity and licentiousness and laziness.

Today's religions have disrespected the unity of the Divine in its principle and its multiplicity in the way that it expresses and manifests itself. God is both One (One Mind) and multiple (One Malleable Thing). It is vanity to believe that any one nation/people are the sole agent of God. The promotion of one exclusive God would prevent the exchange of deities between countries and would extinguish the hope of kinship between peoples.

The works of great writers are more durable than the pyramids. Every one of us has flaws to work on and moments of weakness. That's when evil tries to defeat our consciences and stifle all the goodness in our hearts. Don't give in to the evil, that's what matters most.

"Egypt ... considered life to be everlasting and denied the reality of death ... Pharaoh was not mortal but a god. This was the fundamental concept of Egyptian kingship that Pharaoh was of divine essence, a god incarnate.... It is wrong to speak of the deification of Pharaoh. His divinity was not proclaimed at a certain moment in a manner comparable to the concretatio of the dead emperor by the Roman senate. His coronation was not an apotheosis but an epiphany.

- Henri Frankfort, Kingship and the Gods, 1948

"The figure of Osiris is not exclusively at home in mythology ... Each king, at death becomes Osiris, just as each king, in life, appears 'on the throne of Horus'; Each king is Horus .... The question whether Osiris and Horus are ... gods or kings is for the Egyptian, meaningless. These gods are the late king and his successors; those kings are those gods ...."

- Henri Frankfort, Kingship and the Gods, 1948

"The Egyptians believed that in the beginning their land was ruled by a dynasty of great gods, of whom Horus, the son of Isis and Osiris, was the last. He was succeeded by a dynasty of semi-divine beings known as the 'Followers of Horus', who, in turn, gave place to the historical Kings of Egypt".

- Selim Hasan, The Sphinx, Cairo, 1949

"I am convinced that there are universal currents of Divine Thought vibrating the ether everywhere and that any who can feel those vibrations is inspired"

- ***Richard Wagner***

Chapter Four: The Land Before Time

Although this is a most controversial claim to academics and scholars of these days, I will say that a pre-deluvial (before the flood), civilization existed which was more scientifically and spiritually advanced than the Egypt, Sumer, Greece and Rome that orthodox history celebrates. This high culture which was given to homo sapien sapiens through the ancient Anu, Ptah Daneg people has existed in isolated area since before the end of the last Ice Age, which ended circa 13,000 years ago when the ice caps melted. When this happened, it initiated the end of an age, in which 70% of the life of this planet became extinct. This included plants, animals and humanity. This major cataclysm wiped away the successes of this early high culture, its scientific and spiritual advances leaving only a remnant.

Global Cataclysms:

There are various reasons as to why, periodically, the cycles of life in the planet earth experience global cataclysms or 'extinction-level events' such as the 'Great Deluge' which has been recorded by so many nations and religions. Each 'Age of Man' ends with a major global cataclysm, having experienced many minor ones. The first 'Age of Man' was ended by meteor shower, the second age was also ended by meteor shower, the third (previous) age was ended by the great deluge (water) and we are currently in the fourth age of man, called by some cultures, the fifth 'Age of the Sun'. We are currently upon the doorstep of another major cataclysm which threatens the future of our modern civilization.

It is not my intention here to predict or prophecy how our modern world will come to an end. It is beyond the purpose and scope of this scroll to go down that route. There is more than enough material out there for those of you who want more information on this end of the subject. Whether the next cataclysm will be spawned by a magnetic polar-shift caused by the sun, another global flood, an earthquake, comets or meteors or from self-inflicted nuclear war is not important. What is most important is the fact that the cataclysms are a reality and really do happen and that the life of humans is not as guaranteed as you may be prone to think.

Our current civilization could end overnight if say a comet 1km in size silently and invisibly crept up upon us travelling even 30,000 miles per hour and landing either on land or in the sea. The earth is regularly had near fly-bys which were not picked up until moments before or even after the object has passed. Another K/T Event could happen like it did 65 million years ago wiping out the dinosaurs and 99.9% of the species upon the face of the planet.

A violent solar storm could result in a magnetic polar reversal and kill all life on the planet at any time, overnight. A polar-shift would flip the planet upside down like what happened to Venus circa 3113 B.C.; solar radiation could kill entire populations, comets and meteor bombardment could strip away the planets crust and atmosphere like the planet Mars confirms. Again, the life of humans is not promised. Our civilization is fragile and yet; mankind is playing with fire with the threat of nuclear war upon our doorstep. Despots, dictators and religious fanatics hold so much power, that one push of a button could change the course of history. Men like Donald Trump, Vladimir Putin, Assad, Al Baghdadi, and Kim John-Un to say the least.

Though the experts try hard to ignore it, there is evidence to suggest that ancient man inhabited the earth far back into the Cambrian and Cretaceous periods, inhabiting the world alongside the dinosaurs. Technologically advanced humanoids have been operating here much longer than experts are willing to admit. This is because the experts know that the Kushite evolved not here on Earth, but in another far off solar system in the form of the Anunnaqi/Neteru (Elohim/Malaaikat) before coming to Mars and the planet Earth and genetically engineering modern hominids in a long process of assisted evolution.

The early civilization that was handed down to humanity achieved a 'Golden Age' of marvels which has never left the psyche and memory of humanity throughout the ages. The myths of all the world's nations contain corrupted and mythologized accounts of the coming of the Gods and the Golden Age that followed. The legacy of the Kushite people, the original man, preserved this reality in the eternal stone of the monument and the infinite appeal of the teachings which was dissipated throughout the world culture and religion. Many artefacts have been mentioned, pictured and indeed some even have been found that attest to the scientifically advanced predeluvial civilization which was preserved within the civilizations of Kush, Khemet, Elam, Sumer, The Indus, Xia (China and Mexico), among others.

In 1936 a Parthian device dating between c.248 B.C. to 226 A.D. was discovered. It was a vase-like vessel of light yellow clay containing a copper cylinder held firmly by asphalt. The vase is about 15cm high; the sheet copper cylinder tube with bottom had a diameter of 26mm and was 9cm long. The stopper of asphalt within it, contains a completely oxidised iron rod, the top of which projected about 1cm above the stopper. It is covered by a fully oxidised thin coating of yellowish grey metal resembling lead. The bottom end of the cylinder, upon which has a layer of asphalt roughly 3mm deep.

Wilhelm Koenig realized that when the various parts were put together and examined, that by adding acid or alkaline liquid, the device activated its electrical element. In other words, it was a battery. Dr Arne Eggebrecht duplicated the artefact and added grape juice (alkaline liquid) resulting in the battery generating half a volt of electricity. Along with the 'Baghdad Battery', there is evidence of electro-plating as in the small statue of Osiris in gold plated silver, which remains a mystery and dates back to 400 B.C.

400 B.C. is far from 10,500 B.C. and although by the time we reach back to the 1st Dynasty Kings, this sort of evidence disappears, the inferences of electrical technology remain surprisingly strong. There are also many curious phenomena associated with the design of the Giza pyramids, especially the Great Pyramid of Khufu that are suggestive of electrical sources and properties. It is a known fact that the myserious lights generated at the apex of the Great Pyramid has much to do with the static electricity that it generates, even when an aurora is not present. They are caused by static electricity which manifests itself as an aurora during certain climatic conditions. It's also causes ringing noises, causing the Arab invaders to believe that the pyramid is haunted. This electricity can be demonstrated by using Leyden Jars which store static electricity.

From the vast evidences produced here, it is clear to see that the history of the planet, its people and contributions of certain cultures has been deliberately distorted and suppressed. Too often, alternative views are brushed aside by scholars as pan-African, misguided and even consipiracy-theories, when in actuality the only misguided views are the orthodox official histories taught by the establishment.

The many treasures in the sand attest to the pioneering genius of many cultures especially those of the Anu people and Kushites, whose remains have been uncovered at every major site from east to west and found buried in and around all of the great world monuments worthy of the name. Contrary to what the song sheet scholars deny; the Ancient Kushites were expert seafarers who established a network of trade and spiritual sciences all around the globe, after the great deluge which happened when the ice caps melted last, roughly 13,000 years ago. According to Sumerian records this 'Age of the Deluge' was 10,860 B.C.E. and the Ancient Sig.Gag.Ga – 'Black Headed People' transported civilization from Tama-Re all around the planet from then 10,860 – 8640 B.C.E., which was the 'Age of Leo'. It was during this time (c.10,500 B.C.E.) that Horemakhet (The Sphinx) was erected by the Shemsu Haru also called Ahkus, staring at his namesake, Re-Horakhty – the constellation of Leo, each early morning sunrise, which was in the Age of Leo.

Monuments were erected worldwide in an effort to re-balance the planet by harnessing earth energies and unblocking the earth's chakras and meridians, in the same way that acupuncture works to unblock the energy channels in humans. Monuments were erected in

Africa, the Americas, Europe, Asia and the Far East, all established by the same pioneering people using the sacred spiritual sciences with a full overstanding of the solar forces (the operation of the sun). These were the 'Earth Alchemists'. These metaphysical masters based all of these ancient monuments and sites upon the same divine principles and this is why so many links and connections can be found between them all; Giza, Teotihuacan, Stone Henge, Nabta Playa, Saqqara, Shensi Province, etc., etc. It was originally planned and constructed by the same Neteru, Kushite and Anu people, later being inherited by others who often lost the meaning and technical know-how as humanity regressed through the ages.

The similarities which betray a hidden link between the constructions of various ancient sites are numerous, even though there are many differences that should not be overlooked. Take for example the great Pyramids of Giza which are constructed from large blocks of stone carefully shaped and aligned, while those pyramids of Teotihuacan are crudely built of mudbricks, stones and pebbles. The heights are significantly different at 480ft for the Great Pyramid of Giza and 250ft for the Pyramid of the Sun at Teotihuacan. The Great Pyramids of Giza have a difficult angle of 52°, those at Teotihuacan do not have triangular sides and the stages of the steps start at a much safer angle of 43½ °.

The angle of 52° in the Giza plateau is unique to the Giza complex alone. All other Khemetian (Egyptian) pyramids use the safer angle of 43½ ° like those of Teotihuacan. This is proof and evidence that the Pyramids of Giza were not built by Shekem Ur Shekems Khufu, Khafre and Menkuare or any other Pharaohs, but were constructed c.10, 500 B.C., by Paut Neteru/Anunnaqi and the Ptah Daneg (Anu people) after the great deluge of the late glacial period. The Pharaohs refurbished them during their reigns in the 4th Dynasty and Aaferti (Pharaoh) Khufu states, on a stelae, that the Great Pyramid already existed during his childhood but this stelae is largely ignored as fantasy by song sheet Egyptologists. The Giza complex was used as a part of the altered landing corridor of the Anunnaqi after the first corridor was rendered unusable due to the great flood. The corridor was re-rooted from the Sumerian E.Din – 'Land of the Rocketships', through to the western sites of On (Giza), Jerusalem, Mount St Katherine (Sinai), Baalbek, using the same 45° angles and geodetically linked sites.

Only the bottom half of Pharaoh Sneferu's Bent Pyramid at Ashur began at the 52° angle, but adjusts midway to the safer angle of 43½°. The common belief or lie taught as fact by experts, is that midway during its construction the pyramid began to collapse inward under its own weight, at the tricky angle of 52° and the architects having calculated wrongly, were forced to adjust the angle. In other words, the scholars are saying that it was a mistake on the part of our ancestors and they were forced to resort to the safer angle in order to save it. I beg to differ on that point and would like to state that the Bent Pyramid was deliberately built in that way, for various reasons, as has recently been proposed by many independent researchers.

The Step Pyramid of Saqqara was also built at the 43½° angle during the reign of Aaferti Djoser Neterkeht of the 3rd Dynasty and his Grand Vizier Imhotep, who were both members of the Anunnaqi (Neteru) – the 24 Elders – incarnated upon the earth to help to raise man's consciousness levels back up. The 24 Elders are mentioned within 'The Book of Revelation' as the 24 Thrones. This pyramid is also thousands of years older

None of the similarities between the two sets of pyramids in Egypt and Mexico, and other monuments and sites spanning the globe, is coincidence. Indeed, there is no such thing as coincidence. The pyramids articulate and demonstrate advanced knowledge of the sacred 'Pi Ratio' which is falsely claimed to be the discovery of Pythagoras and the early Greeks. The 52° angle of the pyramids of the Giza complex shows an intense and masterful familiarity of the Pi Ratio and so do the many other pyramids which use the 43½° angles around the ancient world. In the Great Pyramid of Giza, it was realized by giving the pyramid a height (H) equal to half its side length (S) divided by Pi and then multiplied by four (754 ÷ 2 = 377 ÷ 3.14 (Pi) = 120 x 4 – 480ft in height). In the 43½° pyramids, it was done by reducing the height from a final multiple of four to a multiple of three. In both instances, knowledge of the 'Pi factor' is needed, along with the knowledge of the sacred so called 'Fabonacci Sequence' which our illustrious ancestors referred to as 'Divine Numbers'. The Fabonacci Sequence is obtained by a sequence of numbers in which the two numbers before, added together, equal the next number.

Ie: 0, 1, 1, 2, 3, 5, 8, 13, 21, 34, 55, 89..... Etc. and so on

This adds up to the Divine Equation of $9 \times 9 \times 9^9$ holding the secrets of the Infinite. The ancestors also possessed the sacred knowledge of Phi – 'The Golden Section' and more which is demonstrated at Giza, Teotihuacan and even on Mars at Cydonia and Elysium.

This sacred and divine equation governs the construction of all of the matter of the physical creation, from atoms and cells, to animals, humans, plant life, patterns in nature and inanimate objects, giving rise to what is called the 'Sacred Geometry' of creation. Therefore, our ancestors built their lives and monuments in line with the universe(s) and the natural order of things, with an intricate overstanding of God consciousness/Universal consciousness. In this way, the Gods – Principalities of Nature – gave us the sacred wisdom to build structures that would stand the test of time, as can be evidenced throughout the many standing ruins of the ancient world. These monuments held within them the secrets of eternity.

"Everybody fears time, but time fears the pyramids ......"

Far from being the idol worshipping, sun worshipping fools that they are portrayed as, the Ancient people were applied scientific geniuses, of the likes the world has never seen before, never seen since and probably won't see ever again. They overstood not just the gross (visible) physical world, but more importantly had an intricate overstanding of the subtle (invisible) forces that operate beyond matter in the spiritual and mental planes. Our Kushite ancestors have been communicating with this other side of reality since we were gifted by the Gods with civilization, at the dawn of time itself. The science is therefore nothing new.

The monuments left worldwide are 'Books' written in stone that cannot be changed like the pages of man-made scriptures. They cannot be read without the cosmic key to unlock the encrypted 'Higher Knowledge', the *"Truth that Will Make you Free"* (John 8:32). The fullness of this can only be deciphered by true initiates and modern 'Seekers of the Facts'. Our ancestors left these monuments for us in full expectation that we would have the learning and capacity to overstand by way of our enthusiasm. Like I said before, to achieve this you must cease from being lazy and learn to do your own in depth and consistent research because in this current 'Age of Information', the truth is all out there. There's no excuse for remaining ignorant in this day and age of computers, the Internet and Wikipedia etc. As the saying now goes in my circle; *"Ignorance is a choice"*.

There are numerous reasons as to why the Giant Star Clock, known to us as the Giza complex was laid out with its enigmatic monuments, alignments and edifices. Many of these functions are carefully explained in '2mrw Iz 2day Iz Yesterday (Vol II)', by me, Djedefre Memnon KKR 33°/360°. The complex and its higher meaning is a testimony of the Gods and their flock, the Kushite people of yesterday and today. It is for us, our responsibility to re-awaken this African spirituality along with the long sleeping African (sound) mind that pioneered the spirituality and sciences that led to the breakthroughs that we enjoy today. There definitely is nothing new under and above the sun; no new breakthroughs have been discovered since the advent of Kushite civilization. Today nothing new is discovered by the Europeans as they like to make claim, only uncovered after being lost in the sands of time.

"The fabric of existence has many threads. Nothing happens on itself ....."

"…. 'How on earth did the Ancient Egyptians build these edifices without twentieth century technology?' Admittedly, at the time the statues were cut out of the living granite on the spot, but how were the statues of Memnon near Thebes that weigh 600 tons transported or the stone blocks of the terrace at Baalbek, some of which are over 60 feet long and weigh 2,000 tons? And now the sixty four thousand dollar question; who nowadays can still accept the 'serious' archaeological explanation that these stone blocks were moved up inclined planes using wooden rollers? The sides of the stones are dressed so accurately that they were fitted together without mortar. There must have been a tremendous amount of waste material on the work sites. Very little has been found. Why did they not build near the granite quarries? I get no answers to questions like that, so could it be true that extra-terrestrial space travellers helped with their highly developed technology? Yet why did alien spacemen take the trouble? Was it precisely because they wanted to make the children of later millennia ask the questions I dare to ask? ….."

- In Search of Ancient Gods: Eric Von Daniken, Pg 60 (In Part)

So let me now remind you of a much forgotten universal principle of life and existence. This is going to make religious, Abrahamic faiths especially; disagree but I am not writing for you to agree with me. What you may think has no consequence on the facts. So I don't particularly care whether or not you will agree.

You were here on earth before, living a different lifetime. You were here in ancient times, witnesses to the dawn of civilization. You incarnated into human form to learn various life lessons in order to grow and expand in consciousness, increase your electromagnetic spark/ charge thereby adding to the infinitely expanding multiverse of experiences. You see, the Creator, the One – knows everything but hasn't experienced everything.

You are a part of the Creator experiencing itself as a human for a while. You are the universe(s), the electromagnetic spectrum. As waveform energy, you existed before you were born into this physical reality, subtle and invisible, beyond matter and beyond the atom. You are a spiritual entity, with elements recycled.

Each time that you incarnate, you are supposed to 'remember', that each being is responsible for their own actions. You cannot blame anybody else but yourself ultimately. You chose your own circumstances. Each of us has a memory of all of the lifetimes in which we incarnated into forms, beings, humans. But sometime long ago, we humans got disconnected from the invisible, the spiritual aspects of self. For nothing in the universe(s) is wasted or truly expires.

We built the ancient monuments so that we could remind ourselves of this great purpose knowing we would return in the future to relearn the higher mysteries of existence and put together the jigsaw puzzle of life. The oldest stories are written in the stars and the monuments align with and point to them. Your ancestors, the stars, yourself; has something very important to tell yourself; something more powerful than both birth and death. It's time to see through the illusion. Open your eyes.

'Remember to Re-member……'

The laser like precision, accuracy, the exact East – West, North – South alignments, the deeply encoded mathematics and astronomy, rule-out the misguided religious statement which claims that Pharaoh Khufu (Cheops) used condemned Egyptian and/or Jewish slaves in the construction of the Great Pyramid. There is no way in the world that slaves under duress could've achieved this ancient architectural marvel, which in so many ways, still remains an enigma. It is also fact, that by the time of the patriarch Abraham/Ibrahim, the Sphinx was already considered ancient. Those that know, know that the Giza necropolis is much older than scholars will admit, being older than the Pharaonic state of Egypt and therefore established before the Hebrew/Jewish nation themselves. This is therefore just another vain attempt to dampen the glory of the Kushite Tamarean legacy and attribute its achievements to non-Africans as usual. If the Hebrews or Jews did construct the pyramids under Khufu or Ramses or whoever, then how is it that no pyramids can be found in the region of Israel, in Canaan? How come none of the Hebrew monuments such as the famous Temple of King Solomon could similarly stand the test of time having been re-built after its destruction? Exactly! These monuments go back to the Neteru/Anunnaqi, the Ptah Daneg (Anu) and the Shemsu Haru (Ahkus) before 10,500 B.C. Indeed the site of Giza, tracks back with the ancient sites of Anu (On), Men-Nefer (Memphis) and Waset (Thebes) to the Zep Tepi – 'Beginning Times', through the mists of time approximately 17,250,000 years as unbelievable as it sounds.

".... In practice this means any time before 15,000 B.C. – a hunch that West says is based on the complete lack of evidence of a high culture in Egypt in 7000 to 5000 B.C. 'If the Sphinx was as recent as 7000 to 5000 B.C., he argues, "I think we probably would have other Egyptian evidence of the civilization that carved it." Since there is no such evidence, West reasons that the civilization responsible for the Sphinx and its neighbouring temples must have disappeared long before 7000-5000 B.C.: 'The missing other evidence is, perhaps, buried deeper than anyone has looked and/or in places no one has yet explored – along the

banks of the Ancient Nile perhaps, which is miles from the present Nile, or even at the bottom of the Mediterranean, which was dry during the last Ice Age...."

".... Of course it cannot be said that Robert Schoch has proved that the monuments dates back to the epoch of 7000 to 5000 B.C. Nor has John (Anthony) West proved the even earlier date that he favours. But then again neither has orthodox Egyptology proved that the Sphinx belongs to Khafre and to the epoch of 2500 B.C.

In other words, by any rational and reasonable criteria, the jury is still out on the true attribution and antiquity of this extraordinary monument.

The riddle of the Sphinx is still unsolved. And as we see In the next chapter, it is a riddle that encompasses the entire Giza necropolis ....."

- Keepers of Genesis: Robert Bauval & Graham Hancock: Pg 22-23 (In Part)

".... The unifying features of these ancient and anonymous structures are the stark, undecorated austerity of the building style and the use throughout of ponderous megaliths – many of which are estimated to weigh in the range of 200 tons a piece. There are no small blocks here at all: every single piece of stone is enormous – the least of them weighing more than 50 tons and it is difficult to understand how such monsters could have been lifted and manoeuvred into place by the Ancient Egyptians. Indeed, even today, contractors using the latest construction technology would face formidable challenges if they were commissioned to produce exact replicas of the Sphinx Temple and the Valley Temple.

The problems are manifold but stem mainly from the extremely large size of the blocks, which can be envisaged in terms of their dimensions and weight as a series of diesel locomotive engines stacked one on top of the other. Such loads simply cannot be hoisted by the typical tower and hydraulic cranes that we are familiar with from building sites in our cities. These cranes, which are pieces of advanced technology, can generally 'pick' a maximum load of 20 tons at what is called 'minimum span' – i.e. at the closest distance to the tower along the 'boom' or 'arm' of the crane. The longer the span the smaller the load and at 'maximum span' the limit is around 5 tons...."

- Keepers of Genesis: Robert Bauval & Graham Hancock: Pg. 29 (In Part)

".... I'm looking at what you're showing me here and looking at the distances involved. I don't know if we would be able to pick the 200 ton blocks from the positions that I see available to us..... In my business we pick heavy loads and we look to see how heavy loads were picked by other people before us. And seeing how they moved these heavy blocks, 200 ton blocks, thousands and thousands of years ago, I have no idea how they did this job. It's a mystery and it'll probably always be a mystery to me and maybe to everybody....."

- Long Island Construction: Crane Engineer

"..... We are told that King Zoser of the third Dynasty began to build the Step Pyramids near Saqqara around 2700 B.C. Is the building of the pyramids wrongly dated? Are they incomparably older than archaeologists assumes? There is justification for such a suspicion. Abu'l Hassan Ma'sudi is not the only one to assert that the pyramids were built before the flood. Herodotus (484-425 B.C.), the oldest Greek Historian, whom Cicero (106-43 B.C.) called the 'Father of Historiography', declares in chapters 141 and 142 of Book II of his 'Histories Apodexis' that the priests of Thebes had assured him that the office of high priest had been handed down from father to son for 11,340 years. As proof of this claim, the priests showed Herodotus 341 colossal statues, each of which stood for a high priestly generation. And his hosts assured him that 341 generations ago the Gods had lived among men, but that since that time no God had appeared in human form. It is a fact that so far the date of the building of the great pyramids has not been irrefutably proved ....."

- In Search of Ancient Gods: Eric Von Daniken: Pg. 58 (In Part)

".... To put a figure like this into some sort of context, there is more stone in this one pyramid than all the cathedrals and churches built in England over the past 2000 years. Napoleon once calculated that by tearing down the pyramid he would have enough raw material to erect a wall three metres high and one metre thick around the whole of France...."

- Martian Genesis: Herbie Brennan: Pg. 100-101 (In Part)

Other artefacts discovered since 1936 include the supposed model of a flywheel, found in the 5100 year old tomb of Prince Sabu at Saqqara, Egypt. This model made in stone was a type of wheel with a hole through the middle. The archaeologists speculated that they were staring at a model of a flywheel which was supposed to be fitted over an axle. In metal, the artefact has the functional appearance of a light rimmed flywheel developed for transport in 1978, America.

In 1960s, an early fragment belonging to the Olmecs turned out to be part of geomagnetic compass which dated back to 1000 B.C. In 1898 archaeologists turned up a wooden model of an aeroplane dating back to 200 B.C. in a tomb at Saqqara, Egypt once again. It has the same proportions and wing form as concord which renders it a supersonic aeroplane.

Another interesting find at the turn of the twentieth century, off the island of Anti Kythera, brought up in a sunken ship is referred to as the Antikythera Mechanism. This sophisticated mechanical calculator dating back to the first century B.C. was found and recovered by Greek divers. All of these enigmatic finds together with the enigmas of Baalbek, Giza, Teotihuacan, Abu Simbel, Tenochtitlan, Sacsayhuaman, Tiawanku, Nazca, the Piri Reis Map, Machu Piccu, Ollantaytambu, Easter Island, etc., are hard evidence that the engineering skills of the distant past were far greater than the methods of today; evidence of a higher predeluvial civilization? I will leave that to the reader to make up their own minds.

In 1968, a fossilized human shoe print was discovered by a fossil collector named William J. Meister inside a block of split open shale near Antelope Spring, Utah. There were trilobite fossils within the same stone. It was confirmed by Dr Clarence Coombs of Columbia Union College, Tacoma, Maryland and geologist Maurice Carlisle, University of Colorado at Boulder, as a genuine fossil.

Many footprints of modern human specifics have been found all over the globe even in places like Russia, reported by Moscow News in 1983. The one in Russia was reportedly found next to the fossil footprint of a three-toed dinosaur in the Turkmen Republic, part of what was then South – Western USSR.

Most of the evidence is ignored by the establishment because it conflicts with the orthodox consensus taught in the educational mainstream institutions today. In order for them to mis-educate the masses with their distorted timeline of human history, they must blatantly ignore the hard evidence and facts regularly turning up in their faces. Most people swallow this ignorance without ever scrutinizing the facts and figures. This sheep mentality is responsible for the dumbing down and regressing of humanity.

".... The earliest presentation of the Golden Age as an historic fact is in the Dialogues of Plato, a Greek Philosopher who lived between about 428 and 348 B.C. Plato quoted Egyptian sources to describe an advanced prehistoric culture which he believed had developed the ideal political system. He located the home of this culture 'beyond the Pillars of Hercules', and dated its collapse to about 9600 B.C.

This places the heyday of this lost civilization towards the end of the Ice Age, a time when most of us believe the planet was occupied by cave men....."

- Martian Genesis: Herbie Brennan: Pg. 44-45 (In Part)

The Indo-Aryans (Hindus) inherited the Dravidian (Puntite) texts concerning the existence of the cycles. These cycles are subdivided into four stages or epochs, called Yugas: the Krita Yuga (1,728,000 human years), the Treta Yuga (1,296,000 human years), the Dvapora Yuga (864,000 human years) and finally, the age in which we currently are, the Kali Yuga (432,000 human years). As Professor Hermann Jacobi states:

".... The astronomical aspect of the Yuga is that, in its commencement, sun, moon and planets stood in conjunction in the initial point of the ecliptic and returned to the same point at the end of an age. The popular belief in which this notion is based is older than Hindu astronomy ...."

What he means to say is that this mythologized astronomical knowledge goes back further than the Indo-Aryans to the Dravidians (Puntites) who as you can recall from the evidence presented, were Kushites: Eastern Kushites from the Nubian land of Punt. This Ancient Kushite information is related to the precession of the equinoxes, the cyclical process in which the zodiacal constellations slowly shifts against the backdrop of which the sun rises on the Spring Equinox. The 12 shifts of 2,160 years adds up to 25,920 for a full completion of this zodiacal display and this falls into larger cycles such as the sun making its 250 million year cycle around the central black hole in the universe.

The first of the civilizations on earth was generated by and for the Elohim 'Lofty Beings (Gods)', when they left the planet Mars after having lost its atmosphere, humankind was first created to serve these supreme Beings who came from a far off constellation with advanced scientific and mechanical (technological) knowhow.

This is when the Gods lived among man or better man lived among the Gods as their servants, this was the '1st Golden Age' recorded as myth and corrupted through the sands of time. The remnants of this genetic memory are contained within each culture and religion worthy of the name. Every culture worldwide speaks about the same Golden Ages, Cataclysms, Epochs of time cycles and higher spirituality and Gods in their own language and symbolisms. There is no such thing as coincidence and this is testimony to the reality of these Anunnaqi/Neteru (Elohim – Gods), as everybody across the globe could not have generated the same symbols, images, ideas and stories. No chance.

Maxim 42: Epilogue 5

On the duties and destiny of a spiritual son

".... A son who understands is a Follower of Horus and only after having understood will he find fulfilment. He will live to a ripe old age and become a venerable one.

He should hand the same message on to his children, renewing his father's teachings. Every man receives teaching in keeping with his deeds; he should pass this on to his children.

Mould your character as an example, do not give free rein to your destructive tendencies. Reinforce rectitude and you will have spiritual descendants.

As for the first among them to introduce evil, injustice and disorder, let witnesses declare: "That's exactly what we expected from such a wretch." And let it be repeated for those listening: "That's what we expected from such a wretch." Let each and every one see the wise man and then the crowd will be appeased. Without those sages there would be no riches ...."

- The Sage Ptah-Hotep

Roughly about 200,000 years ago, homo sapien (modern thinking man) appeared upon the world scene. After the time of the Paut Neteru – 'Company of Gods', circa 100,000 B.C., civilization was given to modern man in Nubia (Sennar). From its Meroitic origin, it spread into Egypt (Khemet), Arabia, Elam, Sumer, China, Athens, Phoenicia, Cyprus, Crete, Hatti, etc., in no particular order.

This was the time in which the demi-Gods ruled between the Gods and humanity. These demi-Gods were the off-spring of the Gods and human beings, half divine being, half human and half Neteru/Anunnaqi Rulers such as the first Nimrods, rulers such as Gilgamesh, among many others represent this stock spoken of upon many clay tablets and also mentioned in the myth made Bible's, Genesis 6: 1-7 as both Giboreem – 'Mighty Men' of renown and Nephileem – 'Fallen Angels/Giants'.

The Giboreem were spawned from Agreeable deities, while the Nephileem were sired by way of the Disagreeable deities. The Giboreem were hunters of the Nephileem, both being descendants of the Anunnaqi/Neteru (Elohim). It was during this predeluvial epoch, that

Kingship was sent down from heaven, meaning the stars (Illyuwn, Orion, Sirius), along with civilization unto early man. Pa Neter Ptah (Enki), gave the keys of civilization to Tehuti (Thoth, Marduk) amongst the Gods upon earth and circa 30,000 B.C., it was given to the first divine couple born upon and acclimatized to earth; Asar (Osiris) and Aset (Isis) to teach to the humanity in Sennar, Meroe – Nubia and its surrounding communities.

This Kingship and civilization was developed in Mother Africa before the flood circa 10,860 B.C. and spread into Nabatean Arabia, Elam, Sumer, China and the Yucatan Peninsula, etc. after c.4100, generally-speaking. The rapid growth of the Nile Valley population and climate change, and the threat of the Beastman, the descendants of the Ice Men, Cavemen (Caucasians), forced many tribes of people to migrate from the ever encroaching desert regions of the Nile Valley into more fertile and population supporting regions of the planet, and also caused some Nubians to move into and plug the bottle neck gateway of the Sinai Peninsula and other regions.

Now the song sheet scholars are going to try to refute the claim that a pre-deluvial civilization of Africa existed before the end of the last Ice Age, approximately 13,000 years ago. We have already shown that they falsely claim that the Ancient Kushites were not a seafaring nation and therefore could not have crossed the great seas of the globe.

For their own reasons the Anunnaqi/Neteru had to seek other areas to occupy in order to continue their projects before, during and after the great deluge. One of these regions was Atlan and Amexem (North and South America, including the Yucatan). Therefore, we would like to suggest that sites such as San Larenzo, Vera Cruz, La Venta, Tiahuanaco, Tenochtitlan, Ollantaytambu, Nazca Peru, Sacsayhuaman, Machu Piccu, etc.; are far older than the scholars would like to admit. C^{14}, Carbon dating cannot be used to date stone, only organic material, so what these Europeans do is try to date other remains and artefacts in the surrounding area but, that is not a conclusive way to date sites, as it was common for ancient sites to be inherited and used by later tribes and peoples newly coming into the area.

Some of these sites such as Teotihuacan, Tiahuanaco, Sacsayhuaman, etc., have no records of their origin and were already considered ancient by the Nahuatl tribes (Mayans, Aztecs, Incas, etc.) who inhabited them in their own more recent times. All of these tribes attribute the founding of these sites to an olden race of giant God like beings who have irrefutably been proven to be the Olmecs (Xia people) who spoke African languages as has been shown irrefutably.

Almost all of these ancient sites worldwide were later inherited by the northerners, the mountain people; Tamahu (Caucasian) people, who invaded, occupied and forced out the original people of all these civilizations. Those that were left were amalgamated by the invaders which lightened the complexion of the remaining population. This is most evident in the region of India, Pakistan and Khemet of the New Kingdom, 17th Dynasty upwards. Much of the original inhabitants, as always, retreated to the Southern hemisphere region of Africa, i.e. Nubia (Meroe, Ethiopia, Yemen, etc.).

The fact remains that there has never been an ancient civilization, worthy of the name found, that wasn't first inhabited by the sons of the soil, the African Kushite, the original and oldest race of humanity. Only by ignoring the hard evidence can anybody claim otherwise. Again, this is not racism or 'Pan-Africanism', this is hard facts beyond the shadow of a doubt.

The argument most used by experts is that there is no tangible evidence of a high civilization anywhere in the world prior to 4000 B.C., when they speculate that the society of Sumer emerged out of the mists of pre-history. In order to say this, all of the proof is blatantly ignored and corrupted into insignificance. The enigmatic monuments, such as pyramids, megaliths and temples, the astronomy and Innovations, the spirituality, medicine and mathematics, the legal laws and applied sciences and all of the unexplained achievements such as engineering and construction, the precision and the fact that none of this could've been achieved with primitive tools in the hands of primitive minds. We are now in 2017 A.D. of the Gregorian calendar and the world is still in awe of what our ancestors achieved during these 'Golden Ages' of human history. Only now is the glory of the Kushites and their Gods, Paut Neteru beginning to re-surface, in preparation for the Kushites to once again rule the world by spirituality.

".... Scholars have a problem with a crossing of the oceans by boats 15,000 or 20,000 years ago: Man, they hold, was too primitive then to have ocean going vessels and navigate the high seas. Not until the Sumerian civilization, at the beginning of the fourth millennium B.C., did mankind begin to attain the land (wheeled craft) and water (boats) means of long range transportation.

But that according to the Sumerians, themselves, was the course of events after the deluge. There had been, they states and re-stated, a high civilization upon Earth before the deluge – a civilization begun on Earth by those who had come from the Anu Planet continued through a line of long living 'demi-Gods', the offspring of intermarriage between the Extraterrestrials (the biblical Nephileem) and the 'daughters' of man'.

Egyptian chronicles, such as the writings of Manetho, followed the same concept, so of course did the Bible, which describes both rural life (farming, sheepherding) and urban civilization (cities, metallurgy) before the deluge. All that, however, according to all those ancient sources was wiped off the face of the Earth by the deluge and everything had to be restarted from scratch ...."

- Zecharia Sitchin: The Lost Realms: Pg. 39 (In Part)

So, either the ancients don't know what they're talking about concerning their own origin and history and cannot be trusted or the modern day consensus on the origin or history of civilization is seriously misguided. I don't know about you, dear reader, but I'd rather believe that our modern day consensus is incorrect; who better than the ancients, themselves, to tell us the true origin of humanity and world civilizations. For as is evident, this was of the utmost importance to them, as they greatly cherished their roots and sense of origin and identity. The Ancient Kushites all kept detailed records of their history going way back to the Zep Tepi – 'First Times, Beginning', the dawn of time, when humanity was given the gift and tools of civilization such as, reading, writing and arithmetic (communication, language), record-keeping, kingship, penal system, agriculture, astronomy, science, medicine, metallurgy, architecture, arts, etc.

To assume that the ancient ancestors were not of sound mind because their allegorical myths and stories are misunderstood is presumptuous, prejudice and based on nothing but bias. The fact that many of these so called myths have been proven and continue to be proven correct, both historically and scientifically, is more concrete proof of how wrong our perception of the early civilizations of man is. It is now time for this misconception to be replaced with the correct outlook. It is time for the historical timeline to be corrected, readjusted in the light of the hard evidence on the ground, the treasures in the sand. It is the time in which the history of the Kushites, Nubia, Egypt and the wider world must be rewritten, from a Black African perspective. It is the purpose of this book for Black African people to reclaim their stolen legacy, especially that of Egypt which has for far too long been separated from the rest of Black Africa and painted 'White' or 'Asian looking', but also the Indus Valley, the Yucatan Basin, Sumer, Elam, China, Athens and Crete, Nabatean Arabia and Yemen and Phoenicia among others. It is of the utmost importance for the next generation of young Kushite scholars and historians, Khemetologists etc., to see this great work achieved. Otherwise all of the efforts of the ancients and our modern day seekers of the facts such as, Cheikh Anta Diop, Dr John Henrik Clarke, Dr Ben Jochannan, Ashra & Meira Kwesi, Wayne Chandler, Indus Khamit Kush, Druscilla Dundee Houston, Dr Francis Cress Welsing, Ivan Van Sertima, Chancellor Williams and the countless others would've been in vain. The great work of Dr Malachi Z. York, 'The Master Teacher', everything all of the modern black recovered greats would have been for nothing but suffering, so many have suffered just to give us back our true liberating identity. For we are Kushites!

It's time to take off the chains from off of your minds because the 6000 year spell of religion has run its course. It's time to wake up from the nonsense and see through the fairytales. The children are depending on us adults to guide them and point them in the right direction, so that they may never be pointed in the wrong direction ever again. This fourth age of Kali Yuga has been an expensive learning curve, not just for Black people, but for the wider world in general. This new age of Hapi (Aquarius) is ushering in the end of the world (as you know it).

Imagine if a Black person or group for that matter, was to retell the history of White Greece or Rome, Alexander the Greek, or the Caesars while painting them with black skin and woolly hair? What do you think would be the reaction of the Caucasian world? Do you think that they would let us get away with that blatant lie and disrespect to their ancestors? Well, based on that, it's time for us to make a stand against the blatant lies and audacity of the White world. To stop allowing so called religious nut jobs and academics to lie and slander our beloved ancestors, our mothers and fathers because we owe it to them to honour their memory in the correct way and keep their truth, their story alive. It is no longer acceptable to allow others to present them as sun worshippers, atheists, heathens, backward, polytheists and all the rest of the negative names which have been associated with them. If you can ignore your own legacy and allow Mother Africa to be portrayed as the 'Dark Continent', of ignorance, then you are unworthy of the sacred blood running through your veins and the divine pigment (Melanin) colouring your skin.

If you were robbed of your money you'd do your best to see that your finances were recovered. If you were robbed of your car, you'd probably report it stolen as soon as possible and try to get it recovered. If you were robbed of your clothes wouldn't you try to get them back? Then how come so many of you Kushites, having been robbed of your identity and legacy, not try to retrieve them straight away upon learning about the conspiracy being ran upon our people?

You are too busy lying to yourselves trying to convince yourselves that you are an Arab or Hebrew or Christian or that you are English, American, European, Jamaican or Caribbean, even; anything but Kushite (African). You don't wish to know your own culture and contribution to world civilization; your own glorious role as civilizers and pioneers as humanity under your own natural identity and theocracy; before any of these plagiarized religions put you under their spell-binding influence and brainwashing. Well, I want to tell you that the Kushites established the greatest civilizations ever witnessed upon the face of the earth to date.

Now this is what the majority of Egyptologists do to confuse our legacy. Egyptian chronology is founded upon the Egyptian Priest Manetho's writing along with four other sources which, despite minor discrepancies, confirm Manetho's list. These four sources split Khemetian/Khamite (Egyptian) history into three eras. These sources are: 1) Manetho's list, 2) Palermo Stone, 3) The Turin Papyrus and 4) the Abydos King list. The eras are namely:

1) The Era of the Neteru (which end with Horus, son of Osiris and Isis)
2) The Era of demi-Gods (Shemsu Har - 'the Followers of Horus')
3) The Era of the Shekem Ur Shekem (The Pharaohs, beginning with Pharaoh Menes/Narmer).

What the Egyptologists do is ignore the first two eras because the astronomical length of the timeline extends so long back into prehistory, that they refuse to acknowledge them, claiming that they are superstitious myths. Still, at the same time, they base Egyptian chronology on the third year; that of the pharaohs which they presume began c. 3100 B.C., because it is in line with their own world timeline of history.

In this way, they deny the Kushite his true place in world history as pioneer of civilization, claiming that the Ahkus – 'Shemsu Har', are a myth. For them to acknowledge the authenticity of the full three eras, would mean that they would have to rewrite the textbooks on world history, as our legacy would extend right back through prehistory (Neolithic, Mesolithic and Palaeolithic) when they (Europeans) claim that humanity was supposed to be unlettered.

"We feel obliged to point out that this was not at all how the Ancient Egyptians viewed their own history. For them there was never any question of mythical epochs or 'nebulous spiritual forces' lurking in the distant past. For them, to state matters plainly, the 'Followers of Horus' and the geographical landscape in which they had 'ruled', were unquestionable realities to which they were directly and inseverably connected. Indeed, if one takes the Egyptian accounts and traditions seriously what the 'Followers of Horus' begin to sound like is a lineage of real, although 'unnamed' individuals whose function and duty, as Henri Frankfort himself suggested, was to provide the 'spiritual force' behind the monarchy (though by no means in a 'vague' or 'nebulous' manner). The Egyptians' own accounts also invite the conclusion that the role of these 'Followers' may have been to carry down the ages a body of

extraordinary knowledge harking back to the even more mysterious 'time of the Neteru' – i.e. the 'Gods'.

From available primary sources, in other words, the overall picture that emerges is that the 'Followers of Horus' may not have been 'Kings' in the usual sense of the word but rather immensely powerful and enlightened individuals high initiates who were carefully selected by an elite academy that established itself at the sacred site of Heliopolis – Giza, thousands of years before history began. There is much to suggest, too, that the Ancient Egyptian texts are right and that Pharaonic civilization may indeed have owed its unique spark of genius to just such a 'brotherhood' linked to just such an archaic and elite academy...."

- Keeper of Genesis: Robert Bauval, Graham Hancock: Pg. 205 – 206 (In Part)

One must overstand that an Egyptian priest was not any ordinary priest in the modern sense of the word. An Egyptian priest was an initiate into the Higher Mysteries of esoteric knowledge, but no only that. More times than often he was also an alkhemist, mathematician, astronomer, doctor, magician, architect, scribe, greo, geographer historian, among other things.

As stated earlier, the ancient city of Anu/On (Heliopolis) can be rightly considered as the most ancient religious city in not only Khemet (Egypt) but more so, the wider world. It was not only religious in the one dimensional sense, but also the centre of astronomy, medicine, science and history in Egypt. The High Priests of Anu/On was the chief astronomer in the land, having an observatory whereby he chartered and watched the precession of the equinoxes, the zodiacal cycle in which the sun travels through the twelve houses of the zodiac, rising within a different zodiacal sign every 2,160 years. The priests also observed the larger cycle of 25,920 years and the heliacal rising of Sibtu (Sirius) which signalled the yearly inundation of the Mother Nile.

By the era of the Pharaohs, the ancient city of Anu (Heliopolis) was already extended way back to the origin of the land and the beginning of the processional cycles of time (Zep Tepi). Again, this is where Theology and the Khemetian Theocracy began. The oldest creation story in the world is the Heliopolitan creation story. It was here in the sacred city of On (Heliopolis), within the Het Benbennet – 'The Mansion of the Phoenix', that the ancient relics along with the Benben Stone and the Benben (the craft that Re' was said to have descended to earth in) was housed. These relics were on display for the people of Khemet (Egypt) to visit, see and in some cases even touch.

In study the dualistic nature of the stars, 'so above, so below' and the sacred wisdom of Tehuti (Thoth), the writings of the Hermetica – the Emerald Tablet – The High Priest of Anu/the Ahkus were bringing the powers of above, below and grounding it within themselves, people and surroundings creating a literal heaven on earth; for this On (Heliopolis), like Teotihuacán in Mexico was a place where the quest for immortality could be realized; a place where men could be transfigured through this mystical knowledge into Gods (Elohs, Neters).

The knowledge of the stars was that which holds the secrets to eternal life and creation, capable of transfiguring humans into 'Light Beings' at the site of the Giza necropolis with a high science not understood by modern day humans. The Egyptian Mystery system, Alchemy and the Pyramid Sciences stem from here and were the backbone of the civilization from the time of the demi-Gods – 'Followers of Horus' to 332 B.C. when the infamous homosexual, Alexander the Greek (because he weren't great) and Aristotle and them took over.

MAXIM 38: EPILOGUE 1

On the transmission of wisdom, knowledge and sound principles

".... If you listen to the maxims I have just handed to you, all your undertakings will prosper. The wealth of these maxims lies in the extent to which they are sound. They will live on by word of mouth because they are so complete and so consistently expressed. Each of these maxims should be handed down so they never disappear from this land and each maxim should be perfectly expressed so that those high in the land talk of them. This is the teaching a disciple must pass on to posterity. If he listens he will become a good listener, capable of understanding. It is good to lay down this teaching for posterity in the hope that it will be understood.

If a good example is set by the leader, it will be effective for all eternity and all his wisdom will become one with the eternity of the cycles.

The one who knows takes care of his ba – his capacity for sublimation; he makes certain it will survive and be long lasting. Thanks to his ba he is happy on this earth. The one who knows is recognizable by his wisdom and a noble one by way of his acting. His way of being should be the exact expression of his conscience; may his lips be truthful when he expresses himself and may his eyes truly see, may his ears become intent on listening to what is useful to his spiritual son, for the one who practices the law of Maat cannot lie..."

MAXIM 39: EPILOGUE 2

On the need to listen and understand

".... It is useful for a spiritual son to listen. If a person immerses himself in listening, he will start to understand. True listening makes the word valuable. The person who knows how to listen can master what is enlightening and useful. Listening benefits the one who listens. Listening is better than anything – it engenders perfect love. How fortunate when a son can accept what his father says! Understanding the message, he will reach a grand old age. God loves the man who listens but detests the one who does not. The conscience of a man's heart determines whether he listens or not. For a human being this heart conscience is life, prosperity and health.

It is the man who listens who understands what is said. It is the man who loves listening who fulfils what is said. How fortunate when a son obeys his father.

He who listens to the person who hands on this teaching will be well in his innermost self and blessed by his father. His memory will live on in the words of those living on this earth or of those yet to be born..."

- The Teachings of Ptah-Hotep

To learn the secrets of astral immortality, one must learn to listen twice as much as one speaks. For we each have two ears and one mouth. If God intended for us to speak twice as much as we listen, he would've given us two mouths and one ear! Nowadays, too many of us talk too much and are too loud. Practice listening to the wisdom of silence. Quieten the noise surrounding you so that you may be able to hear your own thoughts and the secret voice of the thinking heart, even the hidden voice of the Kosmos, the secrets of the stars.

Study the cycle of the stars and the cycle of our own star, the sun. Measure and commemorate the passage of time and peer into the mysteries of the epochs. For this is how to become an Ahkus once again my brothers and sisters. This is how we can and will become Gods again, meaning, divine beings of light and love. Drop the unconfirmed beliefs of fabricated religions and look into the origin of all knowledge and wisdom for yourselves. For only then will you truly overstand. Sound Right Reasoning.

To chart the movements of the stars takes seriously long spans of stellar observation and more to the point, seriously intelligent men and women. In order for Kushites such as the Khemetian, Egyptians to create the precise records that they possessed, they first would've had to have a long tradition of stellar observation behind them going extremely far back into prehistory (before records began). The same goes for the Sumerians etc.

The technical expertise of such a group as the Ahkus or 'Followers of Horus' is evidently mind blowing and unfathomable to our contemporary society. These great minds of the ancient world would make our best scientific minds today look spastic. All of the world's religions and philosophies today, have their roots in the ancient teachings of the Kushite Kingdoms with no exceptions. Through time and misunderstandings these teachings became diluted into the belief systems we see in all their various forms in the contemporary world today. They all owe a great debt to our Kushite ancestors.

The 'Followers of Horus' (Shemsu Har, Ahkus) brought to fruition the universal blueprint with the intensity of a messianic cult (cultivating our culture). These applied scientist, astrologers, astronomers, solar biologists, astrophysicists, atomic theorists, sages, historians, alchemists, geographers, mathematicians, engineers, doctors, etc. were multifaceted geniuses par excellence, who had been taught this divine information since the Zep Tepi. It was them who were responsible for implementing the 1st Golden Age of humanity which was on a global scale before the great deluge.

They mobilized and united the people of Kush into Kingdoms and were the glue that kept the civilizations and peoples of different tribes together. It was them that initiated the Pharaonic state after the flood, the end of an Age/Era, in a last ditch attempt to preserve the teachings and seal them up, away from the Beast man; until the end of time.

".... But thou, O Daniel, shut up the words and seal the book until the time of the End...."

- The Book of Daniel 12:4

MYTH noun (I) a traditional story about the early history of a people or explaining a natural or social phenomenon, typically involving supernatural beings or events. 2. A widely held but false belief. 3. A fictitious or imaginary person or thing.

- Origin Greek Mutos

As stated earlier, myths are not taken as historical events by scholars, especially Egyptologists who altogether overlook these aspects of Khemetian, Egyptian history. They are of the belief that the so called myths of Egypt are nothing but the fantasies of prehistoric people with unsound minds. Because of this, all of the accounts of a pre-deluvial civilization of high science and technology are quickly dismissed and not taken as historical realities which actually took place on the planet, in times far gone.

The funny thing about this is the fact that our myths and many others have regularly proven to be true, whilst the myth made bible has never been proven to be accurate, in the sense that none of its fictitious, mythological characters have ever been found. Noah's ark has never been found or Noah confirmed. Abraham may have a shrine supposedly housing his remains but his remains have never been confirmed; Jesus, King David, Solomon, Daniel, The Disciples, John, Job, Elijah, Moses, Isaiah, Ezekiel, Isaac, the list goes on. None of them have ever been proven to have ever been real. The exodus has never been confirmed outside of the scriptures because all of these stories are myths which were based on the stories of real Kushite people and civilizations. They were not Jews, Christians or Moslems. They were Africans with African Gods and African customs. The biggest and most persistent myths are the so-called Holy Scriptures. In contrast, Pharaoh Rameses the Great has been confirmed, Pharaohs Kamose and Ahmose, Seti 1st, the sage Ptah-Hotep, Pharaoh Djoser Neterkeht and Imhotep, Sesostris I, Khufu, Khafre, Menkuare, Ankhenatun, Tutankhamun, Gilgamesh, Sargon, Utnapishtim (Ziusudra), Memnon, In all their glory.

The expulsion of the Hyksos (the real Exodus), the Osirion, the sacred city of On (Heliopolis), the Benben, the Labyrinth of Suten Amunemhet III, Nippur, Sippar, Uruk, Eridu, Atlan (Xi Mexico, and North America) etc. These were real folks upon whom biblical and qur'anic myths were based; Black people, who were drastically different to the pseudo-characters that the Bible fabricated with new names. Thus, it has been confirmed, time and time again, that the ancient so called Kushite myths are not myths but realities. One can even go as far as saying that the Neteru/Anunnaqi has been confirmed as realities not myths. Don't believe me, do the research for yourselves!

It is also a fact that the ancient city of Troy, home of the Trojans was also considered a myth along with Minoa (Ancient Crete), until they were unearthed following clues form Homer's Iliad, another confirmation that these myths can and should be taken as historical in most cases. A lot of these so called myths are confirmed accidentally. If you only knew how much time, money and effort has gone into looking for biblical myths and still nothing concrete has never been proven or confirmed. The only myths are the diluted so called 'Holy Scriptures'. For they have not been confirmed historically or scientifically like Kushite myths have and most probably never will be in the way that they are depicted.

To praise the Egyptians for all of their astronomical, technological engineering, spiritual sciences and precision and then with the same breath try to imply that their minds were unsound and superstitious and that their records of their origins cannot be treated as real, is a blatant contradiction. How can a people so frank, so precise and sophisticated be at the same time backward, semi-savages? That just doesn't add up or make any sense.

For them to produce the awe inspiring civilization that they did, the mind boggling span of rulers and great philosophers, sages and art, the mysteries, the medicines and so much more, the ancient Egyptians and their officials must have been astute individuals and critical, practical thinkers, no savages. The fact that much of the Egyptian story still mystifies experts today is testimony to this.

The Zep Tepi, the Neteru, the Ahkus, the Sages, the Pharaohs were real events and people of flesh and blood. Most of the stories of the so called Holy Scriptures are based on the legends of these factual Kushites, which were corrupted with time and turned into corrupted myths. All of the Abrahamic faiths (Judaism, Christianity, and Islam) are based upon the Egyptian and Sumerian Mysteries. The leaders of your institutions know this to be true. The Vatican, the authors of the Torah (the Sanhedrin), the Imams in Arabia, the Knights Templars, the Freemasons, the Theosophists, the Rosicrucians, the priory of Zion, etc., all know this.

There is a conspiracy being run on Kushites of today, to convince you that the Egyptians were sun worshipping Satanists, so that you will never look more deeply into the Egyptian teachings and sciences, to discover the secret of your legacy of spirituality and the Law of the Light. This way they hope you will never re-establish your link with your ancestors and Gods, which will quicker usher in a New Age of Spirituality and Righteousness. When Ma'at reigns again, is when the Nubian/Kushite will rule the world again, as a God and Vice-Regent of Paut Neteru and the Most High, AMUN RA (pronounced Re').

That will be the end of this world (as you know it – Capitalism, Westernism, False beginning of a new 'Golden Age') not just for Kushites, but for the whole human family and the earth itself. This will be a rude awakening, a radical change for humanity which must rediscover its purpose, the purpose of creation in general.

".... Imitate your fathers who lived before you; success depends on your ability to learn. The Sages passed on their teaching in their writings: consult them, study them, read and re-read them unceasingly? ...."

- The Wisdom of the Sages

I will say, that at the start of the New Kingdom, Egypt was in her death throws. She never regained her former glory, becoming only a shadow of herself. The priesthood began to corrupt the priesthood of Amun, the house of Pharaoh began to become mediocre, but for a few great ones. By the end of the Middle Kingdom, it was Egypt in death. Not like the days of those in the 1st, 2nd, 3rd and 4th Dynasties – the 6th Dynasty and the 11th and 12th Dynasty.

Sedjem Ash "He Who Heard The Call"

Practice remaining silent, watching, listening and learning to overstand. Rebelling against the life is pointless. We must learn to accept what it brings. There is a profound symbolism in the transition of day and night. The darkness tries to devour the light. Because it fights so valiantly, the light manages to overpower it. When the sun appears to rise every morning, it is a sign of the triumph of the Light reborn, but most people cannot perceive it.

The beauty of life does not depend on us; it dwells also in our capacity to grasp it. Beauty is not in the eyes of the beholder, but in the object beheld. In order to see the beauty in something, one only has to know how to look at it.

The rectrix, the tail feather which allows birds to direct their flight without error, guides your life in truth, justice and righteousness. Truth is the breath of life in the nostrils of men/women and may she drive away evil from their bodies. Judge the lowly in the same way as the powerful. Protect the weak from the strong and turn away the rage of the evil being from everyone, as a servant of Ma'at. For this is the Law of the Light. Vaster than humanity, she stretches beyond the stars. Ma'at lives and thrives off Love and Light. There is a place of truth within the centre of the heart; the Holy of Holies within the Temple of man/wombman. In order to become a truth-seeker, one must hear the call, from then on, one must shun all falsehood. For falsehood destroys the word. As a servant of Ma'at, it becomes impossible to lie to the self or to others.

When true love unites man and woman, it makes them inseparable. They want to live the same life, in all its dimensions, from the most worldly to the spiritual. Whatever trials they might have to endure, they would never complain or lament and if they must confront the notion of failure, they would not turn away from it. True love shapes eternity as if it were a fabric; Reverence to mother Hathor, Goddess of Love.

Sometimes the call is so close, so close that its power can make you deaf to the call. Listen to the secret voice of the heart; the hidden voice of the Kosmos. The tighter shut you keep your mouth, the better off you are. Within the sacred silence are held the secrets of matter. Truth drives away falsehood, evil-doers are struck down and darkness (shadow) yields to the light.

The Kushites (Egyptians) achieved a Utopian reality before and during the Old Kingdom. The Shekem Ur Shekems (Pharaoh's) duty to his people was to direct the building of 'Heaven on Earth', the cities of God. The power behind the throne was the Ahkus, Shemsu Har – 'Followers of Horus', the officials, the initiate priesthoods, the scribes and craftsmen. Most importantly, the power behind the Utopian state, mentioned by the poet Homer, was 'the Rule' (Maat).

Pharaoh built in accordance with his duty to his people and to prove his beneficence by the works he undertook for the Gods, building their temples and fashioning their images. At Anu/Iunu, Memphis, Abydos, Edfu, Khemenu, Waset, Aswan, Siwa, Bubastis, Pi-Rameses, Elephantine, in both Upper and also within Lower Khemet (Egypt) and throughout the Ancient Kushite Kingdoms. The work was accomplished, progressive and monumental. This gargantuan construction continued in many forms.

At the heart of this work was the Shekem Ur Shekems, 'House of Eternity' (tomb), which was created by the craftsmen of places like 'the Place of Truth' in Thebes (Waset). Each day the craftsmen toiled to vanquish (the illusion of) death; they build for the Ka, that intangible energy which resides within all living things without being fixed within it or dying with it. And it was for the royal Ka which passes from Pharaoh to Pharaoh without ever belonging to any one of them exclusively, that the craftsmen continued to perfect the Houses of Eternity, for the essential mystery from which everything proceeds is the birth of what limited minds consider to be tombs and which, in reality, are dwelling places of light. But what can second rate people overstand of this secret? Simple minds with closed hearts and limited intelligence? Thus, the A'afertiaat (Pharaohs) and other such Kushite rulers could never be the unsound, backward idolaters that they are painted by the misinformed (and Hollywood) to be. The dictators, myth makers and believers of unconfirmed fantasies. They, unlike the Tamahu Greeks and Romans, did not practice back-biting, treason, murder from covetousness and jealousy for the throne and/or crown, slavery for economic reasons and usurping of the throne/crown, but for the few rulers who misunderstood the purpose.

The Kushites did not practice intrigue and deceit to steal the rulership with father murdering son, son murdering father, etc. They did not practice child sacrifice or human sacrifice to appease any fantasy, spook Gods. The theocracies of the Kushites spawned the longest lasting civilizations on earth by light years. They did not impose their way of thinking on others but for the benefit of the entire globe and the propagation of Ma'at into every corner of the world.

The expert and precise knowledge, wisdom and overstanding (Sound Right Reasoning) produced all the major breakthroughs that the world takes for granted and still enjoys today in every field and walk of life, from science to religion. The subtle monotheism of BA KULUWM "THE ALL" is only overstood by those who tune in to the sacred Aum principle, which personifies and expresses itself in the multiplicity of Paut Neteru – 'The Company of the Gods', with AMUN RE "THE HIDDEN ONE" [Revelations 3:14], (ANU "THE MOST HIGH [Psalms 82:1-6]), also known [in other cultures, regions, and languages] as Allah, El Eloh, Yahuwa, Yahweh, Ahura Mazda, God, Theo, El Eloh, The Almighty, etc.; as the Most High.

Any contemporary religion (such as Judaism, Christianity, Islam) claiming exclusivity to God/s while condemning others as invalids has missed the point completely. Man, as has been suggested by experts did not move up a linear timeline from primitive ignorance, to progress smarter and smarter into our contemporary modern world today. Humans were taught by the Gods far back in the Zep Tepi in Africa and after falling further away from spiritual truth after the Golden Age, have regressed and become dumber and dumber with each cycle. The further we get away from the 'Beginning Times', the more 'Sacred Wisdom' that is lost. Thus; the modern religions that you follow are but a shadow of the glory of the ancestors which many today will never know. As the world changes, many are called but only few will be chosen to be here, in the here-after. Although the Pharaohs had achieved many miraculous feats within their illustrious lifetimes, that they had often been the cause to the ceasing of hostilities all over the ancient world, they had not succeeded in wiping out hatred, ambition or the encroaching greed in a fast changing, money orientated world.

They were conscious that only the Goddess Maat, the incarnation of truth, justice and reciprocity, could prevent the human race from pursuing its natural trajectory and tendency to corruption, injustice and its ultimate destruction. Since the Zep Tepi – 'First Times, Beginning', the Pharaonic state had relied upon a brotherhood (Ahkus, Shemsu Har) initiated into the mysteries of life and existence, capable of carving and writing eternity into stone. After the great deluge, it was these remarkable, incorruptible God-Men who took up the truth.

In their sacred moments (logged in time and space), gazing into the distance with a vision that far exceeded that of other men; often, during the courses of their reigns and life, they had intuitive premonitions which enabled them to see through the barriers of the future and to walk outside of the well beaten, well-trodden paths. The A'afertiaat to, were Sedjem Ash 'He Who Heard the Call,' and their thoughts were regularly transformed into creations filled with love and light. They drew their inspiration from the Principalities of Nature. They were Neters incarnate, rather than Abraham and Muhammed, it was these 'Mighty Men' (Giboreem), 'Men of Renown', who were and still are, by far, the best examples of man.

Still, the important thing is a man's worth not his titles. Men of vision, they were clear sighted and most of all, they knew their limitations. They were not defined by their jewellery or vast riches, but by their values, purpose, their undying principles, the Rule. All attempts to depict them as merciless tyrants is being exposed as I write their true story though love, reverence and admiration for my ancestors. For I have put my life upon the line to tell this story. In emulation of them, let us seek to be men of integrity and sincerity.

"Oh heavenly ones, the Neteru, who are the sustainers of all the world's; we do accept the duty you have lain upon us to clean up the filth made by the West and its non-submitting fools. Oh our sustainers, we beseech you, to keep your hands over us, to control the strings of the courses of our lives, our sustainers. And if we do disagreeableness, please show thy divine forgiveness and blessings upon us. For you are the only ones that can lead us true followers of the News-bearers and in thy name we carry on....."

- The Prayer of the Deities

The initiates into the Higher Mysteries had made many discoveries in Egypt (and Sumer, etc.). Many of these discoveries would've been dangerous in the hands of second rate men and women, who could use the power to do harm and forge new weapons. Due to this risk, this sacred knowledge was guarded and kept between the brotherhood, the Pharaoh and initiates of the higher mysteries. Thus, many discoveries made by the Kushites (Egyptians) were later attributed to others, like the discovery of iron and electricity and subatomic science (the splitting of atoms), etc.

Of course, with some properly-done research from yourselves, all can be self-confirmed, without the need of any religious 'Middle-Man' holding your hand, doing your thinking for you. You do not need any Imam, or Sheikh, Rabbi or Pastor to confirm for you what you can confirm for yourselves. Neither do you need the so-called conscious community of late.

Our ancestors were extraordinary people with profound insight. The Higher Mysteries held many secrets of vital importance. Many men tried and failed to decipher the living wisdom of Ancient Egypt. Many men came to Egypt to study under the initiate priesthoods, attend the House of Life and take what they had learnt back to their own areas of the globe. Many were disagreeable in nature and many had nothing but power, riches and self-interests on their minds and we know this.

Some of the students of Egypt established philosophies, academies and religions founded on what was learnt during their time in Egypt. People like Socrates, Solon, Homer, Plato, Aristotle, the Hyksos Kings, Arabs and many others. The appropriation of the Egyptian and Kushite (Nubian) origin of civilization is blatant racism. Because the world at large has still not cleared the hurdle of racism and far right extremism, they (others) do not want to acknowledge the significant contribution Kushites have made to the uplifting of humanity, both then and now. Science and philosophies, religions and spirituality of the East, do not want to acknowledge the roots of their ideas and concepts. They show us no appreciation and this is also the fault of ourselves in allowing our legacy to be tarnished. In 2017 there is no more excuse for us to allow this to carry on unchallenged.

The secrets of eternal life and alchemy were highly sort after secrets of the Ancient Kushites of Egypt and Mesopotamia (Sumer). Even into modern times, this sacred information has been coveted by many men from diverse nations. The sacred wisdom of Tehuti (Thoth) also called Hermes was sealed and hidden from the uninitiated and today the bits and pieces that have been found and deciphered have become the most profound scientific theories, such as sub-atomic sciences and quantum physics and also the Jewish Kabbalah and other esoteric occult sciences.

Many of the secrets were taken into other areas of Africa by those, such as, the Dogon tribes of Mali and the Moors under the camouflage of Sufi Islam. A lot of the tenets of the sacred knowledge were taken into Europe by the Moors which inspired the Renaissance and Enlightenment period of more modern times. Our sacred ancestors and knowledge brought the world out of the dark ages, not once but twice. It was the Moors who freed the Slavic's from their own slavery and initiated them and the Gypsies and others, into masonry and other secret mysteries. The Copts of Egypt and Ethiopia also kept many of the ancient traditions which dissipated into Middle Eastern religions.

If you, Modern Kushites, do not turn back through contemporary religion to retrieve your legacy, then it's nobody's but your loss. If you do not claim your heritage, then others, other than you will claim it, as is being done now by Shashu (mixed people) and Europeans. You now have nobody else to blame and you owe it to the Gods, the ancestors and yourselves to live in the image of divinity awakening from your 6000 years of slumber, to rebuild Africa back into the land of light and the power of 9 Ether $9 \times 9 \times 9^9$, the universal equation.

The Pharaoh and their spiritual descendent are men carved from a different block, poured from a different bottle and cut from a different quality of cloth. Happiness is as fragile as the wings of a butterfly and at the same time, as sturdy as granite, as long as you savoured each moment as though it were a miracle. The first and foremost of virtues is silence. In silence resides the pure energy of creation.

The teachings of the wisdom of Kush teach that a human is not just a human but belongs to the whole of creation and is thus linked to all forms of life. We are all in BA KULUWM "THE ALL". It is the 'Eye of Horus' which allows us to perceive and see the Higher Mysteries and to be in communion with the ascended masters and blessed ancestors who reside in heaven. The teachings inspire both our thoughts and deeds and acts as the rudder for our nation's ship. The Rule is the expression of the Goddess Ma'at, daughter of the Divine Light, the Principle of all harmony and order. Never be negligent; seek what is just, be consistent, pass on what you have received by embodying it in matter without betraying the spirit. The mystery of the 'Great Work' will ever remain hidden to the unworthy, even after it has been revealed. Be silent and preserve the secret. The secret best kept sacred.

Make offerings and prayers to Paut Neteru and the ancestors with reverence and the worship of The Most High, AMUN RE (ANU). Take an interest in your culture, history and root; celebrate the triumph of light over shadow with every new sunrise. Tolerate no ill-will, do not go to any place of worship (Masjid, Temple) if you have acted against Ma'at, if you are in any state of impurity of lies. Learn the Rites of Ma'at and the Living Wisdom of the Sages with fervour. Do not falsify the weight or measure, or the facts. Do not wrong the Eye of the Light, do not be greedy. Protect the weak from the strong, protect the orphan and always respect the Rule (Ma'at), whatever religion you wish to call yourselves. Learn to respond always to the call, pray and work to have access to Neter Tehuti's sacred words and incantations, decipher their meanings, resolve their difficulties and become a master of their secrets. Thus you will become, once again a 'Light Being' (Ahkus) worthy of travelling to the 'Land of Light'; a true servant of Ma'at.

".... If the act of ceaseless listening enters him who listens, he who listens becomes he who hears. When the listening is good, the word is good. He whom God loves is he who hears; he who does not hear is hated by God. It is he who loves to hear who accomplishes what is said. As for the ignorant man who does not listen, he will accomplish nothing. He considers

knowledge to be ignorance, the useful to be harmful, he does all that is hateful, he lives on what causes death. Do not put one thing in the place of another, be aware of the shackles breaking within you, be aware of that which is spoken by him who knows the rites ...."

- The Wisdom of the Sages

".... Remember the rule for a teacher, for him who instructs future scribes: "to be to his pupils a patient teacher speaking gentle words, to earn their respect by awakening their sensitivity, to educate by inspiring love"...."

- Nefer the Silent: Christian Jaq; Pg 227 (In Part)

Never force your views upon anyone and allow each person to be responsible for their own choices. Writing makes abstract things live, reading gives access to the teachings of the sages, but some people choose not to read. Quiet combat can be fought without violence, not by use of the fists, but by way of the mind. Pay homage to the ancestors and pray that they will enlighten our nation. May their example reunite all Kushite people of the African diaspora, so that we can take the role of uniting the wider world. Our predecessors established the spirit of our nation and they nourished its soul with their deeds. We must pass on, in our turn, the things they passed on to us. If you neglect the ancestors, you will become deaf, dumb and blind.

Let your home be a shrine also. Let its objects, furnishings and pictures give it meaning. Ask the right questions, because the wrong ones are sterile. A woman should be able to learn how to introduce her husband to all the games of love with enthusiasm, from the wildest to the most subtle and to channel his Rau/Chi and vice-versa. The intoxicating delights will become inexhaustible pleasures of love and passion. It is pleasing also when a woman's beauty is able to change with the seasons, like the beauty of the sky or the River Nile. Full blossomed, nature beautifies herself for mating in the summer, she is tender, delicate and yielding in the autumn, wild in the winter, lively and sublime in the spring, revealing endless pathways to desire. With this, a man will make love to his woman with all the vigour of a ram and the years will flow by with the sweetness of honey.

It is the works of the beings of light that you must see; those that operate in the invisible world, Paul Neteru. The God's work lasts and continues forever, while the work of men is destroyed with time. According to the sage Ptah-Hotep; *"Listening is the best of all things"*, and it is the heart that enables us to listen. If we follow its commands it will transform us into upright beings. If we do not separate it from our tongues, we will achieve everything that we set out to do.

".... Let there be no compulsion in religion: Truth stands out clear form error: whoever rejects evil and believes in Allah has grasped the most trustworthy handhold that never breaks. And Allah hears and knows all things....."

- The Holy Qur'an: Abdullah Yusuf Ali: Surah 2, Ayat 256

A strong woman, virtuous and obedient to her husband, is a diamond to a man. Trust in a woman's advice and her intuition, for she can decipher fragments of the future with intuition better than men. Trust in the wisdom of her intuition, be it a mother, wife, sister, daughter, aunt, grandmother, etc. Listening is the best of all things.

True happiness is found in righteousness and the love of Ma'at. Ma'at is what Paut Neteru love, the justice of the creative act. Great is 'the Rule', effective and everlasting; she has not changed since the birth of creation, order out of chaos and when all things have passed from this physical creation, she will live on. The Pharaoh's principal duty and function is to replace disorder, injustice and disagreeableness with the Order of Maat. Accomplish Ma'at and she will unveil herself unto you. The divine light lives through Ma'at, justice, thanks to which you will distinguish good from evil. Build your path with the Light of Ma'at and do not forget the smile of Ma'at.

The names of the great authors endure beyond their deaths, even though they did not build pyramids. The most solid of monuments crumbles to dust, but through time, people still remember books. A good book constructs a pyramid and/or temple within the readers' heart; it is more lasting than any pyramid, tomb or temple. What the great authors say is completed. What comes out of their books remains in the memory. They hide their magic power, but we benefit from it when we read them.

Learning is one of the tastiest of dishes. Everything we do should be like the plumb-line, for incorrect conduct never ends in good results. The man who has gone astray is not allowed on the ferry to the land of the just, while the righteous man reaches the other side. Tools can teach us the correct way to behave; they are not interested in our moods or weaknesses. Thanks to them, the pyramids and many other monuments are still standing in the glory of existence.

Each thing will come in its own due time, if we take the right path and align our will with that of the universe(s), the natural order of things. Among all of the marvels the Gods have created a beautiful woman is the most seductive. Life under the watch of the Gods demands more from us than existence. It calls us towards fulfilment and gratitude, meaning and purpose.

The invisible energy is the secret soul of the universe(s) which permeates all things. It is the substance from which light is created to bring matter to life, whatever its nature and form might be. This is the one thing of the Emerald Tablet.

If your hearts are full of love for your work, no misfortune shall break your spirit. A human being can become a goddess when she is reconnected to her Ka – 'Creative Spirit'. Within the company of the Gods, she becomes a divine being once again. This Ka, is nourished by Ma'at. May you be permitted to see, to hear and to feel this secret – mysterious energy, the creative force, a part of the Nun (Celestial Waters), to commune with the stars (ancestors).

The great architect of the universe(s) arranged the elements of life according to proportion and measurement and our world is but interplay of numbers and equations. Geometric thought governs mathematical expression. It is based on the one which develops, multiplies and comes back to itself. Its art is to reveal the presence of unity in all created forms. Your own world exists because it is a collection of proportions and you will need to overstand these principles to become initiated into the higher mysteries of life and creation. But do not study equations for the sake of equations. Those who have been side-tracked in this way have been caught in the trap of sterile knowledge.

In this way the harmony of the human body and anything else in nature, within the universe(s) can be deciphered. There are many grids which reveal the intricate interplay of proportions (Pi, Phi, The Golden Section, The Fibonacci Sequence, etc.).

"....If you want to find the secrets of the universe, think in terms of energy, frequency and vibration...."

- Nikola Tesla

The universe is a gigantic eye, whose parts are separated by our own eyes. Hence the term 'Allah swt (ANU/AMUN RE) sees everything"; into the deepest depths, corners of the human soul, spirit and being. As with 'the Eye of RE', the Gods are always expressing themselves through nature and we must open our eyes and ears wider to see and hear their eternal message.

Great is he whose greatness's are great and venerable is he who surrounds himself with those of noble spirit. She who knows how to carry herself, has a beauty that is more than skin deep. Inner beauty needs no make-up, she who is chaste, belongs to a higher class of sacred feminine, that only the most noble of man is worthy of. She is worth more than (10 of the most aesthetically beautiful women.

The enduring spirit of the ancestors resides within their spiritual descendants. This Ka – 'Creative Spirit', communes with the Ba, soul and motivates its thoughts, feelings and actions. For these few inheritants, no manufactured, sterile religion will sufficeth to fill the void left by the disappearance of Maatian principles, the Rule. All contemporary religions are lacking in their ability to make the person a 'Whole Being', once again. The craving and thirst for the ultimate reality drives the truth-seeker on in their personal legend; their quest for enlightenment and they leave no stone unturned.

The transformative power of these religions, where belief is more important than conduct (Living in Truth), pales in comparison to the Rule (Maat). He who embraces Maat wholeheartedly is given the cosmic key of life to transfiguration to become an Ahkus, Shemsu Har, Eloh also known as Light Being. They turn themselves inside out by way of the newly created Astral/Light Body, within this light body they are housed. The light body has the ability to grow, just as the physical body grows, nourished by the Rule.

Here is wisdom for those that listen, heard, pay heed and answer the call. These are those that will become immortal, eternally remembered when their names are read upon the lips of their future descendants. For when the physical world has perished with everything within it, the tenets of the Rule (Maat) will live on through the spiritual and mental planes of existence. The student and servant of Maat dwells within 'The Infinite Now', a sacred moment in time and space.

This is the subtle, esoteric knowledge of the alchemists; those who realized the magic energy which runs the universe(s). It is the fundamental basis of the Emerald Tablet, the Law of Attraction (& Repulsion). With its knowledge and wisdom overstood; a few people can change a world of many like has been done before and will inevitably be done once again. The time of religious speculation, assumptions and unconfirmed beliefs (dogma) has passed full circle and the time for the rebirth of the Rule is now at hand. Open your eyes and real eyes.

According to the Ancient Egyptians themselves, they referred to their own ancient ancestors of pre-historical times as the 'Souls of Nekhen' and the 'Souls of Pe', Nekhen is an Upper Egyptian (Southern Egypt) town which is now called Kom El Ahmar by the occupying pale Arabs. It was renamed Hierakonpolis by the invading Greeks and is located roughly eighty kilometres South of Luxor. Pe – classical Buto and modern Tell El Fara'in – is a town located in Lower Egypt within the Delta, approximately 140 kilometres to the North of Cairo. Before the unification of the South and North, Nekhen being the older was considered the origin and capital of Upper Egypt (Southern Egypt) with strong links to Nubia. In many Egyptian religious texts, including the Pyramid Texts, it is clearly stated that the 'Souls (Baui) of Nekhen and Pe' indicated that the Ancient Egyptians referred to their earliest ancestors as divine ancestors. These of Nekhen were portrayed as Jackal Headed men, while those of Pe were depicted as Falcon Headed men.

Both were regularly depicted kneeling in the 'huna' potion, with their left hands raised and fists clenched. One can't help but notice the similarities between the huna fists in the air and the 'Black Power' salute which re-surfaced during the Black Power, civil rights movement which erupted in America and Britain and spread around the globe. The kneeling 'huna' position and the gesture with the hand on hearts and the fists were displayed during the Pharaoh's Heb-Sed – 'Regeneration Ceremony'. During this royal jubilee, jubilation was performed by the people beating their chests resulting in a gurgling sound while they were singing.

Nekhen – Hierakonpolis, 'Falcon City' in Greek, was the sacred domain of Neter Haru (Horus). The fact that the Souls of Nekhen were depicted with Jackal Heads is indicative of the fact that they emerged from the desert through Southern Western Egypt (the Western desert). Jackals are desert animals, hence the suggestion. Horus of Nekhen was considered as the last reigning Neter on earth and thus founder of the sacred line of Horus – Kings, as every Pharaoh lived in the image of Horus throughout the time of the whole of dynastic Egypt. Neter Horus (Haru) was also revered and venerated at Pe as well and they too were known as 'Followers of Horus' (Ahkus) and depicted with Falcon Headed masks. The souls of Pe were also sometimes called the souls of Anu (Heliopolis). The fact that this Lower Egyptian people were depicted with Falcon Heads and associated with Nekhen – Hierakonpolis, is evidence of the Upper Egyptian (Southern) origin being that the older Nekhen was the original home of these divine ancestors. Our great ancestor Imhotep, 'He who comes in peace' and his father were both themselves from the sacred town and region of Nekhen as his title, 'Medjeh Nekhen' implies.

"... We have no intention, therefore, of reviewing the laundry list of archaeological prehistoric sites, let alone explaining their names here. Were we to do so, it would require another book at the very least. Suffice it to say that the Nile Valley in Egypt was inhabited by

New Stone Age (Neolithic) people in the region today known as Lower Nubia, when a highly sophisticated black skinned people – bringing along their domesticated cattle, their astronomical know-how and their sky oriented religious beliefs – came in from the Western Desert around the middle of the 4th millennium B.C. It is almost certainly these newcomers who moved northward and unified the whole Egyptian Nile Valley into a United Kingdom. What we need to focus on now, however, is the strong possibility that Imhotep was not just an Upper Egyptian (Southerner), but also a direct descendant of these black skinned ancestors who eventually became the Egyptians. Was Imhotep the 'Keeper', or high priest, of their esoteric and scientific knowledge..?"

- Imhotep the African: Robert Bauval & Thomas Brophy PhD; Pg 188 (In Part)

After the ancient city of Nekhen was first excavated in the 1890's by the British, it has been recognized as the largest pre-dynastic settlement in Egypt. When the British arrived there in 1897, the site was largely untouched by grave robbers and vandals. The dams at Aswan had yet to be built, nor had the deep canals seen at today's Kom el Ahmar been cut. Within the thick walls of Ancient Nekhen were discovered the remains of ancient burial sites and mysterious stone mound that, up to this day, has not been adequately explained. According to the independent researcher and engineer: Robert Bauval, he states:

".... Unfortunately, these early archaeologists were more interested in pre-dynastic graves (some 188 graves were opened according to Garstang) and didn't much bother to record, let alone publish, the architectural details of this enigmatic structure properly. Sadly, because of the modern canals built in the area, the fortress and huge walls of the early dynastic town, some of which were virtually intact in 1897, have now been reduced to shapeless heaps in a mere three quarters of a century by the moisture coming from the canals .....

From Clarke's scant records and from what remains of this building today, however, Egyptologists were able to deduce that there was an outer wall some ten meters high and 2.34 meters thick, as well as an inner wall; the two were separated by a narrow space of about 2.3 metres. The outer wall was plain, whereas the inner wall was built in panels, very reminiscent of the boundary wall of the Step Pyramid Complex at Saqqara...."

Although the British 19th century archaeologists ignored both the pre-dynastic and Neolithic evidence found in abundance at the ancient site of Nekhen, in favour of the more museum lucrative dynastic aspects, some amazing discoveries were still made including the famous

Narmer Palette and the so called 'Two Dog Palette', which dated to 3200 B.C. and are now in the Ashmolean Museum in Oxford.

All of the evidence attests to the reality that a scientifically sophisticated black skinned, Woolley Haired people moved from the Sahara after desertification and entered into the Nubian Nile Valley region from the South West, occupying roughly 450 kilometres of the area from Aswan to Abu Simbel. This Nubian region influenced Qena in Southern (Upper) Egypt and is the origin of the Khamites/Khemetians. Migrations into this area from Tamana (the Sahara civilization) and the South West migrated northward ushering in the Meroitic and Egyptian dynastic states.

Ta-Seti – 'Land of the Bow' (Nubia) was the origin of Khamite civilization of which many elements of the illustrious, enduring culture can still be witnessed throughout the people of this Nubian area and region today. In the eyes of many, the Ta-Seti controversy with the building of the Aswan Dam was a direct opportunity to do away with the abundance of evidence that points to the Nubian, therefore African origins of all civilization.

For those that want to believe in the mainstream, official Egyptological backed story and timeline of the Ancient Egyptian story, Sumerology and the false history of Gods, men and civilization that is entirely up to them. For those that know, we are sure and confident that civilization existed before the great deluge, approximately 13-12,000 years ago, in isolated areas where the Paut Neteru (Gods) from another star system lived together with the humans they had created in their own image and likeness (Gen 1:26).

Over a time period of 49,000 years (7 x 7000), these early humans were upgraded into modern homo sapien sapiens of today by way of gene manipulation and the increasing of our chromosomes through trial and error. Most of the early types of humans, such as Cro-Magnon, Neanderthal, Java man, Australopithecus, Homo Habilis, etc. got absorbed into the homo sapien type and died out as individual species. The first of these modern homo sapien sapiens to be celebrated by Paut Neteru 'the company of the Gods', was the Nubian – New Being – man and woman. Over time they were given the gift of civilization by Paut Neteru themselves, after many years of being trained to serve these Lofty Beings (Elohim in Hebrew [Aramic]). After the rule of the Gods on earth and that of the demi-Gods, kingship was lowered to earth, modelled off of the kingship of the Gods themselves and given to man, humanity after the great deluge and the kingdoms of the Kushites/Nubians spread from Ta-Seti also called Meroitic Sudan (Ethiopia proper) into the wider world springing up as various ancient kingdoms, all interlinked with the same roots of civilization. Each kingdom developed its own character but basically and fundamentally, they were originally one extended civilization of many fruits and flavours. Of this, there is not a shadow of a doubt among honest scholars and those that know. It is only the so called scholars who all sing from the same official song sheets who are forever going to be in denial about the many revelations being made by the author, along with countless other great men and women. Egyptologists know full well that there were many Pharaohs who ruled before Egypt was supposedly unified by Pharaoh Narmer/Menes of 0 Dynasty. These Pharaohs are referred to as the Proto-Dynastic kings and are never really given much relevance in Egyptology. This is because they will certainly lead straight back to the A Group of Nubians from Ta-Seti already spoken of here. The Egyptologists are also aware of the proto-Saharans of the civilization of Tamana/Tama-Re and that the glorious Kushites inherited a fully formed advanced, esoteric knowledge of astronomy, medicine, science, geography, world history, religion, alchemy, architecture and agriculture among other things. The world has owed us Kushites a great, largely unrecognized debt since way before the terribly inhuman Transatlantic Slave Trade, of the late 1500's A.D.

".... In February 1987, the Oriental Institute organized an exhibition titled Nubia – Its Glory & Its People. Concerning the A Group, which was called 'An Early Kingdom in the Land of the Bow' and dated to 3800 – 3100 B.C., the brochure of the exhibition asserted:

Most surprising, evidence that early Pharaohs ruled in A-Group Nubia was discovered by the Oriental Institute at Qustul, almost at the modern Sudanese border. A cemetery of large tombs containing evidence of wealth and representation and monuments could then be identified and in the process, a lost kingdom or Land of the Bow, was discovered. In fact, the cemetery at Qustul in Nubia, could well have been the seat of Egypt's founding dynasty ...."

- Imhotep the African: Robert Bauval & Thomas Brophy PhD; Pg 198 (In Part)

All of this evidence is today buried under the many tons of water within the artificial Lake Nasser. There is no reason why this lost evidence could not have been saved before the construction of the Lake, but if you ask me, the authorities, such as, the Illuminati and organizations, such as, the Egyptian Ministry of antiquities, under the guidance of the racist Zawi Hawass, could not afford for this wealth of pre-dynastic evidence to come forth into the mainstream. Such people will do everything in their power to use excuses to hide your legacy from you of who and just what we are: *"The Flock of the Gods"*.

Still, as is always, the truth must always come to light even when being suppressed from the people of the wider world. The liars and their lies will always end up being exposed because it is the natural way of the universe(s). In these last days and times, now that the seven seals have been opened by him we call 'The Lamb', in 1970 A.D and the Holy Tablets, The Sacred

Records of Neter: Atum-Re' and the Sacred Tablets of Tama-Re have been received and revealed the truth has re-surfaced to erase the falsehood.

The Ahkus – 'Shining Ones, Star People, Venerables, Transfigured Ones', lead back to the same 'Followers of Horus' in Ancient Pe and Nekhen. According to one source, the Ahku, Shemsu Hor reigned after Horus's 300 year reign and their reign lasted 13,420 years; which was followed by another group of Shemsu Hor, without the prefix 'Ahku' and they reigned for 23,200 years; totalling 36,620 years. The plural word 'Akhu', is normally translated s 'Venerables'. Yet, a closer scrutiny of the word and its implied full aspects of meanings to the Ancient Khamites reveals its more esoteric meaning concealed by the word. The deeper meaning of the epithet/hieroglyphs for Akhu can also mean 'Transfigured Beings', 'Shining Ones', 'Shining Beings' or 'Astral Spirits', sometimes confused by Egyptologists as the stars. Other meanings pointed out by E.A. Wallis Budge in his 'Hieroglyphic Dictionary' render meanings, such as 'to be bright', 'to be excellent' and/or 'to be wise' and 'instructed', and is regularly associated with 'those who recite formulae'. These high initiates were deeply enlightened and learned people, an elite of highly initiated astronomer philosophers' way before any rise of Greece or Rome, or contemporary (monotheistic) religions.

From the earliest, primeval times, it was these 'Followers of Horus' who initiated the Horus Kings (Pharaohs) and priests of Khemet (Egypt) into the 'Higher Mysteries' of creation and existence. They were the power behind the monarchs not only Egypt but also in Elam and Sumer, Ta-Seti, Xia and Sheng China and Atlan and Amexem (the Americas). The Ahku were the forerunners of the Magi, Shriners, Wisemen of the Bible, etc., recorded within various religions. These Ahku are the persons responsible for preserving the pre-diluvia civilization of the past by retaining many of the elements of science and spirituality, maths, architecture, penal system, religious rituals and ceremonies, alchemy, architecture and what not. So let us remember our great ancestors for the great men and women that they were and not what the Agents of the Shadows try to programme us to simply believe without knowing. Only in identifying who and what we were and are can we reconnect and re-establish the order.

"Success is not the key to happiness. Happiness is the key to success. If you love what you are doing, you will be successful."

- Herman Cain

Chapter Five: The Kendake' Project

Reawakening of the Mother Goddess Principle:

What if I was to tell you the biggest secret? A secret so explosive, that most people haven't realized its significance and its underlying implications, though the thought may have crossed many minds before. That God, as in the Most High God, is a female and not a male. You'd probably say that I am crazy wouldn't you? But what if all the evidence was out there that attests to this and was, and always has been, staring you in the face? Would you still deny the reality based on your religious upbringing? Or would you consider the facts for yourself and make your judgements based on logic and reasoning?

Now all across the ancient world, Mother Goddesses were venerated and celebrated along with the male aspects. In order to have a God, there had to be a female counterpart or equivalent – the ying to the yang. This is a basic tenet of physical creation and the physical universe(s) all around us; the energy of the universe(s) being twofold; centripetal and centrifugal, masculine (positive) and feminine (negative). Everything in creation contains various degrees of both energies. Based on this reality, the ancient people celebrated a number of Goddesses throughout the world, such as, Nut, Aset (Isis), Het-Heru (Hathor), Tawaret, Nephtys, Neith, Maat, Mut, Ninti, Arishkegal, Ninlil, Damkina, Ishtar, Kali, Athena, Artemis, Aphrodite, Dina, Sekhmet, Amunet, Antum, Venus, Kishar, Ninsun, Asherah, Ashtoroth, etc., etc.

These Goddesses were the counterparts and spouses of the masculine equivalents and being that nature itself is referred to as 'Mother' nature and not 'Father' nature and the universe is known symbolically as the 'Great Womb', which gave birth to creation, the physical universe(s), the feminine aspect of God was always recognized in the ancient world until the coming of the homosexual Greeks, who were 'left brain thinkers'.

Kushite Africans and the peoples of the southern hemisphere have always been matriarchal people, placing their women in the highest esteem and placing their wives and mothers upon a pedestal. This can be witnessed within all civilizations still connected to their Kushite cultural roots, such as Khemet, Ta-Seti, Sumer, Elam, Atlan, Sheba, Black Athens, ancient Minoa, Carthage, Black China, Mesoamerica, Troy, etc. In these civilizations women had as much rights as men to own property, to inherit, to be educated, to have an opinion, to seek divorce and even to rule the throne and crown. The people of the northern hemisphere treated their women totally opposite in their male dominated societies which were patriarchal and nomadic, not agricultural. Even Greece, which the European scholars like to claim was the origin of true civilization in the 5th Century BC (rather late on the timeline), didn't give their women the right to vote or rule independently of men in their so called democracy. Indeed, women in Europe didn't get the right to vote until some women threw themselves in front of running race horses in protest and died in the 20th Century AD. There was no European Kendake (Kentaka) or Candice, Queen of Sheba, Cleopatra, Nefertiti, Ahmes-Nefertari or Hatshepsut, etc. other than the so called pagan rebels, such as Boudica and Joan of Arc, etc. who never really held sway over the entire population and ended up executed. Therefore, the elevation of women and spiritually uplifting society is and always was a Kushite cultural tradition. The Black man of today needs to wake up and start seeing his women through spiritual eyes again, be they Black, White or Asian and stop following White, Arab and Asian male chauvinists.

Today most African Kushites treat their women as possessions, rather than the Goddesses that they are. This is largely because of westernization of the world through male dominated 'White society' and monotheist religions, such as Judaism, Christianity and so called Islam (Mohammadism), but it wasn't always so.

Before the advent of modern (monotheistic) faiths, most of the cultures of old followed what can be termed as 'Earth Religions', heavily connected to nature. The followers were naturalists with a deep reverence for nature, all of creation and the dual aspect of the Mother/Father creator. This is often misunderstood through the eyes of today's monotheism as nature worship or animal worship. The polytheist aspects blind many from realizing that out of the one Mother/Father creator, the invisible and mysterious cosmic energy that generates and constructs the universe(s) by way of the one mind come many different expressions in the form of Gods and Goddesses. The multiplicity of these Gods is mistaken as 'the worship of many Gods' (Polytheism) and so in today's world, religion (monotheism) has given the word 'Pagan' negative connotations, when all the word really means and implies is that one is in tune with nature and the natural pulse of universe(s); the Sacred Aum Principle.

Scientifically, DNA has proven that here on earth, woman could not have come from man because the X chromosome carries more matter within it and is much more complex than the Y chromosome. It has long been realized that the males Y chromosome is actually a shrunken and distorted female X chromosome, with one of the lower legs broken off. A woman can only ever give an X chromosome.

Female X chromosome　　✗　　　✗　　Male Y chromosome

So, science proves monotheism wrong showing that the male Y chromosome is derived from the female X chromosome, the male (man) comes from out of the female (woman) and not the other way around, as the 'fairytale' (myth) of the scriptural Adam and Eve suggest. You can see that woman contains man within herself just by the scrutiny of the word; the first women were capable of producing off-spring by themselves, without a male mate, by producing semen from the clitoris.

Wo (man)   Man

When humans were first created, they were created as Hermaphrodites as can be realized in the Book of Genesis "Genes of Isis", when read with an open mind and within the knowledge of the ancient teachings, where all of the monotheistic religions derived their ideas and concepts. It was the Neteru/Anunnaqi who took the male gene from out of the female hermaphrodites enabling the hybrid called Adamah – 'Earthlings' to procreate and reproduce upon themselves. This is why the man, not the woman determines the sex of the child, as only the man can produce the Y chromosome being XY, while the female only has two XX chromosomes.

"So God created man in his own image; in the image of God he created him; male and female he created them...."

Genesis 1:27. The New English Bible

If you take the time to read and learn the story of 'The Family Triad', Asaru (Osiris), Aset (Isis) and their child Haru (Horus), there comes a part which explain how Aset learns the secret name of Re' by tricking him. In learning the secret name of the Most High Re, Aset then becomes one of the most powerful of the Neteru and her magic words of power, assisted by Tehuti (Thoth) were able to resurrect the slain Neter Asaru (Osiris) from death. Knowing the secret name of Re gives her the rulership upon the earth, but out of love for her son, she hands the power of rulership from herself to her son Haru (Horus), in order for him to avenge his father, Asaru's murder. The significance of this is the fact that the power of rulership was given from woman to man. It was the Netertaat – 'Goddesses' who gave man his strength, muscularity, force, simplicity. This was necessary because as the female is the true God who creates in her own image within the womb, not the male; the man is her protector and enforcer and so would benefit from the extra attributes. In the heavens, the male came first, but upon the earth, it is the woman who came first.

Now these teachings may seem very odd compared to the monotheistic teachings that many have been accustomed to but, these are the teachings of the pioneering Kushite culture which has influenced all others, from then until now. The many Triads almost always consisted of Father, Mother and Child, which is the natural order of things, not Father, Son and Holy Ghost! You cannot have creation without the coming together of both male and female (Centripetal and Centrifugal) creative forces. You can never have creation with all males (men), so as weird as your own culture might sound, you need to wake up and smell what's cooking. It was the hatred of The Mother Goddess Principle and women in general that bred homosexuality and vice-versa.

Still, the Mother Goddess Principle survives even today in camouflage and in a much diluted form. Most monotheistic religions retained it by reducing the role and importance of the female characters. Christianity reduced the role of Mother Mary to just the mother of Jesus, rather than the 'Divine Mother'. I mean ask yourselves; if Jesus is supposedly God, then what does that make Mary? They also distorted the truth about Mary Magdalene as mother of Jesus's children and his wife, who he married at their own wedding, 'The Wedding of Cana'. Within the folds of Islam, the Mary character can be swapped with Saida Faatimah, daughter of Muhammad, while for the Jews, she can be swapped for Hajah and/or Sarah, the wives of Abraham. All of these women were based upon Mother Aset (Isis) and/or Mother Ishtar, just another Egyptian and Sumerian reality turned into mythology.

The fact being, that your scholars have been lying to you all along. They have distorted and now they ridicule your culture and traditional Kushite teachings, spinning around the facts and telling you that the stories your ancestors painstakingly carved into the hardest rock upon earth are myths. The true fictitious myths are the Torah, Bible and Koran which is peddled around as the truth at the cost of so many innocent lives. Well it's time to wake up and end all this senseless religious bloodshed by going back to the truth, that which never failed our people or the world - The Right Knowledge, Right Wisdom and Right Overstanding capable of re-creating heaven on earth.

The Black Madonna

Most people in the world today are familiar with the mother and child statue, said to be representative of Mary and her child Jesus, so often paraded and venerated by various Christian groups. Far less people are familiar with the original statue and the origin of the Mary, Joseph, Jesus story of the Bible's New Testament. Most Christians are still ignorant concerning the origin of Christian and biblical concepts, which predate the Bible by many thousands of years, in this case the statue of Aset (Isis) and Haru (Horus), the child which was adapted and copied into the near eastern and Christian religions. If you were to ask a Christian clergy man about the higher meaning of this representation of mother and child, they'd most probably fob you off with some kind of sterile, religious jargon if anything at all. Ask their learned men about the origin of this artistic idea and see how many of them would honestly reveal the Kushite (Khamite and Si-ga-ga [Sumerian]) idea. Ask them, again, why most Christians in Europe have a Black Madonna statue (statue of mother and child) enshrined within their places of worship, including the Vatican.

Indeed, the Black Madonna statue said to be Mary and Jesus is blatantly copied and based on the statue of Mother Aset (Isis) and Haru (Horus), the child. To the Si-ga-ga (Sumerians), the statue was representative of the equivalents of Aset (Isis), Asaru (Osiris), and Haru (Horus) who would be Ishtar (Inanna), Dummuzi and Tammuz. In Tamarean (Tasetian) cultures, the statue of mother and child, which portrays them in the suckling position, says a thousand things. The higher wisdom implies that the mother's lap is the very first throne of a Pharaoh, King, and Ruler. The child, Haru (Horus) is perched upon his first throne, the throne he occupied before ascending to the throne of Egypt (Kush), which was his mother's lap. Each one of us are Pharaohs, Kings in our own right within our own Kingdoms and our first throne was upon our mother's lap. It implies that the Mother Goddess (female) being closer connected to nature, naturally inherits the attributes of Mother Nature which is to nourish and nurture her creation with love and light. Therefore, she (the female) herself, is the child's first and foremost God and therefore there is nothing in creation more powerful than a mother's love for her child. The word Aset translates as 'Mighty Throne'.

Every Horus King (Pharaoh) cherished this example and placed his mother upon a pedestal. Even after her own reign alongside the Pharaoh's father, the mother of Pharaoh still held a high position and kept a strong hand in advising and passing on wisdom, concerning the affairs of state. She held the same importance as the main wife of Pharaoh and together they often regulated the social aspects of society. Each Pharaoh modelled themselves after Haru (Horus), as the 'Living Horus', beginning with this Mother Goddess Principle. This is the true higher wisdom of the Black Madonna, the Holy Grail, which is not a chalice but rather the females who continue the bloodline, nourish and nurture it through life. It was this spirit of placing women on an equal footing that the Kushite rulers (worldwide) embodied. They knew that women came before man based on the secret of the mitochondria D.N.A. that has now been scientifically confirmed. They knew that having a daughter was just as, if not even more, important as having a son. Therefore, our Kushite societies were matriarchal rather than patriarchal unlike Tamahu (White) and Shashu (mixed) and Namu (Asian) people of the northern hemisphere. The whole story of Mary (the Virgin), Joseph and Jesus (the Messiah), was based on Aset (the Virgin Mother), Asaru (the Sacrifice) and Horus (the Messiah).

So, the next time you see a picture of the famous Madonna statue, whether black or white, remember these facts. Overstand where these ideas and concepts originated. The claim that Asaru (Osiris) sacrificed himself to save others and was resurrected, Aset (Isis) was the virgin mother and Haru (Horus) was the born Messeh 'Messiah' or 'Anointed One', that healed the blind, fed a multitude of people with one loaf of bread, baptized people within the waters of the sacred Mother Nile River and was born on December 25th, thousands of years before any Judaism, Christianity or Islam – Torah, Bible or Qur'aan, can be confirmed and verified with a little research. Don't believe me, check it out for yourselves! All Kushite precepts once again.

".... Ancient Egypt was a Negro civilization. The history of Black Africa will remain suspended in air and cannot be written correctly until African historians dare to connect it with the history of Egypt. In particular, the study of languages, institutions and so forth, cannot be treated properly; in a word, it will be impossible to build African humanities, a body of African human sciences, so long as that relationship does not appear legitimate. The African historian who evades the problem of Egypt is neither modest nor objective, nor un-ruffled; he is ignorant, cowardly and neurotic. Imagine, if you can, the uncomfortable position of a western historian who was to write the history of Europe without referring to Greco-Latin antiquity and try to pass that off as a scientific approach.

The Ancient Egyptians were Negroes. The moral fruit of their civilization is to be counted among the assets of the Black world. Instead of presenting itself to history as an insolvent debtor, that Black world is the very initiator of the 'Western' civilization so flaunted before our eyes today. Pythagorean mathematics, the theory of the four elements of Thales of Miletus, Epicurean materialism, Platonic Idealism, Judaism, Islam and modern science are rooted in Egyptian cosmogony and science. One only needs to meditate on Osiris, the redeemer God, who sacrifices himself, dies and is resurrected to save mankind, a figure essentially identifiable with Christ.

A visitor to Thebes in the Valley of the Kings can view the Moslem inferno in detail (in the tomb of Seti I, of the Nineteenth Dynasty), 1700 years before the Koran. Osiris at the tribunal of the dead is indeed the 'Lord' of revealed religions, sitting enthroned on Judgement Day and we know that certain biblical passages are practically copies of Egyptian moral texts. Far be it from me to confuse this brief reminder with a demonstration. It is simply a matter of providing a few landmarks to persuade the incredulous Black African reader to bring himself to verify this. To his great surprise and satisfaction, he will discover that most of the ideas used today to domesticate, atrophy, dissolve, or steal his 'Soul', were conceived by his own ancestors. To become conscious of that fact is perhaps the first step toward a general retrieval of himself; without it, intellectual sterility is the general rule, or else the creations bear I know not what imprint on the subhuman...."

- The African Origin of Civilization: Myth or Reality; Cheikh Anta Diop

Concerning the Netert 'Goddess' Aset (Isis) herself, it should by now be obvious that we are dealing with a Kushite (Meroitic Sudanese) personality. The fact that she and her husband Asaru (Osiris) were always depicted in various shades of Jet black and coffee brown is again self-evident of their race and origin. She is just another black divinity hijacked by the white world and propagated as 'Caucasian'. It is interesting to note that even the Greeks, who stole their concept of a pantheon of Gods from Black Egyptians and Sumerians, depicted their deities in black colour. Again, the argument put forward by Egyptologists is that the colour black in Egyptian reliefs was symbolic of resurrection and not the race of the subject. This nonsense is perpetuated again and again, throughout text books to the point where Hollywood will cast persons such as Angelina Jolie in the role of Aset (Isis) which is completely disrespectful, ignorant and in denial of the facts. Far from being representative of the black soil of Egypt, Khemet, Khamit, Al Kham was representative of 'The Black People' which populated and originated the civilization.

In the words of Abbe Emile Amelineau (1850 – 1916), a great Egyptologist rarely mentioned, who excavated at Om El'Gaab, near Abydos and discovered a royal necropolis identifying 16 rulers;

".... From various Egyptian legends, I have been able to conclude that the population settled in the Nile Valley were Negroes, since the Goddess Isis was said to have been a reddish-Black woman. In other words, as I have explained, her complexion is cafe au lait (coffee with milk), the same as that of certain other Blacks whose skin seems to cast metallic reflections of copper ...."

He also designates the first Black race to occupy the Nile Valley by the name Anu. He states that these people came down the Nile from the south and slowly founded the cities of Esneh, Erment, Qouch and Heliopolis (Anu), for, as he says:

".... If Osiris was of Nubian origin, although born at Thebes, it would be easy to understand why the struggle between Set and Horus took place in Nubia. In any case, it is striking that the Goddess Isis, according to the legend, has precisely the same skin colour that Nubians always have and that the God Osiris has what seems to me an ethnic epithet indicating his Nubian origin. Apparently this observation has never been made ....."

So worldwide, the so called 'Fertility Cults' of the maternal Mother Goddesses were initiated by (southerners) Kushite. Nubian peoples who migrated from out of the Motherland Africa into the wider world, at various different times over roughly the last 100,000 years. The evidence of both before and after the 'Great Deluge' shows us that, at that time and from then on, Kushite Negro Africans left Africa and became indigenous to the whole planet. They installed matriarchal, agricultural societies throughout world civilization which was usurped by patriarchal, nomadic northerners many millennia later. 100,000 years ago humanity began to adapt to the cold regions after becoming trapped by the ice through the 4th Glaciation period. These are the usurpers.

MAXIM 21

On the Love & Respect, Due to a Wife

".... If you are a man of quality, build your house, love your wife intensely, marry her according to the customary law, nourish and clothe her. Oil is a remedy for her body. Make her happy all her life; she is the fertile earth, useful to and a light for her husband.

Don't get involved in legal conflict with her so as not to provoke intense rage. Her furious looks can make the storm worse. Act to keep your wife in your house. If you reject her, she will weep. Feminine energy is what feeds her being; what she asks is that a channel be created for the energy of her love to flow ...."

- The Wisdom of Ptah-Hotep

In today's westernized world, women have only recently began to regain some form of equality. Though the form of equality is often corrupted in the form of Feminism and often women and men today are confusing each other's roles, the fact that the re-emergence of the importance of the divine feminine is being felt and recognized, can only be a good thing for mother earth. Once we identify the reality that a woman cannot and will never be the same as a man and vice-versa and stop looking at homosexuality as something that is natural and normal, once we realize and acknowledge that sex changes (transgenderism) also, is the result of an imbalance of hormones, recessive genes within the D.N.A. and counter-productive to society, then women can once again become women and men can return to being men.

We men must respect the divine feminine as the equal of the sacred masculine, two aspects of the Mother/Father creator, which are opposites in all details, but equal in measure and importance. Kushite men especially and all men in general need to embrace the ways of the ancient ancestors and go back to the principles which made us become known as 'blameless', beginning with how we treat our women; mothers, wives, daughters, sisters, etc., for this is the standard of measuring whether a civilization is great or savage, not technological developments or materialism. If you want to know the state of a society anywhere you travel, observe the condition of the women; the way they are dressed, the way that they are treated, if they are educated and well-spoken and whether they are spiritually or sexually-inclined. Through these few things you can gauge everything you need to know about the mind and psychological state of the whole society.

Look at those who keep their women intellectually and aesthetically suppressed and restricted. Those like the Mohammadans, are those who are incapable of seeing the human body and sex through the spiritual eye. Ancient Kushites were a spiritually inclined people. The human body, love and sex was not seen through the carnal eyes, but rather through the spiritual eye. The society was not based on sexual perversions, women were not seen as sexual objects to be possessed and vice versa, but spiritual beings, vehicles of light and agents of the purpose of nation building. There was no need to cover up the breasts or laugh at the erected phallus of say Neter Min (Amun in his fertility role), or Neter: Atum. The human body was appreciated and admired for the beautiful creation that it was and still is. It was thus adorned with perfume and oils, hairstyles and jewels and make-up, to accentuate that beauty as a celebration and gratitude of life. The beauty was realized from the inside-out, rather than the outside in, as it is seen and viewed today cosmetically. The sexual perversions of today are largely due to the eradication of the divine feminine and the Mother Goddess Principle done by the northerners, patriarchal societies who put down their women, placing men above them in all degrees. The women of these Greco-Roman and barbaric vandal and Goth like societies were viewed carnally, materialistically as nothing but objects of pleasure and sexual gratification and it is this way of thinking that after the Trojan War in the 1200's BC, began to spread south and overpower the Old World Order of Kushite Africans and their matriarchal civilizations. After the failure of Hannibal and the fall of the mighty Carthage, generations after, the Black world had no way of keeping the northerners from flooding into Mother Africa. The seed of sexual perversion and accepted homosexuality, was planted by the Greeks when Alexander the Greek (Macedonian) and Aristotle, invaded and conquered Persian occupied Egypt in 333 B.C. Egypt, then long ruined, never regained its independence. The mantle of sexual abominations was inherited by the Romans, after the reign of the Greek Ptolemy.

".... Perhaps the most ambitious attempt to reconstruct African history has been the numerous writings of Cheikh Anta Diop. Diop has a theory that there is a basic global division of peoples into two kinds: the Southerners (or Negro Africans) and the Aryans (a category covering all Caucasians, including Semites, Mongoloids and American Indians). Each grouping has a cultural outlook based on response to climate, the difference between them being that the Aryans have had a harsher climate.

The Aryans have developed patriarchal systems characterized by the suppression of women and a propensity for war. Also associated with such societies are materialist religion, sin and guilt, xenophobia, the tragic drama, the city state, individualism and pessimism. Southerners, on the other hand, are matriarchal. The women are free and the people peaceful; there is a Dionysian approach to life, religious idealism and no concept of sin. With a matriarchal society come xenophilia, the tale as a literary form, the territorial state, social collectivism and optimism.

According to Diop's theory, the Ancient Egyptians, who were Negroes, are the ancestors of Southerners. This bold hypothesis, which is not presented without supporting data, has the interesting effect of inverting Western cultural assumptions. For, Diop argues, if the Ancient Egyptians were Negroes, then European civilization is but a derivation of African achievement ...."

- Immanuel Wallerstein

".... According to Strabo, Susa had been founded by a Negro – Tithonus, King of Ethiopia and father of Memnon. In fact, it is claimed that Susa was founded by Tithonus, Memnon's father and that his citadel bore the name Memnonium. The Susians are also called Cissians and Aeschylus calls Memnon's mother, Cissia. Cissia reminds us of Cisse, an African family name ...."

- Cheikh Anta Diop: The African Origin of Civilization

History, when read in the correct way, without programmed prejudices, shows that the world was dominated by a (Kushite) - Egypto-Phoenician; black-skinned, woolly-haired people who were matriarchal within their culture and traditions. These multi-national people are those responsible for transmitting civilization into the Mediterranean Islands before, during and after the settlement of Caucasians into the region.

After learning the fruits of civilizations from the Egypto-Phoenicians and accepting being ruled by foreigners, the Caucasian – Greeks rebelled against their Kushite rulers and made war, expelling them back across the sea. This general pattern of civilizing blacks and rebelling inhabitants was repeated all over the globe. Again I will turn to the words of Cheikh Anta Diop (JTV), who sums up the situation more precisely, than myself:

".... The Greeks say that Cadmus introduced writing, as we would say today that Marianne [symbol of the French Republic] introduced railroads into French West Africa."

Greek traditions place the installation of Egyptian colonies in Greece at approximately the same time; Cecrops settled in Attica; Danaus, brother of Aegyptus, in Argolis; he taught the Greeks agriculture as well as metallurgy (Iron). During this Sidonian epoch, elements of Egypto-Phoenician civilization crossed into Greece. At first the Phoenician colony held the upper hand, but soon the Greeks began to struggle for liberation from the Phoenicians who, at this period prior to the Argonauts, possessed mastery of the seas as well as technical superiority.

This conflict is symbolized by the fight between Cadmus (the Phoenician) and the serpent son of Maus (the Greek); it lasted about three centuries.

The dissension thus aroused among the natives by the arrival of the Canaanite (Phoenician) settlers is represented in mythical legend by the combat waged by Cadmus and the Spartans. From then on, those of the Spartans whom the fable allows to survive and become the companions of Cadmus, represent the principal Ionian families who accepted domination by the foreigner.

Not long does Cadmus rule his empire in peace; he is soon chased away and compelled to retire among the Enchelians. The indigenous element regains control, after having accepted the authority of the Phoenicians and receiving the benefits of civilization it rises up against them and tries to expel them.....

All that we can discern in this part of the narrative concerning the Cadmeans is the horror that their race and religion, still impregnated by barbarism and oriental obscenity, inspired in the poor but virtuous Greeks whom, however, they had taught. And so, in Hellenic tradition, a superstitious terror is attached to the memory of the Kings of Cadmus' race. They provided most of the subjects for antique tragedy.

At this point we have indeed reached a period of demarcation when the Indo-European world was freeing itself from the domination of the Black Egypto-Phoenician world.

This economic and political struggle, similar in all respects to that which colonial countries are now waging against modern imperialism, was supported, as it is today, by a cultural reaction caused by the same reasons. To understand the Orestes of Aeschylus and Virgil's Aeneid, we must view them in context of this cultural oppression. Instead of interpreting, as Bachofen and others believe, the universal transition from matriarchy to patriarchy, these works mark the encounter and conflict of two different conceptions: the one with deep roots in the Eurasian plains, the other embedded in the heart of Africa. At the outset the latter (matriarchy) dominated and spread through the Aegean – Mediterranean thanks to Egypto-Phoenician colonization of populations, sometimes even White populations, but whose inconsistent culture permitted no positive reaction at the time. This was perhaps true of the Lycians and several other Aegean groups. Yet, the writers of Antiquity unanimously report that ideas never really penetrated the White world of Northern Europe, which rejected them as soon as it could, as notions alien to its own cultural conceptions. This is the meaning of the Aeneid. In its forms most foreign to the northern mentality, Egypto-Phoenician cultural imperialism hardly survived economic imperialism.

The history of humanity will remain confused as long as we fail to distinguish between the two early cradles in which nature fashioned the instincts, temperament, habits and ethnical concepts of the two subdivisions before they met each other after a long separation dating back to prehistoric times. The first of those cradles, as we shall see in the chapter on Egypt's contribution, is the valley of the Nile, from the Great Lakes to the Delta, across the so called 'Anglo-Egyptian' Sudan. The abundance of vital resources, its sedentary, agricultural character, the specific conditions of the valley, will engender in man, that is, in the Negro, a gentle, idealistic, peaceful nature, endowed with a spirit of justice and gaiety. All these virtues were more or less indispensable for daily co-existence.

Because of the requirements of agricultural life, concepts such as matriarchy and totemism, the most perfect social organization and monotheistic religion were born. These engendered others: thus, circumcision resulted from monotheism; in fact, it was really the notion of a God, Amon, uncreated creator of all that exists, that led to the androgynous concept. Since Amon was not created and since he is the origin of all creation, there was a time when he was alone. To the archaic mentality, he must have contained within himself all the male and female principles necessary for procreation. That is why Amon, the Negro God par excellence of the 'Anglo-Egyptian' Sudan (Nubia) and all the rest of Black Africa, was to appear in Sudanese mythology as androgynous. Belief in this hermaphroditic ontology would produce circumcision and excision in the Black world. One could go on to explain all the basic traits of the Negro soul and civilization by using the material conditions of the Nile Valley as the point of departure...."

All of the evidence indicates that civilization spread from the Southern Kushite Kingdoms of Nubia, Northward into the Arabian Peninsula, the Middle East and the Mediterranean basin. The Kadmonites/Phoenicians and the Egyptians, both Negro peoples were both responsible for the spreading of this Egypto-Phoenician civilization and culture. After the Trojan War in the 1200's B.C. and later when the Nabatean Arabian Negroes were forced to evacuate Arabia in numbers, they fell back to Egypt venturing further north establishing Kushite nations in Italy, Sicily and the Greek Islands and mainland. The last colony established by these Black Egypto-Phoenicians was the famous Carthage of Generals Hannibal and Hamilcar Barca in 814 B.C. When Hannibal lost the war against Rome, it was the end of the spread of Kushite civilization throughout the Mediterranean area. The memory of the Kushites and the Etruscans was erased leaving no trace of language or monuments.

Indeed, all of this is well known and documented by European scholars but is deliberately left out of text books and the national curriculum of education. The Phoenicians have been proven to have travelled as far north as Brittany from where they got and traded tin. A stop off colony on the way to Brittany was established in Spain and this is the true reason why Europeans, such as Sicilians, Italians, Greeks, Spaniards, Portuguese and others, are more swarthy (have darker features and skin complexions) than northern Europeans. Even the French, the Nazis claimed, were well mixed with Kushite blood. The most unmixed of the Europeans were indeed the blond-haired, blue eyed Nordics, but what they failed to mention was the fact that the Italians themselves had undergone many generations of racial mixing due to Kushites coming from the South. Something Hitler's sidekick Benito Mussolini and his fascist government might have already long known.

"All things considered, when the Nazis say that the French are Negroes, if we disregard the prerogative intention of that affirmation, it remains well founded historically, insofar as it refers to those contacts between peoples in the Aegean epoch. But that is true not only of the French; it is even more applicable to the Spaniards, Italians, Greeks, etc., all those populations whose complexion, less white than that of other Europeans, has wistfully been attributed to their southern habitat....."

Cheikh Anta Diop: The African Origin of Civilization

The Kushite colonies of the ancient world had magnetic effect and influence upon the savage tribes of barbarians surrounding the magnificent city centres that developed in all of these northern countries. The barbarians were attracted to the innovative ease of living that was created by the industries of trade they developed. Roman and even Greek colonization into the world only supplanted Egypto-Phoenician colonization which is much older in antiquity. These days most everyday people, both black and white are still ignorant of these historical certainties; so many people still ignorantly believe in the false notion of the so called 'White man's burden' and the lie that says that Black people have always been slaves and primitive minded naturally.

Imagine the effect on people if they knew, collectively, the African origin of all civilization, science, architecture, medicine, religion and spirituality, metallurgy etc.? Imagine the neutralizing effect it could have on today's racist organizations, such as the Ku Klux Klan, British National Party, English Defence League, etc.? Imagine the effect it could have on self-righteous religious groups such as Mohammadist Moslems, Jews and Evangelical Christians, knowing that their teachings were not original but borrowed from Black people. The same can be said for science, the Military (indeed Hannibal is said to have been the greatest Military leader ever), Medicine, etc. This Right Knowledge has the power and potential to change the world if and only if, it is passed on to the next generation, the young people and children, as well as the adults. In order for us to change this current corrupted reality and the rulership of the Elite, this is our most fundamental challenge and purpose; the purpose of both sides of the coin if we are to overthrow the order and create a better place. Not for no revenge for the in-human atrocities of the Trans-Atlantic Slave Trade but, more to bring back the harmony of the human family and to raise the vibration of the entire planet into a higher density which is worthy of the Age of Hapi (Aquarius). For this may be our last chance as humanity to make this transition happen successfully and with a utopian ending.

The Mixing of the North & South

These Kushite colonies and their trading expeditions resulted in building intimate bonds and economic relationships between the natives and the traders. The material wealth generated at these industrial centres, making life much easier, were well sought after by the inhabitants of the land and this is a well-known trait of the effect of civilization on barbarism globally. Within this general pattern, it comes to a point where after the natives develop a strong reliance on the manufactured goods produced by these trading industries, a new cultural awareness of life develops and rather than merely supplying the raw materials for the traders to manufacture into the well needed goods, the native inhabitants themselves seek to learn the secrets of industry and manufacture for themselves. In this respect, something from the knowledge and culture of the civilizers is always inevitably borrowed.

In this way, civilisation passes its torch from the civilizers to the uncivilized imprinting upon the latter, their ideas, their religions and their philosophies. But it is not only economic relationships that result from this meeting of societies. Sexual and intimate relationships also result from this. It is well known on both sides of the historical story that upon these Egypto-Phoenician trading parties, that the supplying of White-skinned women to Black-skinned colonist was a trade unto itself. White women were traded and even kidnapped onto ships and taken back to Kushite Kingdoms to be sold to high officials, nobles, even the Pharaoh himself, had to pay high prices for these beautiful White women. These women so different to what they were accustomed to see in their beautiful Kushite women were usually assigned the role of concubines under the main wives who were almost always Kushites. The role of the concubine of Caucasian women played a huge role in lightening the complexion of the Egypto-Phoenician Kushites of the colonies, who usually depicted themselves in the copper-tone, reddish brown hue seen painted upon so many monument walls. Many of these amorous liaisons have been well documented in the pages of history. The fact that the bloodline travelled through the Kushite woman and not the man, meant that the core identity of the Kushite Kingdoms were protected from these amorous trysts on the part of the Kushite men. The heir to the Kingdom was thus always produced via the main wife, the Negro woman, who was more times than often, the half-sister of the ruler having the same father, a theme borrowed by the scriptures concerning the Prophets. It was therefore forbidden for a Kushite (Egypto-Phoenician) woman to marry any other than an Egypto-Phoenician man, but the Kushite ruler usually had a harem filled with various different women from different parts of the planet under his main wife. This is the way it has always been. The same cannot be said of the White man, who again was/is patriarchal, the importance given to the father. Any similar situation with the men co-habiting with Kushite women changed the structural fabric of their kingdom by the fact that the off-spring produced could make the claim of being the heir to the homeland kingdom, like was the case with Caesar, Cleopatra and their son Caesarion, who was killed.

Kushite civilization was almost always polygamous kingdom in which nation building was and is paramount to progress and continuity. Bearing the right personalities within the next generation was of the utmost importance. It was vital that able rulers were produced to enable the unbroken chain that allowed the Kushite Kingdoms to flourish for many thousands of years. It was not just based upon the carnal pleasure, but purpose. This is very important, because in today's world, the polygamous inclination of Black men makes them the targets of insults and misunderstanding. We are called 'players', 'unfaithful', 'cheats', who are incapable of making a whole hearted commitment to our partner. I can speak from experience in saying that often we don't overstand ourselves and so make it harder for others to overstand us. We do not help the situation in our ignorance and identity crisis. Africans from the Motherland more often embrace this Kushite cultural condition, sometimes even when they have been 'westernized' by Christianity and its monogamous doctrine. Those of us born in the West have been converted and brain-washed into 'Negropeans', shunning our own and embracing the White man's monogamy, when the fact is that most of us are not wired that way. The Black man was not created to be monogamous but to be fruitful and multiply. We are amorous, hot blooded beings, capable of loving more than one woman. We are not Neanderthals (the European's ancestors) who were largely impotent and often witnessed one woman sexually intimate with 3 or 4 brothers. Something which can still be observed as the norm when watching any soap drama, such as, EastEnders, Coronation Street or Emmerdale and Hollyoaks. Even today we regularly see and hear how one White woman might be sexually involved with two brothers, or two friends and this is normal behaviour in our modern over-sexualized society. People hardly bat an eyelid. And so now the Negropean is also tainted by this 'Sex and the City' slut culture of the West, enforced upon us as the social-norms. Both our men and women believe that this is the right way of the world, with no knowledge of culture or purpose. Today many are turning to the abomination of homosexuality and lesbianism and the sacredness of the family unit has been compromised. Many women today do not want to have children, before having fun or a career, etc. Civilization lost its way long ago.

But it wasn't always like this. Sex, in the ancient Kingdoms, was largely seen as a gift from the Gods (Paut Neteru), a spiritual act with the added bonus of pleasure. With it came responsibility and a duty of care, physically, mentally and emotionally. The story of Adam and Eve, carries within it the echoes of the carnal corruption of the sacredness of sex by the servants of the serpent. The severity of this is recorded among the Sumerian stories of the Anunnaqi (the Tablet of Atra-Hasis, the Book of Enki, the Epic of Gilgamesh, etc.) which filtered down into the scriptures (the Torah, Bible and Koran) within the story of the myth made characters; Noah and Abraham and Lot, etc.

The spiritual science of Kula Yoga, also referred to as Tantric Sex (Tantra), kept sex sacred between man and woman. It was used for purpose as much as for pleasure and a skilled partner knew how to harness the 'Life Force' (Rau/Chi) or Shekem in order to create, or to heal, or in psychic phenomenon, spiritual cultivation and/or magic. Sex was as much based upon a 'Crown Chakra' vibration as today's sexual unions are largely based upon 'Base Chakra' vibrations. The women of the ancient world was not as jealous, emotional and selfish as they are today in western societies. They were not brainwashed by the 'One and Only' tradition of Europeans, but wanted for other women, close to them like their friends – what they wanted for themselves. Even today many African traditional women will choose other women for their husbands that they think will be a benefit to the bloodline. The women and not the men alone, chose who they wished to cohabit with, for the chief purpose of nation building and the continuation of the healthy society and bloodlines. Today it is, in the western world, all based on pleasure and not purpose. There is no spirituality involved in the majority of sexual unions and flings of the modern free world today. One night stands, bed hopping, teenage pregnancies and rape and abortions have become the order of the day. The 'Gay Agenda' is making sure that homosexuality is normalized, globally and anybody who disagrees is labelled homophobic. This word 'homophobic' is being used in the same way as 'anti-Semitic' is used to discredit those who are speaking out against 'Zionism'.

The Black man and all others must cease from these sexually perverse and alien practices taught to him as a Negropean and once again embrace the sacredness of both the Mother Goddess Principle (fertility) and the Kula Yoga, which must once again be learnt and re-mastered. The Black woman and all other women, must free their lovers from the 'Curse on Love' being called monogamy. They must do this by dealing with their own fear of loss and insecurities which result in the over attachments to their lovers and also men must cease from being dishonest and having secret liaisons and affairs and learn to speak to their spouses about polygamy and everything that it involved. The feminist must stop thinking that men and women are equal in the sense that a woman can also have multiple partners if a man can. This is sexually unclean as it is the man who ejaculates and leaves his (germ) print on the woman and not the other way around. It is unhygienic for a woman to have more than one lover at once. It is not in their nature to live in this way. It is for a woman/wife/concubine to hold on to the security, stability and love of her man in an unselfish way, in order for us to conquer the sexual perversions rife in today's new Sodom and Gomorrah. You all must see past your emotions to see this logical truth. This should not be taken lightly by either man or woman; the fact that there are way more women in the world than men? Nature, my brothers and sisters, is never wrong.

Until the Black man and woman of the diaspora, (especially the US and UK), once again takes a passionate interest in relearning and redefining our culture for and by ourselves, identity and purpose, the modern Nubian Nation will never awaken and rise from their thousands of years of sleep and slumber, for she is the 'Mother of all living' humans and also the first school of humanity and its children. Until Black men and women lead the way in empowering each other once again using the spiritual sciences and becoming the blameless examples that the world needs more than ever right now, humanity will continue to drown in the wave of its own potential and the shadow of the greatness of our ancestors.

The new pseudo-culture of celebrity and sport must be disposed of in the light of these words. We must prioritize the re-education of our children with Right Knowledge, Right Wisdom and Right Overstanding (Sound Right Reasoning), racial and religious tolerance to neutralize the atmosphere of religious fanaticism which is causing terrorism and the spilling of innocent blood. Our people in the West must become family orientated and forget about fame and the pursuit of wealth at the cost of purpose. It is time for all women, Black woman and otherwise to stop flaunting themselves as sexual objects of pleasure to be possessed, but rather as 'Vehicles of Love and Light'. It will take a hug effort on the part of us men to stop viewing woman simply as sex objects because it is killing our divinity. Humans 'Love to Lust and Lust to Love'. If we are to advance into Light Beings (Ahkus) and evolute in the next stage – 'Homo-spiritus', this must be achieved within the shortest time possible, because time is running out on us. The attention must be turned to the inside rather than the outside. It's no point glorifying aesthetic beauty when the inside is ugly. Until we can look inside and penetrate the darkest recesses of the self, we will not be able to see outwardly clearly into the world, in the correct way. Therefore, this current trend of cosmetics and surgery is nothing but an illusion perpetuated upon broken people who do not love or view anything realistically. The people who create the market for these soulless trends are severely damaged people psychologically, the result of the spiritual void of the modern, technological world. The speed at which technology is advancing is doing nothing to help improve the spiritual health of humanity or to erase the suffering of the poor, the unfulfilled, the diseased, etc., etc. All of this technological and material wealth does nothing but make the world further detached from reality, from the purpose and meaning of creation. All of this is largely anchored upon the desire of sexual gratification. What a horror show!!!

".... For all our scientific achievements, great discoveries and the many convenience comforts of the modern western world, there remains a pervading sense that civilization has taken a wrong turn somewhere down the line. Secrets and lies seem rife within governments and institutions, countries go to war on very shaky grounds and an agenda of control and surveillance appears to have replaced the relative freedom the West once knew. Fear of climate change, fear of terrorism, fear of flu pandemics, fear of poverty, fear of immigrants and outsiders, fear of almost everything; all these threats seemingly dangled above our heads and actively inflated by media shock merchants mean we increasingly act from a place of threatened security rather than from expansion and joy. The prevailing impression is that we are poised on the brink of political, economic, spiritual and social breakdown as the family unit dissolves and the old foundations of respect and a sense of the sacred dwindle away into disorder, systematic corruption and crime. Meanwhile, the savage austerity measure seen in several countries amidst the current economic turmoil have focussed many minds on loss (or, in some cases, simply the fear of loss), rather than abundance ....."

- The Truth Agenda: Andy Thomas; Pg 19 (In Part)

This Orwellian picture which was painted by Andy Thomas put it perfectly. The fact is that society civilization took a wrong turn when the matriarchal spirituality of the Ancient Kushite Kingdoms, such as, Khemet (Egypt), turned into the rise of the patriarchal, materialistic Kingdoms of homosexual Greco-Rome. The materialism, male chauvinism and inhuman barbarity that these civilizations wrought upon the original people and cultures of the planet, from then until now, have been the worst blight that humanity has ever had to face. The inhuman nature of the European peaked not with the holocaust of the Nazi fascists (which killed 6 million), but with the trans-Atlantic Slave Trade of the 1500's (which killed 100 million on the ships alone). This was the worst atrocity on humanity, not the holocaust, for which no one has been held responsible, or no official apology has been given or compensation been paid.

The raping of Mother Africa, her resources, her women (our grandmothers), not to pass on civilization, but only to increase Europe's material wealth, the Willie Lynch Syndrome encoded into us and its psychological implications, have never been addressed by today's elite (the descendants of the slave masters). The 'White man's Burden' is used as an excuse for it.

The good news is that the outcome can still be swung in our favour. It is possible for us to control our sexual urges and to purify ourselves; mind, body and soul. The re-emergence of the tantra is paramount to the success of humanity. The liberation of love and the overstanding of the meaning of the spiritual traditions of the Kushites is a must for this to work out in humanities favour. Those who still believe that European society today is the pinnacle of humanity and that the European way of viewing and doing things is the only relevant way need not concern themselves in these matters. These words are for the 'chosen few', who hold the power and key to the salvation of the planet earth. Out of the many called, these 'chosen few' (144,000 elites) will each affect up to 750,000 people within their radius, thereby awakening the Love and the Light, embedded deep within the subconscious of all of humanity, for we are all the children of BA KULUWM "THE ALL". Our job is to destroy the illusion presented to the masses as reality, in order for the servants of the serpent (Leviathan) to dim the light and truth of Paut Neteru/Anunnaqi (Elohim). This 6000 year spell of sleep (of racial and spiritual blindness) should've run its course in 2003, but today in 2017 AD, it is still holding the majority of the world under its spell. The planet has been so thoroughly conditioned, that most folks cannot see behind the physical world, they cannot perceive the war being fought in the spiritual realm for the minds of men and women. The over-exertion of perverse, carnal and lustful sex has the world trapped within its own vanities and iniquity. Fellow Lightworkerz; don't give up the Good Fight!

".... Consequently, Van Gennep's notion that Egyptians, who often married their close relations, especially their sister's, could not be totemists, is definitely refuted here. Marriage with one's sister stems from another cultural trait equally pervasive in the Black world; matriarchy, which will be discussed shortly ...."

- Cheikh Anta Diop: The African Origin of Civilization; Pg 135 (In Part)

The Black man (Kushite) proper, has long become an endangered species, especially here in the West. Today the West is manufacturing Negropeans and Neutranoids, tailor made to express White and Western ideals. Men such as Barak Obama, the ex-President of the United States himself, who claimed that he was not 'Black', but mixed-race. Many other high profile blacks have made this claim such as Tiger Woods, the disgraced golf player.

Without returning to the Kushite (African) concept of matriarchy, the Black man is doomed to fail in all of life's endeavours. A return to the sacredness of the family unit, the response-ability of taking an active role in the upbringing and emotional support of our children is fundamental and paramount to the reawakening of the African mind laying dormant within the DNA of all Black people of the diaspora. Otherwise the long sought after unity of African peoples and humanity in general will never happen within our lifetimes and the lifetimes of our children and grand-children. The better utopian world we envision for them will remain a psychological fantasy.

It all starts with us Kushites taking the leading role, by reclaiming our stolen legacy in all of its glory. We must recognize and re-identify with our Kushite roots and resurrect a culture and tradition that never failed us, but which we failed to hold on to. Being family men, we must re-educate our women and ourselves in the image of our own true and living Black Gods and give the White supremacists back their fake Gods and false Christs, in all of their various 'isms and schisms – Judaism, Christianity, Islam, the whole lot. Only in this way can we end the identity crisis affecting our people for so long. Again, the eminent Cheikh Anta Diop puts it perfectly when he stated:

".... This identity of Egyptian and Negro culture, or rather, this identity of mental structure, as observed by Masson Oursel, makes Negro mentality the basic trait of Egyptian philosophy; .... [one that] should be obvious to anyone of good faith.

The oneness of Egyptian and Black culture and race today all Negroes can legitimately trace their culture to Ancient Egypt and build a modern culture on that foundation. A dynamic, modern contact with Egyptian Antiquity would enable Blacks to discover increasingly each day the intimate relationship between all Blacks of the continent and the Mother Nile Valley. By this dynamic contact, the Negro will be convinced that these temples, these forests of columns, these pyramids, these colossi, these bas-reliefs, mathematics, medicine and all this science are indeed the work of his ancestors and that he has a right and a duty to claim this heritage ...."

"From now on, in this type of research so invaluable for the investigation of thought, we are beginning to perceive that a great part of the Black continent, instead of being unpolished and savage, as was previously supposed, has cast its influence in many directions across the immense isolation of desert or forest, an influence which came from the Nile and passed through Libya, Nubia and Ethiopia ...."

".... A people without the knowledge of their past history, origin and culture, is like a tree without roots ...."

- Marcus Mosiah Garvey

Matriarchy served as the base and foundation of Ancient Kush and Black Africa which were industrious agricultural civilizations. The fact that this matriarchal system still exists and can be found in many areas of Black Africa today, attests to the endurance of Black African, social structure. The only places where the ties to the Nile Valley civilization has been cut, is places that have been usurped by outside influences such as Christianity and Islam. And we should make note again that Greco-Rome never attributed any pre-eminence or importance to its women, they never, in the case of Greece, really had any notion of monarchical rule but were more like warring city states and also never had any Queens among them. Greece was never really a fully united kingdom in its heyday. The perfect utopian society reported to have been achieved by 'the blameless Ethiopians' (i.e. Kushites) has never been achieved by the Caucasian and his materialist societies of have and have-nots. The world that we live in today is irrefutably the result of the Caucasian taking civilization down a completely different route, since the defeat of General Hannibal in 814 B.C. and the usurpation of Black African, matriarchal civilization globally. The absence of spiritual principal, such as Ma'at, the inhuman, barbaric events passed off as sports, the homosexual activities, repression of the female principle and the material greed for wealth, resources and technological advancement, created the void which is swallowing the world and humanity today.

In the Light of the Sun, (Paut Neteru) created in their image and likeness, the Kushite is the Vice-Regent of the Most High, ANU (AMUN) upon the earth. Until we awaken from this 6000 year Spell of Sleep, of Ignorance (racial and spiritual blindness), nothing in the world will change. We will keep on falling victim to men, such as, Adolf Hitler, Lenin, Stalin, Napoleon Bonaparte, Saddam Hussein, Benito Mussolini, Bin Laden, Assad, Al Baghdadi, Vladimir Putin and now Donald Trump. What kind of world are we handing to our children? Continuing down this path what can the future of humanity hold but peril and tribulation? Stop waiting on some spook, mystery God and/or Messiah to float down out from the sky and save you and become the change that you want to see. Be the example and influence that the world needs, because it is more powerful and influential than you may think. The power of God/s (divinity) is embedded deep within all humans and all life. The spiritual awakening from within us is ready to happen, but we must eradicate the atmosphere of fear and control. Listen to the wisdom and intuition of your mother, your wife, etc. Reclaim your legacy and wake up!!

I hope that these words of wisdom are not taken as an attempt by the author to try and justify the sexual appetites of men, but the need to replenish and nourish society with able minds to ensure its continuation and expansion, in order that civilization might flourish. Of course there are people, men who may want to have sexual relations with one woman during their lifetimes, but it is the duty of all men to supply the nation with children in the image and likeness of their ancestors (the Gods), contributing to the production of a strong population with a healthy outlook on life is not an option but a duty. In this way, the strong, family-orientated man must place purpose before pleasure, always. Because of the mental condition of Black people today, this is more needed than ever. The emotional and psychological state of modern Kushites, both men and women, requires for a reawakening of the Maatian mind, in order to counter-act the 'mentality of death', being called the western way of life, the free world.

Kushite (Black) women are still being programmed to hate their African features and beautiful kinky hair, being bombarded constantly with the white standard of beauty by the media. Perming and relaxing their hair is evidence of the pressure that our women feel to conform to that white standard. Blue eye contacts, blonde wigs, hair extensions and skin bleaching are traits of the ongoing conflicts occurring within their minds. The self-hatred is evident. While you Kushite Queens are trying so hard to conform to their standard of beauty, they themselves are paying hundreds of pounds and dollars to look like you and claim your spot. They all are deforming their mouths and lips with lip-fillers, etc., to create the so called Angelina Jolie look, they are paying for bum implants to improve their bums to look like Black women and have the voluptuous hour glass shape of the African woman. They are breeding with Kushites and it is evidently improving their aesthetic form compared to fifty years ago. While you are busy bleaching your beautiful melanin skin whiter and whiter, they are obsessed with sun beds, spray (bottle) tans and the likes, like never before.

The images of beauty portrayed by the mainstream through Hollywood, the music industry and magazines, such as FHM favour light skinned Black women, mixed-raced and white women with European features, long hair blowing in the wind (machine), at the expense of the supernatural African Kushite Goddesses. Constantly bombarded with these tailored edited images creates a psychological conflict within the minds of the Kushite. They want for you to believe that the 'Bust of Nefertiti' (which has been whitened) is the only image of African beauty, never giving any recognition to exquisite images of beauty, such as the sublime beauty of images, such as the 'Bust of Queen Tiye' (mother of Pharaoh Akhenaton), a true Wasetian (Meroitic Sudanese) Kushite woman. Of course, all of this is done deliberately by blond haired, blue eyed Pleiadians, those who are in control of the world and all its industries and institutions currently.

All humans are beautiful in their own ways. Black people are a shining example of the beauty and origin of the human aesthetic form. This cannot be denied or overstated and they know this. The most they can do is blind you to the beauty that permeates from within yourselves, expressing itself in so much variety and physical diversity. The dynamism of the Kushite man and woman is the origin of all beauty in all human beings, as the Mothers and fathers of all. The only way to destroy the insecurity we feel about ourselves at the moment is to reconnect with the beautiful images of our ancestors displayed throughout the ancient and modern Kushite (African) kingdoms and especially where our children are concerned. We must teach them to see beauty not just aesthetically, but in spirit and personality. We must teach ourselves to see beauty holistically, within all colours and creeds. Indeed, this must start by limiting the time and content of what ourselves and our little ones are viewing on T.V. so many people are wasting countless hours watching celebrities, reading gossip and all types of other pig shit, with no interest in anything beneficial or intellectual, just cosmetic, shallow fashion, materialistic garbage. If people spent half as much time studying knowledge and wisdom, as they did on celebrity crap, we would develop the overstanding needed to raise the density and vibration of the planet in no time.

Its time now for women to make a choice, you can continue to live in a climate of intimate fear of betrayal and fear of loss or begin to overstand and see past your own emotional content, allowing your husband's to perform their duty unto the Gods and their Black nation and live free without the fear of an emotional back lash. This doesn't mean that men should be free to have no strings attached relations and one night stands with whoever they lust over, but allow them to be free to love more than one woman, bring through children and look after them, spreading love and not restricting love because more love is needed in the world. Stop cursing this abundance of love and start to share and embrace it throughout society. Every woman shares her man mentally and physically, knowingly or unknowingly. Repressing men creates problems and has consequences in society. Would you as a woman rather share your man knowingly, knowing who he has relations with sexually are of sound body and mind, or unknowingly, while he is cheating with any old female behind your back? Would you rather assist your friends by offering them the love of a man you know from experience is responsible and decent, or watch them get hurt by excuses for men who are only out for their own sexual gratification and not interested in nation building and taking an active role in raising his children? What I am saying is nothing new, but only that which was once established globally and worked for us; it's time to take off the blinkers of the tunnel-visioned western world and embrace your own heritage, cultivate your own culture and reclaim your stolen legacy brothers and sisters.

In this way we will make the Gods and our ancestors proud and celebrate life rather than be burdened by it because life is meant to be a celebration of 'Love, Peace and Happiness', a gratitude to AMUN RE. Us men have a lot of work to do to put things right, but a lot also depends on the women too. It's too easy to blame everything on the men without recognising the failure of the women and the importance and role they play in establishing a spiritually sound modern civilization. Without both sexes recognizing what they have got to do, the utopian reality cannot and will not be achieved ever again. It is up to all of us to do what we have to do and play our parts to heal the damage that has been done to humanity and civilization by the hand of the 'Agents of the Shadows', the 'Servants of the Serpent'. May the Ancestor-Gods be with us ALL.

That brings us to the end of the first section of this scroll (the foundation). Now I feel that upon this foundation of Kushite origin and culture, we are in a good position to take an intimate look upon the personages of Pharaonic Khamit (Egypt), upon the Shekem Ur Shekems (Aafertiaat), 'the Pharaohs' themselves, their divine purpose, legacy and principles; so that us Kushites today might pick up the torch after so long, resurrect and continue the great work - The Good Fight. I hope that you enjoy the reading and learning, as much as I have enjoyed the researching and writing. Hotep.

WARRIORZ OF THE LIGHT

"LIGHTWORKERZ"

Section II: The Example

"Beauty is not in the face, beauty is a light in the heart"

- Khalil Gibran

Timeline and King List

c. 17,250,000 B.C	The first coming of Paut Neteru from Nibiru. Ba Rashunaat 'Ogdoad' (Sacred 8) crash down in Nile River 2,250,000 B.C. (1st Adamah Project – Ptah Daneg). Migration from Zimbabwe through Uganda.
c. 450,000 B.C	Landing of ENKI and 49 Anunnaqi, (staying on earth) : Zep Tepi 'Beginning' 1st Golden Age – Predeluvial (Gods end with Horus)
	Adamah Project Pt: II (Kadmon and Nekaybaw)
c. 100,000 B.C	Time of Shemsu Haru (Ahkus – demi-Gods)
	Shemsu Haru (Ahkus) reigned 13,420 years
c. 50,000 B.C	Shemsu Haru 2nd group 23,200 years
	Migration further up the River Nile
	Priest – Kings
	Ancient Sages – descendants of Ahkus/Shemsu-Haru
c. 12,000 B.C	Concentration in and around Nubia (Nile Valley)
	Great Deluge: climate change, social upheavals, population growth
	Concentration of Proto-Sahara (Aqualithic), migration into Asia
c. 10,860 B.C	Dynasty O (Nubian Pharaohs): Sennar – Egypto Nubian
	Late pre-Dynastic: Capital at Nekhen (Hierakonpolis)
c. 4,000 B.C	Nekhen Pharaohs – Pharaoh Scorpion, Menes (Narmer),
4,000 – 3,100 B.C	Tera-Neter, Men-Thiou, etc.
	Dynasty I (Pharaonic Khemet): Egyptian Independence
	Early Dynastic (1st dynasty). Thinite Dynasties (3,000-2,778 B.C)
c. 3,800 B.C	Capital transferred to Thinis
3,100 – 2,900 B.C	Aha
	Djer
	Djet
	Qa'a, etc.
	Dynasty 2
	Hetepsekhemury
c. 2,900 – 2,778 B.C	Peribsen
	Dynasty 3 (Centralization Complete) – OLD KINGDOM (Golden Age: 2,640-2,040 B.C)
c. 2,778 – 2,613 B.C	Djoser Neterikeht & Sage Imhotep
	Sekhemkhet
c. 2,723 – 2,648 B.C	Khaba FEUDALISM EVOLVING
c. 2,648 – 2,640 B.C	Huni
c. 2,640 – 2,637 B.C	
c. 2,637 – 2,613 B.C	Dynasty 4
	Sneferu
c. 2,613 – 2,494 B.C	Khufu FEUDALISM PEAKING

c. 2,613 – 2,589 B.C	Djedefre	
c. 2,589 – 2,566 B.C	Khafre	
c. 2,566 – 2,558 B.C	Menkaure	
c. 2,558 – 2,532 B.C	Shepseskaf	
c. 2,532 – 2,503 B.C	Dynasty 5	
c. 2,503 – 2,498 B.C	Userkat & Khentkaus	
c. 2,494 – 2,345 B.C	Sahura	PEAK OF FEUDALISM
c. 2,494 – 2,487 B.C	Neferirkara	
c. 2,487 – 2,475 B.C	Shepseskara	
c. 2,475 – 2,455 B.C	Raneferef	
c. 2,455 – 2,448 B.C	Nyuserra	
c. 2,488 – 2,445 B.C	Menkauhor	
c. 2,445 – 2,421 B.C	Djedkara Isesi (Ruler during life of the sage Ptah-Hotep)	
c. 2,421 – 2,414 B.C	Unas	
c. 2,414 – 2,375 B.C	Dynasty 6 (Capital relocated to Men-Nefer/Memphis) Nubian	
c. 2,375 – 2,345 B.C	Teti Kushite strong connections	
c. 2,345 – 2,181 B.C	Userkara	
c. 2,345 – 2,323 B.C	Pepi I	FEUDALISM DECLINING
c. 2,323 – 2,321 B.C	Merenre	
c. 2,321 – 2,287 B.C	Pepi II (Longest reigning Pharaoh)	
c. 2,287 – 2,278 B.C	Nitigret	
c. 2,278 – 2,184 B.C	7th – 8th Dynsties – Numerous Pharaohs from Memphis, often called	
c. 2,184 – 2,181 B.C	Neferkara	
c. 2,181 – 2,160 B.C		
	FIRST INTERMEDIATE PERIOD (collapse of Feudalism) Asiatic Invasion	
	9th & 10th Dynasties	
c. 2,160 – 2,055 B.C	Khety	
c. 2,160 – 2,025 B.C	Merikara, etc.	
	Early 11th Dynasty	
	Sehertawy Intef I	
c. 2,125 – 2,055 B.C	Wahankh Intef II	
c. 2,125 – 2,112 B.C	Nakhnebtepnefer Intef III (End of Autonomous Governments) Revolution	
c. 2,112 – 2,063 B.C	of People	
c. 2,063 – 2,055 B.C		
	MIDDLE KINGDOM: (Re-emergence from Southern Homeland)	
	Later 11th Dynasty – Capital at Waset (Thebes)	
c. 2,055 – 1,650 B.C	Mentuhotep II (clearly Wasetian Kushite features)	
c. 2,055 – 1,985 B.C	Mentuhotep III	
c. 2,055 – 2,004 B.C	Mentuhotep IV	
c. 2,004 – 1,992 B.C	Dynasty 12 (Introduced Co-Regencies)	
c. 1,992 – 1,985 B.C	Amenemhet I	
c. 1,985 – 1,773 B.C	Senusret (Sesostris I) "Greatest ruler of Middle Kingdom"	
c. 1,985 – 1,956 B.C	Amenemhet II	
c. 1,956 – 1,911 B.C	Senusret (Sesostris II)	
c. 1,911 – 1,877 B.C	Senusret (Sesostris III)	
c. 1,877 – 1,870 B.C	Amenemhet III (Famous for his Labyrinth)	
c. 1,870 – 1,831 B.C	Amenemhet IV	

c. 1,831 – 1,786 B.C	Subekneferu (Queen)
c. 1,786 – 1,777 B.C	Dynasty 13 (More than 60 imposters)
c. 1,777 – 1,773 B.C	
c. 1,773 – after 1,650 B.C	SECOND INTERMEDIATE PERIOD 14th Dynasty
c. 1,700 – 1,550 B.C	*Hyksos Invasion (Greek, Syrian, Arab mixtures)
c. 1,700 – 1,650 B.C	15th Dynasty Salistis
c. 1,650 – 1,550 B.C	Khyan } Hyksos Pretender Pharaohs Apepi (Apophis), etc. 16th Dynasty Resistance under:
c. 1,650 – 1,580 B.C	Osortasen II Osortasen III (Nubian ancestor of Pharaoh Shabaka) 17th Dynasty: Liberation from Hyksos Occupation Intef IV
c. 1,650 – 1,550 B.C	Seqenenre-Taa Taa & Queen Ahhotep (Liberators, Instigated Hyksos War) Khamose (with Queen Ahhotep he defeated Hyksos cowards)
	NEW KINGDOM 18th Dynasty
c. 1,550 – 1,295 B.C	Ahmose (Built on his brother's success & drove out the defeated Hyksos)
c. 1,550 – 1,525 B.C	Amenhotep I & Mother Ahmes Nefertari
c. 1,525 – 1,504 B.C	Tehutimose (Thutmose) I
c. 1,504 – 1,492 B.C	Tehutimose (Thutmose) II
c. 1,492 – 1,479 B.C	Tehutimose (Thutmose) III "Warior King' called Egyptian Napoleon
c. 1,479 – 1,425 B.C	Hatshepsut (Confusion & strife with co-regent Tutmose III)
c. 1,473 – 1,458 B.C	Amenhotep II
c. 1,427 – 1,400 B.C	Tehutimose IV
c. 1,400 – 1,390 B.C	Amenhotep III & Queen Tiye' (New Kingdom Golden Age)
c. 1,390 – 1,352 B.C	Amenhotep IV/Akhenaten & Nefertiti/Neferneferuaten "Aten Religion"
c. 1,352 – 1,336 B.C	Tutankhaten (Tutankhamun)
c. 1,336 – 1,327 B.C	Ay Capital at Akhetaten } Armana Period
c. 1,327 – 1,323 B.C	Horemheb Tel El Amarna
c. 1,323 – 1,295 B.C	19th Dynasty
c. 1,295 – 1,186 B.C	Rameses I (Army General of non-royal blood)
c. 1,295 – 1,294 B.C	Seti I (Renaissance of Khemet)
c. 1,294 – 1,279 B.C	Rameses II (The Great) 1275 Battle of Kadesh
c. 1,279 – 1,213 B.C	Meneptah (c. 1209 claims victory over Sea Peoples)
c. 1,213 – 1,203 B.C	Seti II (Civil War with his son Amenmessu – lasts 3 years)
c. 1,203 1,194 B.C	Amenmessu
c. 1,203 – 1,200 B.C	Saptah
c. 1,194 – 1,188 B.C	Tausret (Queen, wife of Seti II)
c. 1,188 – 1,186 B.C	20th Dynasty
c. 1,186 – 1,069 B.C	Sethnakht
c. 1,186 – 1,184 B.C	Rameses III (Defeats invading Libyans & Sea Peoples 1180, 1174, 1177

c. 1,184 – 1,153 B.C	BC)
	Rameses IV
c. 1,153 – 1,147 B.C	Rameses V
c. 1,147 – 1,143 B.C	Rameses VI
c. 1,143 – 1,136 B.C	Rameses VII
c. 1,136 – 1,129 B.C	Rameses VIII
c. 1,129 – 1,126 B.C	Rameses IX
c. 1,126 – 1,108 B.C	Rameses X
c. 1,108 – 1,099 B.C	Rameses XI
c. 1,099 – 1,069 B.C	
	THIRD INTERMEDIATE PERIOD: LIBYAN DYNASTIES
c. 1,069 – 715 B.C	21st Dynasty
c. 1,069 – 945 B.C	Smendes
c. 1,069 – 1,043 B.C	Amenemnisu
c. 1,043 – 1,039 B.C	Psusennes I
c. 1,039 – 991 B.C	Amenope
c. 993 – 984 B.C	Osorkon I
c. 984 – 978 B.C	Siamun
c. 978 – 959 B.C	Psusennes II
c. 959 – 945 B.C	22nd Dynasty
c. 945 – 715 B.C	Sheshonq I
c. 945 – 924 B.C	Osorkon II
c. 924 – 889 B.C	Sheshonq II
c. 890	Takelot I
c. 889 – 874 B.C	Osorkon III
c. 874 – 850 B.C	Takelot II
c. 850 – 825 B.C	Sheshonq III
c. 825 – 773 B.C	Pimay
c. 773 – 767 B.C	Sheshonq V
c. 767 – 730 B.C	Osorkon IV
c. 730 – 715 B.C	23rd Dynasty: Many more puppet Kings, from different centres
c. 818 – 715 B.C	24th Dynasty
c. 727 – 715 B.C	Tefnakht
c. 727 – 720 B.C	Bakenrenef
c. 720 – 715 B.C	
	*EARLY 25th DYNASTY: Re-establishment of Kushite Roots (Nubian)
c. 747 – 715 B.C	Piy/Pianki, Kashta, Alara, etc. (728. Piy's victory stelae)
c. 747 – 715 B.C	LATE PERIOD: (founded by Alara & his son Kashta)
c. 715 – 332 B.C	*LATER 25th DYNASTY: from Napata, Nuri, Meroe, etc.
c. 715 – 656 B.C	Shabaka (c. 711 Shabaka unites Khemet & Kush – Shabaka Stone Stelae)
c. 715 – 702 B.C	Shabitqo (confronts Assyrians at Eltekeh in Palestine, 701 BC)
c. 702 – 690 B.C	Taharka (C. 671 flees Memphis from Assyrians, recaptures Northern
c. 690 – 664 B.C	Egypt c. 669)
c. 664 – 656 B.C	26th Dynasty: Ashurbanipal invades from Assyria
c. 664 – 525 B.C	Psamtek/Psammiticus I
c. 664 – 610 B.C	Nekau II
c. 610 – 595 B.C	Psamtek II

c. 595 – 589 B.C	Haaibra
c. 589 – 570 B.C	Ahmose II
C. 570 – 526 B.C	Psamtek III
c. 526 – 525 B.C	27th Dynasty: Perisan Fools
c. 525 – 404 B.C	Cambyses
c. 525 – 522 B.C	Darius I
c. 522 – 486 B.C	Xerxes I
c. 486 – 465 B.C	Artaxerxes I
c. 465 – 424 B.C	Darius II
c. 424 – 405 B.C	Artaxerxes II
c. 405 – 359 B.C	28th Dynasty
c. 404 – 399 B.C	Amrytaios
c. 404 – 399 B.C	29th Dynasty
c. 399 – 380 B.C	Nepherites I
c. 399 – 393 B.C	Hakor
c. 393 – 380 B.C	Nepherltes II
c. 380 B.C	30th Dynasty
c. 380 – 343 B.C	Nectanebo I
c. 380 – 362 B.C	Teos
c. 362 – 360 B.C	Nectanebo II
c. 360 – 343 B.C	31st Dynasty: 2nd Persian Occupation
c. 343 – 332 B.C	Artaxerxes III Ochus
c. 343 – 338 B.C	Arses
c. 338 – 336 B.C	Darius III Codoman
c. 336 – 332 B.C	
	PTOLEMAIC PERIOD
c. 332 – 30 B.C	Macedonian Fools
c. 332 – 305 B.C	Alexander the Greek (because he wasn't great)
c. 332 – 323 B.C	Philip Arrhidaeus
c. 323 – 317 B.C	Alexander IV
c. 317 – 305 B.C	Ptolemaic Idiots
c. 305 – 30 B.C	Ptolemy I Soter I
c. 305 – 285 B.C	Ptolemy II Philadelphus
c. 285 – 246 B.C	Ptolemy III Evergetes I
c. 246 – 221 B.C	Ptolemy IV Philopater
c. 221 – 205 B.C	Ptolemy V Epiphanes
c. 205 – 180 B.C	Ptolemy VI Philometer
c. 180 – 145 B.C	Ptolemy VII Neos Philopater
c. 145 B.C	Ptolemy VIII Evergetes II
c. 170 – 116 B.C	Ptolemy IX Soter II
c. 116 – 107 B.C	Ptolemy X Alexander I
c. 107 – 88 B.C	Ptolemy IX Soter II
c. 88 – 80 B.C	Ptolemy XI Alexander II
c. 80 B.C	Ptolemy XII Neos Dionysos
c. 80 – 51 B.C	Cleopatra VII Philopater
c. 51 – 30 B.C	Ptolemy XIII
c. 51 – 47 B.C	Ptolemy XIV

c. 47 – 44 B.C	Ptolemy XV Caesarion (son of Cleopatra & Caesar)
c. 44 – 30 B.C	

ROMAN CRACKHEADS
Examples: Augustus, Vespasian, Trajan, Hadrian, Constantine I, Theodosius, etc.

7th Centures: Mohammadan Invasion

Modern Times: European Invasion: Armenians, Turks, Syrians, French, British

*As with my other writings, the list of Pharaohs (chronology) used from the Dynastic period of c. 3,100 B.C, is the official chronology used by mainstream Egyptologists. Those that know, know that this chronology is largely based on the assumption that the Pharaohs reigned one after one in that particular order but that is just speculation. More times than often, official history has proven to be wrong as C^{14} carbon-dating cannot be used to accurately date stone monuments. Any attempt to use it to date the remains of those buried around these sites is flawed because the ancients constantly built new temples on top of the older temple and many people buried themselves near to or on earlier ancient sites, to be near to divine persons and places. Together with the fact that the antiquity of Kushite people is so remote, that white historians (Indo-Aryans) try to bring them up to historical times, to fit into their official world timeline, it means that the true timeline of human events is downplayed. The noble: Amunnubi Rooahkptah stated that all of the Europeans dates is missing a zero and that is not hard to believe. Adding an extra zero to every date given by official (Indo-Aryan) Egyptologists yields a more accurate measure of the timeframe.

Still, I have decided to keep things simple and use the 'short-count', the Egyptological timeframe because I know how hard it will be for this book to be taken seriously, even using the standard chronology, never mind the long count which is supported by ancient writers, Egyptian and otherwise. I leave it to the reader to add a zero themselves, or not, but I have included the time of the Gods (Zep Tepi) and the time of the demi-Gods because in the eyes of our ancestors, this was a reality, not a myth. Any attempt by song-sheet Egyptologists and others to refute this in 2017 A.D, is just blatant denial and an attempt to discredit the ancestors and their authenticity. By now everyone should know that Egyptology is a front to disclaim the Kushite African origin of Khemet/Egypt just like Assyriology does to its namesake and etc.

Now that we have familiarized ourselves with the history of Kushite culture, we are in the best position to take a closer look at the formidable and dynamic leaders of men that the 'Shekem Ur Shekems' (Pharaohs) were and realize that they definitely were the best examples of human beings that we have. It was them and not the fictional prophets of fabricated religions that we should seek to follow honour and emulate in the way they never failed to apply the rule (Maat) or shy away from response-ability. Only our illustrious ancestors can show us how to stand up and be counted, bearing the weight of the world upon our shoulders to come up with realistic solutions to the age of problems Kushites of the diaspora and the wider world still face today in 2017 A.D. It is our intention in this scroll to erase the false image of the Shekem Ur Shekem, perpetuated by religion, official history and Hollywood of the Pharaohs as tyrants, Satanists, philanderers, despots and dictators, ungodly 'Servants of the Serpents', etc. So let's dance.

The Qualities of Leadership

A great leader must view leadership as an honour and not only possess good organisational, communication and managerial skills, but must assume great response-ability and provide consistent, inspired and principal centred leadership for the group being led. They must be born with or develop the ability and courage to lead by example, in order to gain the respect and confidence of the masses. It is self-discipline that enables them to hold others accountable for their actions, because obviously, if you as a leader do not turn up on time for work, then you cannot expect anybody else to be punctual either. Why should they be?

No country, nation, group or organization can rise above the quality of its leadership. There are important decisions and personal choices that both new and experienced leaders must make on a regular basis, because leadership is indeed a position that must be earned day in and day out. Efficient leaders are therefore, first and foremost, effective and efficient people because personal ethics cannot be separated from professional ethics. This means that the natural character of the leader is essential to the role.

Leadership is not an exact science, leadership is an art and the contrasting difference between a dynamic and superior leader and short term motivator is to be discovered in the personal decisions an individual makes when choosing to live his or her life. Strict and determined dedication and long term commitment to various principles will produce an effective leader and over time, an inspired organization and/or institution.

".... Begin with the end in mind ... "

- Stephan Covey: The 7 Habits of Highly Effective People

Effective leadership is based in the fundamental ability to believe in yourself. It incorporates a maturity, conviction and expertise that envisions a purpose and direction. It is this 'Clear Vision' (Clairvoyance) that empowers great leaders with the courage and confidence to take on the role of transmitting their motivation, self-esteem and teamwork to others. As visionaries, they are calculated and disciplined thinkers and confidently trust their own intuition. These men and women of higher ken fully overstand their environment, transforming situations to attain established visions. They can combine change with growth, take prudent and calculated risks, adapt to situations and demonstrate innovative problem solving skills. True leaders worthy of the name believe in and invest time, love and energy in people and are sensitive to others needs and appreciate other people's core values. They will actively remake a challenge in order to yield productive outcomes by creating an organizational structure that develops and fosters success. The question often debated is; "Are leaders born or are leaders made"? The answer is both! They are both born and made, with traits and skills that can be learnt and together with direction, encouragement, reinforcement and guidance, can produce outstanding and astute individuals.

There is no general consensus on what makes an effective leader. Essentially outstanding leaders become a precise balance of traits, behaviour, abilities, and sources of power and aspects of the situation. These are the determining factors of the ability to influence followers and accomplish the objectives, goals and vision. Dynamic leaders formulate an idea and then work through the details committing every thought, feeling and living emotion, knowing that they can portray it with purity and confidence. Leadership incorporates attitudes which determine the attitude, values and a mind-set that will facilitate commitment, dedication and transformation and begins by developing a vision, a passionate desire to succeed in the now and in the future.

To overstand the behaviour and traits of leaders such as the Shekem Ur Shekems (Pharaohs) and others, we need to look at their underlying character, the 'Man behind the Mask' so to speak. We need to stop looking at them through the eyes of official history; Hollywood and religion, as emotionless robots and static humans and look at their physical stamina, energy levels and stress tolerance. We also need to look at the political situations that they inherited and created and use what was written about them in credible records so that we can establish fact from fiction and opinion. Leaders undergo unrelenting demands that require physical and mental vitality and an incredibly high degree of emotional stability and resilience. It requires the ability to problem solve and lateral thought to creatively resolve issues along the way. A leader needs to be adaptable, flexible with ideas and open to a variety of viewpoints and eventual outcomes and solutions. The key is to 'see the forest through the trees' and have the mental ability to project through a variety of circumstances and obstacles, but holding focus on the vision.

The absence of a clear vision (Clairvoyance) is one of the major reasons for ineffective leadership. Regardless of the situation, a true leader needs to be able to communicate their ideas clearly and effectively and commit themselves to the outcome. They must also be able to transform and adapt their vision to a more inclusive position by gaining the trust and commitment of those needed to fulfil their objective. Once formulated, the vision represents direction but must be reinforced by consistent and reliable actions of the leader. Earning the respect and gaining the trust and commitment of those individuals, who will contribute in the process of realizing the objectives and vision, requires that they must be dedicated to the task. If the leader is unable to gain the commitment and earn the respect of others and can only achieve compliance, then the ability to succeed is greatly compromised.

Leaders also need the confidence to build self-esteem in others and still hold a strong degree of integrity in themselves. This includes the ability to influence people up, laterally, below as well as internally and externally. You must be able to gain the approval of all involved to make an idea reality. People skills are needed to develop cooperative, working relations, to be a team player and to create an atmosphere that encourages a natural sense of togetherness. This is the mark of a true leader.

Another one of the biggest challenges of leadership is the ability to motivate others, often over long periods of time and guide others effectively. Interaction with others is paramount to effective leadership. Leadership is not so much an individual's directing and/or ordering, but more a cooperative effort fostered by 'Active Listening', gathering a variety of opinions, assessing effective strategies, and thus generating a clear vision. Leadership is 'the process of influencing' the activities of an organized group toward goal achievement, as well as, the process of giving meaningful direction to collective efforts and achieving your objectives.

".... Leaders are people who do the right thing; managers are people who do things right ...."

- Professor Warren G. Bennis

Although there are thousands of documented definitions of what leadership is, it essentially always involves the ability to influence other people with the objective of achieving an intended goal. The dictionary definition of leadership is 'the behaviour of an individual when he is directing the activities of a group with a focus on a shared goal'. It is defined by the process of influence that in many cases is situational. The success of a leader depends on his/her ability to achieve a goal through the actions of those involved. It depends on the dedication and commitment of others to implement a leader's vision and goals. Society and organizations must have effective leadership in order to successfully achieve their objectives, primarily because it is vital for growth and the overall well-being of society. Make note and remember that leadership needs to be constantly developed, adapted and reinforced with the changing times and be able to effectively attract commitment around it.

A leader needs to achieve tough, demanding goals that they set themselves personally, in addition to those set by an organization, and be dedicated and committed to surpassing both objectives. Flexibility and entrepreneurial spirit are both needed. When people are committed to their leaders, individuals will more readily agree with the vision and ideas and will make the greatest effort to execute this vision and these ideas effectively. Mobilizing their kind of commitment from others must be achieved early and with clear understanding that their involvement is a fundamental part of any success achieved. This goes together with trust, which is the vital link. Trust is indirectly proportional to risk, because leadership depends on minimizing risk to guarantee that the trust and confidence factor is solid. The ability to maintain high levels of trust comes through consistent actions, honesty, expertise, confidence and clarity. The most significant factor is probably the dedication to values and principles, (in this case the propagation of Maat) that are exhibited by the leader's own behaviour and the method by which they reinforce this behaviour in others. Obviously, dynamic leaders are intelligent enough to overstand the needs of others, they know the necessity of commitment, they are energetic, possess the courage of conviction and have a sincere and innate integrity. What can be expected of others is nothing less than what should and can be expected of themselves.

Therefore, any member of any group, at any one time, may assume a leadership role, given any degree of innate traits and the circumstances surrounding the event. A wise man once said recently that the time for leaders has passed for black people and it is time that individuals lead themselves. Look at what happened to most of the 'Black Power Movement' leaders and civil rights leaders of the 60's and 70's. Look at the irresponsible people and role models that our nation has for leaders today?

We are all capable of responsibly leading ourselves nowadays. Different persons who can effectively lead by influencing what a group does, how it is done and the method by which the group interacts with one another could carry out various forms of leadership. The examples left to us by the ancients: the Shekem Ur Shekem especially, but also the Memnons, Nimrods, Lugals, Negast, Rishis, etc. can teach us a lot about ourselves and our Kushite identity. People don't change much. People are the same yesterday as they are today, governed by the same likes and dislikes, slaves to the same flaws and vices. The Pharaoh was the 'Servant of Maat', along with the sages and the sons of the green light, in a war with the ever encroaching 'Servants of the Serpents', the Sons of the Amber Light (fire), those of the shadows. The Kushite institutions, the house of Pharaoh was the Temple, the Light of the entire world, from then on until it fell after the 25th Dynasty.

".... If you can become the leader you ought to be on the inside, you will be able to become the person you want on the outside. People will want to follow you. And when that happens, you will be able to tackle anything in this world ...."

- John C. Maxwell

Suten: Men, Menes, Narmer: Bold Strategist & Innovator

As evidenced earlier on, the great A'aferti Menes, the unifier of the two lands; Upper and Lower Egypt, migrated down the Nile River from Nekhen (Hierakonpolis) 'Falcon City', in southern Egypt. He was a Nubian from the A-Group which due to either political upheaval or over population of the area moved into Northern Egypt and established Men-Nefer (Memphis) with his people in Middle Egypt. Contrary to what official Egyptologists claim, the Giza complex and the great Sphinx already existed in the time of Pharaoh Menes and this is depicted upon the Narmer Tablet in the form of the pyramid symbol. After the great deluge (C. 10,860 B.C), Northern and large parts of Middle Egypt became unliveable and both the Ptah Daneg/Anu/Twa (Pygmies) and the Kushites were forced to the Southern areas of Khemet (Egypt). Around 4100 B.C. the Nubian A-Group decided it was time to reunify Egypt, after an influx of Indo-Aryans (Neanderthals, Caucasians, Cavemen, Behaymaw) began to infiltrate the area of the Delta (Northern Egypt) pushing further and further south into the region. Mud from the Niles inundation filled in the land.

A'aferti Menes (Narmer) was a warrior Pharaoh, who sailed his army of Kushites down the Nile and engaged the foreigners on all fronts. This sudden and momentous move obliterated the Indo-European (Asiatics) and the bold event is commemorated in sequence upon the Narmer Palette and others. The unifying of Upper and Lower Khemet (Egypt) and the founding of Khemet's own Pharaonic state, modelled on that of the Pharaonic state of Meroitic Sudan (Ethiopia proper), began the Egyptian (Khemetian/Khamite) Kushites as their own unique entity as opposed to the Sudanese (Meroitic) Kushites, their ancient ancestors in the south, Ta-Seti "The Land of the Bow", in Nubia.

Egyptologists constantly try to differentiate between the two but they are as much different as Nigerians are to Ghanaians. Being a Kushite Nubian, Pharaoh Menes replicated the Meroitic Pharaohs in every detail in establishing kingship north of Nubia and maintained the southern identity and link. Thus, Menes inherited a fully formed model which included writing, cultural customs language, political structure, spirituality, administrative structure, science and astronomy, agriculture, architecture and everything else included within a civilization. The Khemetians thus became another branch of the Kushites just as the Elamites, Sumerian - Si.ga.ga, Phoenicians, Xia, Nabateans, Sabeans would become a little later on, due to migration. The evidence, treasures in the sand, is irrefutable proof of this. Menes was an ambitious, dynamic leader who was honoured and held in high esteem by every other ruler who sat on the throne after him and by all Kushites in general. He set the standard for all other Pharaohs up to the reign of Djoser Neterikeht of the 3rd Dynasty. It was Pharaoh Menes who initiated the Thinite Dynasties (Dynasties 1 & 2) with the established capital at Thinis, near Abydos. Memphis was established by diverting the Nile to create dry ground, at a strategic site, as a garrison fortress city and protected from invasion by high and thick white walls. Thus it was nicknamed the 'City of White Walls' and assumed its role.

In summary, Pharaoh Menes was an intelligent and innovative, accomplished military commander and leader who defied the odds with his vision to establish an independent state. His vision allowed his branch of Nubian people to grow and prosper into arguably the greatest branch of the greatest civilization the world has ever known; the Kushite civilization. Khemet as its own independent entity flowered and prospered for over 3,000 years in an unbroken chain. The close connections of three different regions in Menes' Khemet are undoubtable and obvious evidence of Kushite Nubian origin. Nekhen in the South, Naqada and Abydos further north. Menes (Narmer) was buried in Abydos, but his most significant monuments were in Nekhen (Hierakonpolis). The process of (Re) unification and growth was a rapid process compared to other ancient peoples. Territorial expansion was achieved in only a few centuries which is unprecedented.

The unique ideological foundations of Nubia and Khemet focus on the divinity and personage of the King and the 'Divine Right to Rule', given to man by Paut Neteru. Visual commemorations represent the Pharaoh as much larger than others, as he was the sole agent between the Gods and humanity. The emphasis on his supernatural personage and royal Ka (spiritual essence) permeates all levels of early Khemetian (Egyptian) society and is the main ideological pillar of Meroitic and Khamite culture that endured throughout the region's ancient histories. Kushites formulated a vision of the world that was fundamental and inherited by all that followed in later millennia. This ideology was immortalized with established rituals and procedures and tools as the foundation of official and state life. It would sometimes adapt and evolve in later times, but it always remained foundational and paramount to Khemetian identity. This high exultation of the Pharaoh has its roots in the proto-dynastic period. There was no distinction between religious and secular affairs and the Pharaoh was at the very centre of all aspects of life. He was seen as the physical incarnation of Horus on earth, as the God was his patron, thus, he was no mere human being; he was seen as a part of the divine manifestation of the Gods. It was his duty to maintain order and balance (Maat) in the universe(s) between the Gods and the dead and the living, for the rest of humanity. At his ascension to the throne, the Pharaoh received a Horus name, which appeared upon all his monuments. The Pharaoh's duties included the support of the priests and temples and the Pantheon of the Gods transcended all political boundaries making the system work for all.

".... Leadership is the capacity and will to rally men and women to a common purpose and the character which inspires confidence....."

- Bernard Montgomery

Pharaoh was the glue that held the nation together. Just like the Meroitic Sudanese monarchs, Pharaoh, Menes and those who ascended the throne after him were known as the 'Falcon/Hawk of Nubia'. The Nubian Serekh, one of the symbols of kingship in Ancient Egypto-Nubia translates as 'to proclaim'. The Serekh is an upright rectangle with vertical lines in the bottom half. On top of the rectangle sits the symbol of Horus, as the perched falcon/hawk. The earliest Serekhs are empty, but by dynasty O, the names of the Pharaohs were written inside of them. The Serekh continued to be a powerful symbol throughout the dynasties: some large stele of the 1st Dynasty was decorated with only the Serekh, which is an eloquent symbol of royal authority.

The Pharaoh's position at the centre of the nation was founded in its (Khemet's and Nubia's) ideology about the Neteru 'Company of the Gods' and a divine view of the universe(s), the world. These 'Principalities of Nature' (Neteru) were the manifestation of natural, universal forces that had to be appeased. Regions, tribes, families and communities had their preferred deities.

The Pharaoh's powers derived from his identification with the Neter: Horus, a view that was valid throughout the whole region of Kush and Khemet and this is why the concept worked nationwide. Each town and trade had its own patron God that was the house of that God's main temple. Still, the pantheon of Kushite deities was unified from prehistoric times, as has been confirmed. Both Horus and Seth were connected to Pharaonic kingship and a few pharaohs of the early dynasties and two of the 19th Dynasty chose to identify themselves with Seth. The people of the glorious Kushite Kingdoms had unique connections to nature and the Kosmos. This was expressed through their religious rites, the Principles of Maat and the visionary arts that decorated baes-reliefs and monuments. The Shekem Ur Shekem (Pharaoh) was a great man: with serous face, penetrating gaze, powerful personality, resolute character and life giving words of power. It is important to remember that the word Pharaoh – 'Great House', includes all of the people that made up this great organization, without the 'Divine Feminine' (the main wife and others), the A'afertiaat – 'Male Rulers' (Pharaohs) would be nothing more than a sterile group of men, incapable of carrying out the 'Great Work'. The Pharaoh's path was traced by the Gods. The Shekem Ur Shekems possessed a deep intuitive insight with an acute sense of danger. This was formed out of an alliance with nature.

The qualities of the great rulers and wisemen included the ability to do what is righteous and just, to be coherent, silent and calm, to have a firm character capable of bearing both happiness and sadness, and a vigilant heart and tongue which knew when to observe and listen to silence. 'You won't find perfection among men, but you can find it in their works. If you give them an ideal and enable them to achieve it, they will overcome their weaknesses'.

1. Character
2. Actions are the main indicator of character
3. Talent is a gift, but character is a choice
4. Character brings lasting success with people
5. Strong character is the foundation on which to build success.

The Thinite Dynasty (Dynasty 1 & 2)

The capital of these dynasties was transferred to Thinis near the sacred site of Abydos. The period of the first two Thinite Dynasties was c. 3,100 – 2,778. The rulers of this dynasty cemented the unification which was begun by Pharaoh Ta Nefer and Pharaoh Scorpion and realized by Pharaoh Menes of Dynasty O. The cemetery of these first kings was located at nearby Abydos and people were buried there in large tombs even before the unification period. Tomb U-J is dwarfed by other nearby tombs who occupants we can name from inscriptions. They include 3 rulers from Dynasty O, six rulers and one Queen from the 1st Dynasty and two rulers of the late 2nd Dynasty. The rulers of these two dynasties kept close contact and trade with Nekhen (Hierakonpolis), Waset (Thebes) and the Meroitic Sudan.

Suten Djoser (Neterikeht): The Alchemist

"…. By the Third Dynasty (2,778 – 2,723), centralization of the monarchy was complete. All the technological and cultural elements of Egyptian civilization were already in place and had only to be perpetuated. For the first time in Egypt, Pharaoh Zoser introduced architecture in hewn stone. His strong Negro face with characteristic features dominated that period. In reality, the other Pharaohs of the dynasty were no less Negroid; Petrie affirmed that this dynasty, the first to give Egyptian civilization its almost definitive form and expression, was of Sudanese Nubian origin. It was easier to recognize the Negro origin of the Egyptians when the initial display of their civilization coincided with an unquestionably Negro dynasty. The equally Negro features of the proto-dynastic face of Tera Neter and those of the first king to unify the valley also prove that this is the only valid hypothesis. Similarly, the Negro features of the Fourth Dynasty Pharaohs, the builders of the Great Pyramids, confirm this".

- Cheikh Anta Diop: The African Origin of Civilization

As Cheikh Anta Diop went on to state, during the Old Kingdom before the widespread contact with white skinned Indo-Aryans from in and around the Mediterranean, the Black Khemetian – Kushite was practically unmixed. One only has to look at the portraits of the Old Kingdom Kings to identify Black Africans.

The 24 Thrones/Elders: Revolutionary Pharaoh

Aafeerti Djoser/Zoser Neterikeht was one of the 24 Elders who incarnated upon earth to help to raise man's consciousness level. Together with the High Priest Imhotep, who was also one of the 24 Elders, they raised the standard of Kushite (and Khemetian especially) spirituality, science, architecture, medicine, governmental administration, social organization, etc. which improved every aspect of people's living conditions since the foundation of Pharaonic Egypt. The high level of Pharaoh Djoser surpassed that of Menes and both Djoser Neterikeht and Imhotep were deified by the Khemetians.

Their crowning achievement was the Saqqara (Sokar) complex with its beautiful Step Pyramid and court, which is said to be the first stone complex of its kind and a true work of genius that can still be visited today, at least 4,000 years to the day it was erected. The lead architect was Imhotep of Nekhen (Hierakonpolis), who modelled the complex on an earlier complex built at Nekhen (Hierakonpolis). The Ziggurat type pyramid of Sokar is just as enigmatic as the pyramids of Giza and many debates have been had over where it fits into the chronology of the pyramids. Some scholars believe it was the very first stage of pyramid by building mastaba on top of mastaba (rectangular tombs) in smaller and smaller stages, before the sides were inclined and smoothed to achieve the form of the true pyramid. Some scholars are convinced it is older than the time stated, while others believe the Great Pyramids are older than the actual entire Pharaonic system.

From the 3rd to 5th Dynasties much time and effort was spent on erecting and refurbishing pyramids and other monumental and awe-inspiring monuments which despite the ravages of time, still astound experts today. More than 20 Pharaohs diverted enormous resources, time and energy to recreate heaven on earth. As the Neteru (Gods) had done earlier, the Khemetians were bringing in the power from above and grounding it on earth to create another Utopian reality. The technical ability given to the Anu/Twa and their descendants, the Kushites, the organizational skill of the Pharaonic state is unmatched throughout the history of the planet earth and man. Experts are still puzzled at just how the feats of engineering, including the pyramids were achieved.

During time, when the illustrious Pharaoh Djoser mounted the throne, the capital of the kingdom was moved to Memphis. Administrative centralization erased the noble and privileged class, although the priesthood, guardian of Maat that determined the Pharaoh's authority was in a league of its own, well organized and independent. Until that time, the priesthood had exercised its spiritual guardianship at the Pharaoh's coronation in the temple at Anu (Heliopolis). But, to make his power absolute, the Pharaoh Djoser Neterikeht discarded this tradition, clashed with the clergy and from then on the Pharaohs renounced the Heliopolis coronation in favour of their own place at Memphis. In the Memphis palace, the Pharaohs proclaimed and reinforced the 'Divine Right to Rule', added 'Great God' to their titles and was free from any human or priestly control. Therefore, the Pharaoh was not a puppet ruler controlled by others in any shape form or fashion. Still, the Ahkus, Shemsu Haru and the Anu (Heliopolis) priesthood always recognized the authority of the A'afertiaat rulers Pharaohs and pledged their allegiance to the Gods and therefore the crown and vice-versa. Even though sometimes the relationship was distant and strained. The advent and Golden Age of the fourth Dynasty, with the refurbishment of the Giza complex, is evidence that the monarchy had reached its pinnacle. Along with the zenith of the arts, the engineering and architecture never again attained that level of perfection. After the sixth Dynasty, the end of the Old Kingdom, Khemet went into decline and in many ways, it never fully recovered.

Both Pharaoh Djoser Neterikeht and Imhotep established the masonic order of the 'Sons of the Greenlight'. The colours that they wore were white and blue, symbolizing the White Nile (Pishon) and the Blue Nile (Gihon). These agreeable sons of the greenlight was Lightworkers, alchemists who came up with solutions to humanities problems and innovated many breakthroughs and new ideas in areas, such as architecture, medicine, astronomy, etc. The 24 thrones are mentioned within the Injiyl, given to John of Zebedee by the Anunnaqi Nusqu (Gabriy'El).

El's Holy Injiyl – "The Book of Revelation': 4.4 (In Part)

4. In a circle around this throne were twenty four other thrones and on them sat twenty four elders, robed in white and wearing crowns of gold.

- The New English Bible with Apocrypha

The richer one is, the more generous one must be. A true leader must be a servant of Maat and 'Live in Truth'. The Brotherhood (Sons of the Crystal Greenlight of Amun-Re) must pilot the ship and handle the rudder without weakening. If the Pharaoh commands an imbecile or an ignorant man to carry out work which the imbecile is unable to do, then he himself is unfit to rule. The overseer who acts like a tyrant, or amasses wealth and privileges to himself; he too is unfit to rule. The hive is more important than the bee.

The teachings have power. Man/woman harnesses that power. The actions of the sages/pharaohs/wise ones were constantly linked to the movements of the heavens, so as not to lose their integrity; for the universe(s) is intelligent and it is that which creates and designs us. Life comes from this seemingly limitless space, our parts (gross matter) is manufactured within the stars. Therefore, we are the 'Children of the Stars'.

The architecture of Khemet (Egypt) was a ground map of the heavens, hence all the stellar alignments and emphasis on astronomy. Various other Kushite sites were arranged on a similar plan, a map of the stars in the sky. The divine order and harmony of the heavens was thus brought down to the terrestrial sphere. In many ways this was amplified by Pharaoh Djoser Neterikeht, the 3rd, 4th and 5th Dynasties. Pharaoh Djoser was immortalized by all other Pharaohs after.

The Fourth Dynasty: Giza & Beyond

So much has been written about the 4th Dynasty, referred to as the 'Pyramid Age', largely because of the association of 3 of its most famous rulers with the building of the 3 pyramids of Giza. Let us begin with the founder of the 4th Dynasty who is known as Pharaoh Sneferu. It is Pharaoh Sneferu who is credited with perfecting the true form of the pyramid, with its smooth sides and triangle shaped sides. What's interesting is the fact that Pharaoh Sneferu is associated with 3 separate pyramids built at Dashur and Meidum and so if the pyramids were built as tombs and only tombs, as the main function, as is suggested by mainstream

Egyptologists, then why has one man (Pharaoh) constructed 3 tombs for himself? Exactly. This alone should tell the critical thinker that the pyramids were not primarily constructed as tombs. It is outside of the scope of this scroll to go over the real purposes and functions of the pyramids but this discussion can be found in '2mrw Iz 2day Iz Yesterday' (Vol II), written by myself. So let us continue on our current discussion.

Pharaoh Sneferu was a monumental builder who built on a massive scale, experts say his was the next crucial revolution in engineering and architecture in the development of pyramid building. The combined mass of the 3 pyramids associated to Sneferu dwarf the efforts of every other Pharaoh. The earliest was the Step Pyramid of Meidum, erected 28 miles to the south of the Memphis tombs. Experts say that upon the 7th layer, an 8th layer was added and a smooth outer casing was applied giving the appearance of a true pyramid, but at some point the casing fell away, collapsed and left the monument looking more like a tower. It is surrounded by a heap of debris. Others have claimed that this was not ever a true pyramid but rather an astronomical observatory.

The next pyramid associated with A'aferti Sneferu is referred to as 'The Bent Pyramid', which was built just south of Sokar (Saqqara) at Dashur. The bottom half of the pyramid has the 52° angle, while the top half has the angle of 43½ °. Experts claimed that the architects made a mistake in the construction and the monument began to collapse, so they had to rectify this by adapting the design to the much safer angle. Recent investigations have revealed evidence to suggest that far from collapsing underneath its own weight, the monument was deliberately built this way.

Two kilometres to the north stands what is referred to as the first true pyramid by Egyptologists. It has an inclination of 43½ °. Built of red limestone, it is referred to as 'The Red Pyramid' and measures 220 by 220 metres at the base and was surpassed only by his son's (Khufu's) associated pyramid of Giza. The Red Pyramid of Dashur is much less well known to people than those of Giza because it is mostly closed to the public due to Arab-Egyptian, modern conflicts in the area.

Just as the story of Abraham, the biblical fictional character was based on elements of Pharaoh Djoser and Imhotep's lives. The story of the biblical fictional Enoch (Adafa) was based on elements of Pharaoh Sneferu's life. Sneferu was credited with creating fish-net tights for the women of his harem. The Pharaoh was a charismatic, big thinker and he also led military campaigns into Nubia to subdue those elements of Nubia that had begun to rebel against Khemet. It's important to know that not all of the tribes of hostile areas of

Nubia were civilized. It didn't make the Egyptians any different in race to the Nubians, just like it didn't make the Romans any different in race to the vandals.

Pharaoh Sneferu was a powerful leader; stern, strong, with martial authority and his reign left the kingdom in good health and spirit. Pharaoh Sneferu like Menes and Djoser was another revolutionary of his time. No statues or images of the ruler have been fund to date but we know of his reign through other inscriptions and sources.

A'aferti Khufu (Cheops): The Enigmatic

I'm sure that this Pharaoh's name rings many bells whether in the form of Ahket Khufu or the Greek rendered Cheops. Being associated with the Great Pyramid of Giza, which is classed as one of the 7 wonders of the ancient world (and the only one still standing today), his fame has been guaranteed throughout the last few millennia. With a base of 230 by 230 metres and a height of 480 ft (146 metres) high, it is the highest pyramid of its kind. Without sounding repetitive, the structure contains roughly 2,300,000 blocks of stone with an average weight of 2½ tons each, some weigh up to 16 tons. If Ahket Khufu (Pharaoh Cheops) ruled for 23 years as is recorded by the Turin Papyrus, this would equate to 100,000 blocks daily – 285 blocks being quarried, transported, dressed and hauled into place every two minutes of day light for 23 years. That's if and only if the monument was built using ropes, ramps and pulleys by men dragging these blocks phenomenal distances. Anybody with the least common sense knows that theory is just ludicrous.

Anyway, moving on from the mesmerizing features of the Great Pyramid, Ahket Khufu has been slandered as a tyrant, a cruel ruler who forced his subjects to carry out these impossible workloads. The Greek writers and others suggest that Pharaoh Khufu used slaves, whether Egyptian, Hebrew or otherwise to construct his so called tomb. These tales may have come about because of the sheer size of the Great Pyramid and the inability of late period Egyptians and foreigners like the Greek historians, Herodotus and Diodorus of the 5th and 1st century B.C., to find a satisfactory explanation for its construction. Herodotus claimed that Khufu forced tens of thousands of men to work on the pyramid, brought misery to Egypt and shut down temples. He even claimed that Khufu prostituted his daughters to help finance the project. Both historians portray Khafre in the same way, claiming that the people hated these two tyrants so much they threatened to destroy their corpses. This is nothing more than gossip and slander created to fill the void, as no significant details of them existed. They are shrouded in mystery, especially where foreigners were concerned and didn't reveal these specific details to the uninitiated.

Stories about Khufu's grandson, Khafre's son Menkaure were less harsh and the assumption was that he was a benevolent ruler who cared about his people. These enigmatic pharaohs have influenced a lot of debate and discussion in an attempt to overstand the past and fill in the blanks in the sands of time. Later tales about the Old Kingdom contained a lot of fantasy and magic. The name of the founder of the fourth Dynasty, Sneferu was rooted on the word 'Good', and he was said to have been benevolent and charismatic.

Two forgotten sons of Pharaoh Khufu are Kawab and Djedefre. Kawab died before his father Khufu and Djedefre decided to separate himself from his father Khufu, because he didn't agree with the way that his father ran the kingdom. The pyramid said to have been built by Djedefre was located at Abu Rawash, 8 kilometres to the north but this pyramid was destroyed many centuries later and lies in ruins. Djedefre reigned for approximately 8 years before the reign of Pharaoh Khafre.

The last ruler of the 4th Dynasty was Shepseskaf who built his monument at the Saqqara site, a tomb shaped like a sarcophagus. From Djedefre on up to the 6th Dynasty, so called scholars say that a 'Sun Cult' emerged from around the Sun-God, re. The Pharaoh's connection to the Sun God, Re is said to have found its strongest expression in the monuments of the 5th Dynasty.

So Pharaoh Djoser Neterikeht was immortalized for his monument at Sokar which became a site of pilgrimage well into the New Kingdom. Many visitors left graffiti and in the Turin Royal Canon his name and title 'Ruler of Upper and Lower Egypt' is written in red ink, an indication of the reverence that the author gave him as the initiator of a new era. Imhotep was crucial to this Pharaoh's legacy. Tales of Pharaoh Sneferu were popular during the Middle kingdom and he was remembered as a visionary, seer who could predict the future. He was remembered as an astute individual who loved to relax in the company of beautiful women. He too was honoured as a god. The Westcar Papyrus contains the stories of Sneferu and Khufu, his son. It relates stories of Khufu and his son, Hardjedef, the Sage and the magician. Pharaoh Userkaf, Nyuserra and Unas of the 5th Dynasty also are associated with pyramids and temples of Saqqara, Abusir and Abu Ghurab. The earliest form of the famous pyramid texts are preserved upon the inside of the pyramid of Pharaoh Unas. The pyramid texts are incantations which the deceased Pharaoh recited upon his soul's journey to the afterlife. They are excerpts from the Book of the Coming Forth by Day (into the Light).

The stories of the prophets of Abrahamic faith are really the manipulated stories of the Pharaohs, sages, priest, demi-Gods, etc., of Khemet and Sumeria. These stories were plagiarized by Indo-Aryan Babylonians during the 2nd Babylonian Empire and spread like wild fire throughout the Middle-East. In the 2nd millennium B.C., the Indo-Aryans from the Caucasus regions of Russia came out of the Steppes running through China, India and the Middle East (Mesopotamia). They are the usurpers of the Kushite civilizations in these areas and they inherited a horde of knowledge by penetrating the Kushite mystery schools creating the Babylonian brotherhood. These servants along with their Black (Kushite) devil counterparts intended to misuse the power of the esoteric knowledge from their very beginning. They are the Servants of the Serpent, meaning the Draconian Reptilian race. It is them that control the world today.

It was pharaoh Khufu who reversed the laws of the land in Khemet (Egypt), just as Sargon (Nimrod) had done in Sumeria and Akkad (Mesopotamia), that allowed the Tamahu (Indo-Aryan), white-skinned people to enter into Khemet and live amongst the general population. This was the beginning of the build-up of the Heka-Khasut (Hyksos) 'Shepard Kings – Foreign Rulers' inside of Khemet. Centuries later this would result in the Hyksos wars with Pharaoh Seqenenre-Taa and Queen Ahhotep. Pharaoh Khufu did this because one of his other sons named Rahotep, married a Hyksos woman called Nofret and was thus expelled from Egypt. Since the Asiatic invasions in the delta region generations before, the law of the land stated that no foreigner could enter Khemet (Egypt) unless they had woolly-hair, melanated skin and brown eyes. So Pharaoh Khufu reversed the laws to allow his son Rahotep to be allowed to re-enter the country. Upon re-entering the country, Rahotep brought his wife Nofret and she, herself brought many of her people with her. Over the Centuries word spread and many, many more chose to move into Khemet. Sargon of Akkad did a similar thing in Mesopotamia allowing the 11 tribes/sons of Canaan, who were Caucasians, to live amongst the Kushites. The Canaanites worshipped him as their God, but all this is another story for another book.

The Pharaoh Djoser Neterikeht and the sage Imhotep foresaw all of this in their time, gazing into the future; the mystery schools were formed to keep the power of esoteric knowledge out of the wrong hands. The wisdom of Tehuti (Thoth) was sealed up and sent underground for initiates only. Pharaoh Djoser and Imhotep fought against many sorcerers in and outside of Egypt (Khemet) and there are many Indo-Aryan, Arab, Greek and Roman tales based on this reality. Imhotep was a student of the Neter (God) Tehuti/Thoth and Imhotep was the teacher of Pharaoh Djoser. The order of the 'Sons of the Crystal Greenlight' is known by many other different names, in many different languages and places. Some of these names are: A.E.O. – 'Ancient Egyptian Order', A.N.O.M.S. – 'The Ancient Nobles of the Mystic Shriners', A.M.O.M – 'the Ancient Order of Melchizedek', or simply the 'Egyptian Shriners'. Imhotep was the son of the creator God Ptah and his cult spread from Memphis all around Egypt, on all levels of society. He was identified with the symbol of the Ibis bird which was indicative of him being a student of Tehuti, whose symbol was the Ibis.

The social organization of Khemet – Nu – 'the Black People' is the same now throughout Black Africa; as it was in Ancient Khemet (Egypt). In Egypt of ancient times the stratification was as follows:

Peasants,
Skilled worker,
Priests, Warriors and Government Officials,
The Shekem Ur Shekem (A'aferti/Pharaoh).

In the rest of Black Africa and other Kushite colonies, we have:

Peasants
Artisans or Skilled worker,
Warriors and Priests,
The King.

There were many, many officials of the government in the Old Kingdom, Khemet. Their numerous inscriptions can be found within their tombs and they combined various titles representative of their functions; scribes were particularly important due to the necessity of bureaucratic records. The Egyptians state depended on written records to record everything from resources, to transactions of trade, religious texts, laws of the penal system, astronomy, mathematics, king lists; absolutely everything was recorded in writing. Thus, the number of scribes increased substantially to cover all of the massive projects because at this early time, not everybody was able to read and write the hieroglyphs. Only various levels of society were able to read and write, this is why the scribes were highly valued members of the general population.

Since even before the time of Pharaoh Djoser and the Vizier Imhotep, the Vizier acted as the rulers 'go-to-guy'. It was the Vizier, a kind of Prime Minister, who oversaw all the affairs of the administrative state on behalf of the Pharaoh. Up to the 5th Dynasty, most high officials were blood relatives of the Pharaoh which kept the centre of power within the Pharaoh's family. Administrators were highly rewarded and thus their burials were often funded and supported by the state. The officials were given offerings to support them in the afterlife, just as the Pharaoh was. The entire nation was supportive of the Pharaoh and his officials, in life and in death and this was the axis of Khemetian political ideology. The administrative centre of the state received the largest share of the country's resources which was stretched with the growth of the bureaucracy. This system depended on a precise and airtight process of social organization. This social organization has its roots way back in pre-dynastic, Meroitic Nubia and was perfected during the time of Pharaoh Djoser and the 3rd Dynasty. It reached its height during the time of the 4th Dynasty and early 5th Dynasty which allowed for a Golden Age before the stagnation of the feudal system sent the Old Kingdom into decline resulting in the anarchy at the close of the 6th Dynasty. The social cohesion of Khemetian administration depended upon the sub-division of Khemet into nomes. The Pharaoh was connected and recognized as absolute in every nome. Agricultural estates within the nomes supported the administration, priesthoods and Pharaoh with food etc. The entire country supported the court. The main population centre in each nome became a regional capital, with the local nomarch the representative of the state within the region.

Although the system was long in place and the large administration was stable, over the long centuries, many changes took place. The role of the Pharaoh was always at the centre to give the state authority, but around his personage minor adaptations were made to increase the efficiency of the administration and to iron out any problems it encountered. There were also a few periods in which the Pharaoh's authority was challenged by the priesthood and the army, but Khemet never became a republic, secular state in all its history. The people believed in the Shekem Ur Shekem – 'Great Power of Powers'.

Within the provinces, the nomarchs represented the Pharaoh's interests, although during the intermediate periods, they took their independence. The administrative centre was very large with many layers. The military and the priesthood had their own hierarchy within them to achieve their own objectives. The high priests were the head of the religious administration, with each region having its own patron god and temple. Still, as the pantheon of Gods was unified nationally, the Sedjet – 'The Ennead' of 9 Neteru were recognized and venerated throughout the kingdom. The Gods, Amun-Re, Osiris and Horus took precedence over others because of their connections to the Pharaoh during his life and death. Many officials were astute, multi-talented persons who combined several titles and assumed multiple responsibilities.

From the 4th Dynasty the regime evolved toward feudalism. The courtiers made up a special group of dignitaries which made itself hereditary by usage and then by right. The history of Ancient Khemet ended without ever developing secular thought. Egypt was a 'Theocracy', following the rule and law of the Neteru/Anunnaqi (Gods). Feudalism flourished during the 5th Dynasty and peaked during the 6th Dynasty. It was at the end of the 6th Dynasty that the first popular uprising in Khemetian history occurred, when the country plunged into anarchy. The texts describe how insecurity reigned.

The Old Kingdom reached a pinnacle which was never achieved again during the Middle and New Kingdom periods. In fact, from the old kingdom, Zenith, Khemet went into decline and the further away we come from the Old Kingdom, the less sublime Khemetian civilization becomes in terms of literature, arts – sculpture, architecture, etc. The Middle Kingdom is inferior to the Old Kingdom and the New Kingdom inferior to the Middle Kingdom. More and more of the wisdom of before the flood was lost and hidden. In no other world culture did this happen other than in Kushite (Khemetian and Sumerian) culture. These cultures began fully formed.

2. Charisma

".... How can you have charisma? Be more concerned about making others feel good about themselves than you are making them feel good about you...."

- Dan Reiland

"....When it comes to charisma, the bottom line is other mindedness. Leaders who think about others and their concerns before thinking of themselves exhibit charisma ...."

- John C. Maxwell

Pepi I, Pepi II & Merenre: The 6th Dynasty

The beginning of the 6th Dynasty looked fine at the outset, after the reigns of 5th Dynasty Pharaoh, such as Djedkare, Isesi and Unas. From Teti to Pepi I was a period of prosperity, but by the reign of Pharaoh Merenre, the cracks beneath the surface of the administrative centre began to appear. Pharaoh Ahket Khufu of the 4th Dynasty was a strong, able ruler but some of the decisions that he made during his time had lasting consequences which festered into problems for later dynasties. The nation's social cohesion and support for the administration began to wane. Social upheavals and the threat of invasion in the delta, the breakdown of feudalism and the poverty of the people all contributed to the coming anarchy.

As early as Pharaoh Pepi I, white skinned women were imported into the country and sold to nobles and even the Pharaohs themselves. The times between the 4th and 6th Dynasties are when cross breeding between Indo-Aryans and Kushites, in Egypt (Khemet) began. Before this time, the Khemetian population was largely unmixed. In Nubia, another tribe of Kushites we can refer to as the C-Group began to rise to prominence. This happened because of the void left by the A-Group, who migrated further and further north in Upper Egypt and became the Wasetian (Theban) Egyptians under Pharaoh Menes (Narmer), the 1st and 2nd Dynasties. The nomadic C-Group Nubians settled the deserted areas and established the kingdom of Kerma in Nubia. The relationship between the Nubian A-Group and C-Group was hot and cold and at most times, very icy towards each other. The remnant of the A-Group that remained in Nubia came under the protection of the Khamite Pharaonic state in the north. Several expeditions were carried out by Harkuf and his son under the Pharaohs Pepi I, Merenre and Pepi II. They travelled through Nubia to their ancestral home of Yam in Meroitic Sudan (Kush), south of Jebel Uwainat and the region of the Tibesti highlands of north east Chad. The expeditions carried out under the early 6th Dynasty were largely trading expeditions.

During the time of Merenre and Pepi II, the Pharaoh's importance declined and the power of nomarchs increased along with their wealth. The Pharaoh's unique position was being challenged by provinces. The last great ruler of the Old Kingdom was Pepi II who came to the throne at the tender age of 6 years old and lived and reigned until he was 100 years old. His was the longest reign in Khemetian history. The successors of Pepi II were insignificant going into the 7th and 8th Dynasties of Memphis. This was a time of economic collapse and political friction. During these times royal power was dissipated amongst regional nomarchs.

".... So the first cycle of Egyptian history ended with the collapse of the Old Kingdom. It had begun with the feudalism that preceded the first political unification; it closed in anarchy and feudalism. Monarchy sank into feudalism without being attacked. In fact, the principle of Monarchy could not have been greatly threatened. Perhaps there were a few timid attempts at self-government in the Delta cities, as at Sais. But this was probably a temporary solution dictated by the suddenness of the crisis and the lack of public authority that followed the invasion of the Delta by the Asiatics. Cities on the invasion route were abruptly compelled to assure their own safety as they faced the common enemy. Confronted by the situation the former provincial governors in Upper and Middle Egypt set themselves up as independent feudal lords, freed henceforth from any royal overlordship, though they did not ever question the principal of monarchy itself...."

- Cheikh Anta Diop: The African Origin of Civilization

Dynasties 9 and 10 passed in more or less the same way, neither re-establishing full rulership over Upper and Lower Khemet (Egypt). Approximately 2181 B.C, the Heracleopolitans claimed kingship at Heracleopolis at the entrance of the Fayyum. These Pharaohs saw themselves as the heirs of the Old Kingdom but their power was limited to small areas of Middle Egypt. Their war and struggles with the legitimate Wasetians from the south (Upper Egypt), ended the first Intermediate Period c. 2055 B.C.

The 11th Dynasty Sutens & the Solid Montuhotep: The Redeemer

3. Commitment: Doers and Dreamers

- To the boxer, it's getting off the mat one more time than you've been knocked down.
- To the marathoner, it's running another ten miles when your strength is gone.
- To the soldier, it's sailing down the Nile to engage in a war of which the outcome is unknown.
- To the leader, it's all that and more because everyone you lead is depending on you.

Even though the virtues of Khemetian social organization were abundant, it eventually resulted in intolerable abuses and intense uprisings of anarchy as with many other cultures but the sheer size of the kingdom inevitably killed-off the insurrections in advance. During the period of anarchy, most of the Khamite cities created temporary autonomous governments which disappeared with the revival of the 11th Dynasty and Pharaoh Mentuhotep II.

The Great Shekem Ur Shekem, Mentuhotep II again was a Wasetian (Nubian of Sudanese origin) who came to power in Waset/Thebes, the 'City of 100 Gates' in Upper (southern) Khemet. In the south (Upper Egypt) where Kushite political power had prospered since the early dynasties a new capital developed which would hold the reigns of power for many centuries. Waset (Thebes), the city of Amun – 'King of the Gods' merged with the population of Luxor under the Priest King Intef. Approximately 2125 B.C. he initiated a rival dynasty to the Heracleopolitans further north. This rival Dynasty has become known as the illustrious 11th Dynasty.

The basis for his inauguration is claimed to be unknown by Egyptologists but the truth is that he was the liberation of the kingdom, which in times of trouble always came from the Kushite south. Being close to the ancestral home of Kush (Nubia) and unifying the whole of Upper Khemet by pacification, it legitimized his rule and that of the 11th Dynasty. Pharaoh Intef started a sequence of strong, able and lengthy rulers with a durable base at Thebes. From Thebes his successors began their push north, reclaiming the territory claimed by the Heracleopolitan pretender kings. It was, as always, the Kushites (Wasetians) who restored the prestige and unique position of the Shekem Ur Shekem, the Pharaoh. The administration, priesthood and army acknowledged his legitimacy, their dependence upon him and the Pharaoh once again returned as the recognized sponsor of monument building throughout Upper and Lower Khemet.

Even though, the 2nd king of the 11th Dynasty Wahankh, Intef II took the title of Pharaoh of Upper and Lower Egypt, it wasn't until the successes of Pharaoh Mentuhotep II that these aspirations were fully realized. With this achievement, the first Intermediate Period ended and the era of the Middle Kingdom properly began. Pharaoh Mentuhotep destroyed the army of the Heracleopolitans and desecrated their royal tombs. In year 20 of his reign he adopted the title and Horus name – 'Divine of the White Crown' and in his 39th year of reign he took the title, 'Uniter of the two Lands'. His accomplished reign ushered in a new era and the Khemetians of later times never forgot this. He rebuilt the lustre of Khemet with numerous monuments of remarkable craftsmanship and beauty and his statues depict him as a true Wasetian as black as the night. Egyptologists have tried to down play this by claiming that he depicted himself jet black to symbolize the totality of regeneration, as they say of the Gods, but any sensible person can know what Thebans and Khemetians in general look like through their own woolly haired depictions. Pharaoh Mentuhotep II is the same tribe of Nubian – Wasetian as Queen Tiye of later times, the wife of Amunhotep III and mother of Akhenaten. One only has to look at the famous bust and know, without a doubt, that it depicts a powerful Black woman. It is the same with all of the 11th and 12th Dynasty, all having Nubian features.

Pharaoh Ramesu (Rameses II), the Great of the 13th century B.C., honoured him as the creator of the liberated Middle Kingdom. We Kushites of today remember him in the same vein as Menes and Ahmose, as liberators of our people. After his death a cult developed around his memory and a relief from his mortuary temple shows the statues of Menes, himself and Ahmose all together as Unifiers of the Old, Middle and New Kingdoms respectively.

Mentuhotep II was remembered as one of the greatest Pharaohs who returned Khemet to its former glory in Middle and New Kingdom literature. Although it did not reach the heights of the Golden Age of the Old Kingdom, the Middle Kingdom was a time of much creativity in arts and architecture. It was seen as the classical era for literature. The admonitions of Ipuwer are dated to this period.

Mentuhotep II's reunification lasted nearly 400 years up to the 2nd intermediate period. The defining role for the Middle Kingdom was to re-establish the Kushite cultural dominance and origin. It was a period of innovation and transition. Influenced by the memory of the Old Kingdom and the First Intermediate period, the administration of the Middle Kingdom put in place many laws and practices that were the foundation and anchor of later times. This is especially true for cultural, administrative and foreign policy. The Middle Kingdom achieved the completion of processes envisioned many centuries before and this inspired and motivated the Khemetians for more than 1,500 years.

Most people are familiar with the 4th Dynasty Pharaohs as they are famously associated with the Giza complex and New Kingdom Pharaohs and personages, such as Pharaoh Akhenaten, King Tut, Nefertiti, Rameses II, etc., but not with Pharaoh Mentuhotep II, Amunemhet, and Sesostris etc. Egyptologists down play the glory of the 11th and 12th Dynasties just like they do with the 25th Dynasty because all of their features and facts betray their Nubian (Black) origin and race and it is not as easy to explain this away as it is with the Pharaohs of the New Kingdom. These kings penetrated into Europe and Asia.

Also the fact that pyramid building resumed after having ceased halfway through the 6th Dynasty, it suggests that these Pharaohs were absolute in power once again, regaining the social organization only attainable by receiving the complete support of the entire nation. The precision of the organization of the people and administration, the complete control of the economy and the resources testifies to the grandeur of the 11th and 12th Dynasties. Pharaohs like Amenemhet I, II and III and Sesostris (Senusret I, II, and III) were fantastic leaders who took the 'Cult of the Benben' stone to its zenith along with the legend of the Binnu Bird (Phoenix), which is the forerunner of the Islamic Black Stone rituals. The amazing Labyrinth of Amenemhet III, the site of Deir-el Bahri, AMUN's temple of Karnak, campaigns in Lower Nubia, the new capital at Itj-tawi, the building of new pyramids is the legacy of the 11th and 12th Dynasties. Centralization of the monarchy was again done. King Senusret III was remembered as 2nd to only Alexander the Greek in his military exploits, another fact that scholars like to overlook.

"... A man has perished: his corpse is dust,
and his people have passed from the land;
it is a book which makes him remembered
in the mouth of a speaker.
More excellent is a (papyrus) roll than a built house,
than a chapel in the west.
It is better than an established villa,
than a stele in a temple,
Is there any like Hardjedef?
Is there another like Imhotep?
There is none among our people like Neferty,
Or Khety their chief.
I shall make you know the name of Ptahemdjehuty and Khakheperresonbe.

Is there another like Ptahhotep,

or likewise, Kaires?

- Praise of the Scribes (originally written during the Middle Kingdom)

After the 11th and 12th Dynasties revival, the country suffered a 2nd Intermediate Period which included the rise to power of the Heka-Khasut (Hyksos) Kings in the North (Lower Egypt). I'm not going to go into detail of how brutally barbaric these Indo-Aryan Hyksos people were because enough has been written about these brute by myself and many other authors. What I will briefly say is that the expulsion of the Hyksos back into Canaan, spawned the fabricated story of the biblical Exodus, being that the Hyksos (Greek Syrian) mixtures were the same Habiru (Hebrew, Gews) who today have become known as Jews both Ashkenazim and Sephardim. These Hasidic Jewish bible authors twisted the facts of the Hyksos expulsion into the story of Egyptians enslaving 'God's Children' who are supposed to be 'the Children of Israel'. This fantasy has no evidence to support it outside of the Bible and Qur'aan and the lie has been perpetuated for many generations. For the evidence of the truth; the explusion of the barbarian Hyksos shows that these hostile invaders are the ones who oppressed the Kushite – Khemetians and not the other way around. I repeat; the Exodus of the Old Testament is a gigantic hoax.

Anyway, the breakdown of the Pharaonic state into the 13th Dynasty persisted through to the 17th Dynasty in the 1500's B.C. so keeping to the topic, we will pick up the theme of the great Pharaohs with Pharaoh Seqenenre-Taa and the formidable Queen Ahhotep. After the rise of the Hyksos northern threat in the delta of Avaris, etc., the capital once again relocated to Thebes where the Wasetians once again waxed strong enough to initiate a great war of attrition with these 'Servants of the Serpent'. They had shed enough blood, disrespected the Kushite culture and desecrated the land and our ancestors took a stand to bring liberation to the land and its people once again.

* The Hotep Family Superherus: Pharaoh Seqenenre-Taa, Kamose, and Ahmose & Kendake' Ahhotep: The Unbreakable

The delta city of Hutwaret (Avaris) was founded on the eastern branch of the Nile by Pharaoh Amenemhet I. It was inland, but close enough to the sea to act as a harbour and had overland routes into the Sinai. When the Asiatics infiltrated the area and the 13th Dynasty moved south back to Thebes, the Indo-Aryan Asiatics took over the city and developed it into a fortress or citadel of massive proportions, 50,000 square metres large, on 12.35 acres of land. The pretender King Nehesy of the 14th Dynasty used it as his capital in the north before the Hyksos serpents set up house their too. Avaris and the northern Kingdom of the Hyksos stretched to Memphis and Middle Egypt at its zenith and traded with the rest of Egypt, the eastern Mediterranean and Kerma in Nubia. Avaris was impressively wealthy as can be witnessed from Pharaoh Kamose's accounts of when he raided the city and looted many riches and booty. It was a formidable stronghold which gave the Kushites from Thebes many problems to overcome. It was a constant headache and a thorn in the side of the 17th Dynasty especially. The city had thick brick walls built up around it and bastions and it was constructed in the most strategic of positions to defend against attacks from the south. For a time it was almost tolerable, until Avaris started to compete and threaten to invade Thebes. These aliens (foreigners) developed a hybrid culture merging Asiatic and Khemetian elements and traditions which appalled and insulted the native Khemetian (Kushites). They used hieroglyphs and mocked the very tradition of the Pharaohs, even taking on Egyptian names and claiming themselves Pharaohs.

Pharaoh Seqenenre-Taa: The Real Martyr!

".... You must embrace yourselves, only then can you unlock the doors to your full potential. When you embrace who are. As did the Great Pharaohs....."

- Ali Shahiyd Ashshuuaara 33°/360°

4. Courage: One person with courage is a majority

".... Courage is fear that has said its prayers ...."

- Karl Barth, Swiss Theologian

".... Courage is doing what you're afraid to do. There can be no courage unless you're scared...."

- Eddie Rickenbacker

Let us speak about Pharaoh Seqenenre-Taa, the brave. He who died a violent and honourable death at the hands of the Hyksos hordes, aged between 30-40 years young. He died from fatal blows received to the head from several axes and his face and skull was smashed in. He was honoured as one of the most courageous of men who put his life on the line and was martyred for his beloved country and people. The inscriptions on his sarcophagus call him – 'The Brave'.

The struggle between Thebes and Avaris was seen as a struggle for liberation and it was a long, drawn out conflict initiated by the great Shekem Ur Shekem – Seqenenre-Taa. The diplomatic insults of the Heka-Khasut (Hyksos) and the atrocities and threat to Theban supremacy had gone too far. The antagonism of the pretender Apophis (Apepi) had to be met with force, although Pharaoh Seqenenre-Taa knew that it was always going to be an uphill struggle with all the odds stacked against the courageous Thebans. When the Great Pretender, Apepi, insulted the traditions and culture of Khemet by sending the message blaming Hippos for his sleepless nights, the people interpreted the message as a challenge to Seqenenre-Taa. The Pharaoh then prepared for war by setting up a frontline at a location called Deir El-Ballas today. During this tense time our ancestors were forced to apply a centralized system of rations with supplies coming from Thebes. Thebes had to be protected, at all costs. What's more, Thebes was also under threat from the Kingdom of Kerma in the south. The C-Group Nubians saw the advantage to invade and gain an upper hand in Lower Nubia (Northern Nubia) and Upper Egypt (Southern Egypt) and they were in contact and coalition with the Hyksos north. Thebes was in a dangerous position being wedged in between Avaris in the north and Kerma in the south. For the survival of Khemet, these were indeed the most dangerous of times. We honour Pharaoh Seqenenre-Taa and his brave soldiers because he initiated a battle with the Hyksos that he knew full well he couldn't possibly win. He may have lost the battle, but he never lost the war because it was his spirit and determination that transferred into his son and successor Pharaoh Kamose, the last Pharaoh of the 17th Dynasty and the one who stopped the Hyksos advance. A'se to Pharaoh Seqenenre-Taa! A'se to the ancestors.

"....You gain strength, courage and confidence by every experience in which you really stop to look fear in the face. You are able to say to yourself, 'I lived through this horror. I can take the next thing that comes along'. You must do the thing you cannot do...."

- Eleanor Roosevelt

In this way, Pharaoh Seqenenre-Taa did not fail. His intention and deeds of bravery inspired a down trodden nation to stand up against oppression. He made them realize, 'Oppression is worse than slaughter'. He raised the self-worth and esteem of all the people – to live and die for Egypt.

Improve your commitment

- Look at how you spend your time, are you really committed or do you just say you are?
- Know what's worth dying for.

- Practice the Edison method. Make your plans public, then you might be more committed to follow through.

Suten Kamose: I am my Father's Son

The Great Shekem Ur Shekem Kamose picked up where his father left off. He was determined to avenge the death of his father at the hands of the Hyksos. When Seqenenre-Taa passed on, Kamose was forced to become the man, the Pharaoh overnight being still adolescent himself. Contemporary evidence for the struggle for liberation dates to the equally courageous reign of Pharaoh Kamose, for he reported on his actions in vivid accounts. The account begins with Pharaoh Kamose sitting in his council as reported on Page 33, Chapter 1.

After listening to the Elders in the council, he decided against them and chose to sail north with his army and soon reached Avaris. Pharaoh Kamose plundered the city whose inhabitants were paralyzed with fear and plundered Avaris. He also intercepted and caught a messenger from Avaris on the way; the ruler of Kerma. The pretender of Avaris, Apophis wanted the ruler of Kerma to engage Thebes from the south and join forces with him to crush Pharaoh Kamose's campaign. This is the letter intercepted by Kamose (In Full):

Aauserra, son of Ra, Apepi greets my son the ruler of Kerma. Why have you arisen as ruler without letting me know? Do you see what Egypt has done to me? The Ruler which is in her midst – Kamose – the – Mighty, given life! Is pushing me off my (own) land! I have not attacked him in any way like all that he has done to you; he has chopped up the two lands to their grief, my land and yours and he has hacked them up. Come north! Do not hold back! See, he is here with me: there is none who is expecting you here in Egypt. See, I will not set him free until you arrive! Then we shall divide the towns of Egypt and Khenthen Nefer (Nubia south of the 2nd cataract) shall be in joy.

So after Pharaoh Kamose had attacked the rebellious kingdom of Kerma in the south, in his 3rd year, the pretender Apepi tried to appeal to Kerma to join forces with him and launch a surprise attack from the south, but intercepting the messenger from Avaris, the plan was thwarted. A substantial garrison was left in Thebes in any event of this happening.

Kamose dealt a serious blow to Apophis and Avaris before which the Thebans were seen as a puppet, rag-tag army by the Hyksos forces.

His account ended with a description of the widespread joy and euphoria of Khemet's population and the royal instruction to commemorate all of these great events in stone. Carrying on in the spirit of his father, Seqenenre-Taa, Pharaoh Kamose laid the foundation for the eventual expulsion of the Heka Khasut (Hyksos) from out of Khemet (Egypt). With Pharaoh Kamose's defeat of these barbarian Indo-Aryans, began the reunification period of the defeat of foreigners, the beginning of the Imperial Age of the New Kingdom when Khemet's international prestige was taken to its zenith. Pharaoh Kamose did not live to see the expulsion of the Hyksos for whatever reason that is not clear. But he achieved the impossible and he remains legendary along with his brother and successor Pharaoh Ahmose.

Kendake' Ahhotep & Pharaoh Ahmose: Exodus

5. Competence: If you build it, they will come.

".... Competence goes beyond words. It's the leader's ability to say it, plan it and do it in such a way that others know that you know how and know that they want to follow you ...."

- John C. Maxwell

Keys to cultivate high competence:

- Show up every day and come ready to work.
- Keep learning, growing and improving.
- Follow through with excellence.
- Accomplish more than expected.
- Inspire and motivate others.

Now as the late Great El Malik Shabazz, better known as Malcolm X said:

'The Black woman is the most disrespected, neglected and overlooked Being on our planet. As the 'Mother of Humanity', she is seldom given the reverence and acknowledgement that is due to her. Our strong and beautiful Black women have made the greatest contributions to civilization with spirituality, wisdom and the love and nurturing that they have given to the Great Rulers and Leaders. They were and are, 'The Light Shining in the Darkness', giving so much of themselves and receiving little or nothing in return. Sometimes, more times than often, they have not even received any acknowledgement. There is no better example to

illustrate this than the enduring Queen Ahhotep, wife of Pharaoh Seqenenre-Taa and mother of Pharaoh's Kamose and Ahmose.'

After the loss of her husband, Pharaoh Seqenenre-Taa to the barbarian brutes, she did not lose hope or spirit. She communicated a message of liberation and redemption to herself most importantly and to her two young sons and her people. She guided and inspired the struggle to continue in the spirit of Seqenenre-Taa nurtured and motivated all levels of the movement. The resistance could never have realized its full potential and achieved its goals without her commitment and dedication. She was a wife, a mother, a Queen, a leader, a people manager, the heart of Khemet and the voice and resolve of the people. This warrior Queen prepared Pharaoh Kamose to assume the role of Pharaoh, premature as it was. When Pharaoh Kamose died unexpectedly, she also had the young Pharaoh Ahmose in a good position to overstand what would be expected of him in the shadow of his legendary father and brother.

During these transitions of power she would've had to act as co-regent and assist these two young Pharaohs with sound advice, trust to make the right decisions, constructive criticisms and encouragement constantly. They and the kingdom could not have had a better role model and guide than Mother Ahhotep; for she was bred from the noblest of Kushite lineage and assumed her response-ability in the most impeccable and admirable manner. I cannot find the words to praise her enough. There are not enough words in the vocabulary of the English language to do this or any other language for that matter, even the most eloquent of languages. It is Goddesses (yes, Goddesses) like her, Queen Sobekneferu, Queen Ahmes-Nefertari, Queen Tiye, Queen Nzingha, Queen of Sheba Makeda and such like Queen Kentaka (Candice) that are the foundation of the greatness of our people. This strength of character they have inherited from the Mother Goddesses themselves.

Queen Ahhotep held on to the long established traditions of the white crown of Upper Egypt and the Red Crown of Lower Egypt. She kept the rituals alive, the Rites, the Rule and made the ancestors smile proudly down on her. When the liberation lost hope, she restored it again and again. No mention of her is made by Egyptologists in their writings on the Hyksos period, only of the men, Seqenenre-Taa, Kamose and Ahmose. Out of all of that family, it is she who is the true hero. An example for the Black woman of today and even all these words fall short and are inadequate of her legendary memory. The Khemetians of the New Kingdom honoured and venerated her and Queen Ahmes-Nefertari, as do I. A'se to this liberating family. A'se to Queen Ahhotep!

Pharaoh Ahmose took over where Kamose left off. Having dealt the Hyksos scumbags a disastrous setback in their plans to crush Thebes and the resistance, Pharaoh Ahmose took advantage of the situation. After he forced the Hyksos to retreat out of Egypt back into Canaan, the fortress of Sharuhen, the 2nd Intermediate Period ended and the era of the New Kingdom began. As the first Pharaoh of the 18th Dynasty, Pharaoh Ahmose set the standard that all New Kingdom Pharaohs would follow. The relationship that Khemet had with its neighbours profoundly changed. The attitude taken towards them by the Pharaohs of the Middle Kingdom (11th and 12th Dynasty), was intensified and the decision to extend Egypt's borders by creating 'Buffer Zones' began all around.

"....The two Dogs palette and other similar palettes of the Early Dynastic Period found in Upper Egypt and Nubia certainly indicate, if not prove, that the pre-dynastic and early dynastic Egyptians are none other than the Black Skinned people depicted on the rock art in south western Egypt. And if so, could these ancestors have been the souls of Nekhen – the elusive ancestors also called the 'Followers of Horus and/or Seth'?

Nubia Today

".... When we take foreign visitors to Aswan today, we make sure to visit the Nubian village that is near the first cataract on the west side of the Nile. The journey is usually made by local felluca boats; visitors sail slowly upriver past the lovely Elephantine Island and through the gentle rapids of the cataract flanked with tall reeds and glistening outcrops of granite boulders. There are fine sand beaches along the way and they sometimes swim in the cool, refreshing waters of the Upper Nile. It is on these occasions that you can sense how the Ancient Egyptians lived along this sacred river and why they developed such a great respect and veneration for it and the nature nearby. Seeing the Black Nubian children playing and swimming, you are struck by a sense of timelessness as you contemplate the descendants of the Black African Egyptians of thousands of years ago.

There is now a small modern concrete jetty at the edge of the Ancient Nubian village for disembarking. From there, you go up a wide concrete stairway to be greeted by dozens of Nubian women and young girls selling handmade wooden dolls and bead necklaces. Black skinned and with gleaming white teeth, the Nubians are a very beautiful people ...."

" .... Throughout this book, we have shown evidence of a black pre-historic people that developed a high knowledge of astronomy and methods of cattle domestication and breeding and began a cult with complex rituals related to the stars and seasonal rhythms of the rainfall in the open Sahara. These myserious people also developed the social sophistication and knowledge to move huge stones, shape and sculpt them and place them to mark the rising points of special stars and constellations to indicate the yearly cycle of the sun. The evidence is overwhelming that they made contact with the Nile Valley at the very time and place of the origin of the pharaonic civilization and more pertinent to our quest, where Imhotep started his life and acquired his amazing knowledge. An intellectual and spiritual bridge was thus created whereby the knowledge acquired by these pre-historic Black African forefathers could legitimately be transmitted into the Nile Valley, allowing us to see Imhotep, not just as an Egyptian, but also as an African who first carried that ancient knowledge and memory from whence it came to the plan of Saqqara to ensure its survival in the Great Step Pyramid complex ...."

- Robert Bauval & Thomas Brophy PhD: Imhotep the African: Conclusion (In Part)

The great Shekem Ur Shekem Ahmose didn't allow the Hyksos to re-cooperate in Palestine, he led a long siege of the fortress of Sharuhen and the surrounding areas which ended the Hyksos threat permanently and discouraged others from attempting to invade by demonstrating the strength of the re-organized Khamite forces Pharaoh Ahmose also stifled the Nubian threat of Kerma in the south and strengthened Gebel Barkel (Napata), Meroe of Wawet (Lower) Northern Nubia, between the first and second cataracts.

The political situation of the time, the 16th century B.C., called for the strengthening of Khemet due to the turmoil and chaos of the whole Mesopotamian and Middle Eastern region. The migration of the Indo-Aryan Steppes people, from the Caucasian mountains region, down into China, India and Mesopotamia had drastically changed the political and cultural situation. Word of these strange Ice Men usurping various Kushite Kingdoms, such as Sumer and Akkad (Babylonia), Colchis, the Indus Valley, China, Elam (Western Iran), Assyria, etc., had long circulated amongst the Kushites. Therefore the interactions that Egypt made with its surroundings were drastic, to say the least. The world had changed profoundly across the borders and the ideal of the best defence is offense, foreign conquest became paramount. The New Kingdom turned this cautious Middle Kingdom defence into aggressive imperialism establishing Buffer Zones and tributaries with Khemetian outposts throughout Syria and Palestine. Pharaoh Ahmose laid the groundwork on which later Pharaohs would build and amplify. Ahmose managed to turn Egypt's situation around from being an oppressed dying civilization, extending its life for another 1,500 years. Because of those like him and his family, our legacy as Kushites (Nubians) was preserved before the inevitable prophecy of the seers manifested and fulfilled itself. That is the prophecy of the Kali Yuga Cycle and the Ice Men inheritors coming from the north and reducing all the original civilizations including Egypt into ruins in the sand. Pharaoh Ahmose was the third liberator in the Triad of liberators with Pharaoh Menes and Pharaoh Mentuhotep II of the Old and Middle Kingdoms. A'se to them all!

Once again just, as always, the liberation came from the south, the ancestral home of Nubians just as with the foundation with Narmer (Menes) and the stabilizing with Mentuhotep II. It once again affirms the Black origin of the Pharaonic institution, even at the beginning of the New Kingdom c. 1550 B.C. Those scholars who spend their whole life trying to prove an Asiatic and White origin are deluding themselves and their readers through blatant stereotypical racism. They can claim we are 'Afrocentric' all that they want because 'the truth is the truth', and many Caucasian authors who cannot be 'Afrocentric', have stated the same. The jury is in dear reader, so I rest my case. For the writing is on the wall and you shall 'know the truth and the truth will make you free' (John 8:32). As the ancestors always taught; 'Know Thyself' fellow Kushites.

".... With all the evidence and clues that we have investigated in this book, we have reached a point where we must, at least for now, pause in our search for the real Imhotep and his Black African ancestry. From now on, we will always think of him above all else as African – a sage among the greatest of sages, immensely wise and learned and constructively influential

in the development of humanity. It is a testimony to his name that his legacy at Saqqara is still universally admired after more than 4,500 years. All Africans, be they on the mother continent or in the West among the diaspora of African Americans and Afro-Europeans, should be proud of such an illustrious ancestor – one known to the sages as He Who Comes In Peace ...."

Imhotep is rightly regarded today as Father of architecture, inventor of medicine and inventor of the calendar. His magnificent Temple of the Stars at Saqqara still awes and thrills visitors from all over the world. With this present book however, it is our hope that a new epithet be added to his name.

- Robert Bauval & Thomas Brophy PhD: Imhotep the African:

6. Communication: Without if you travel alone:

- Simplify your message – It's not what you say, it's how you say it.
- Really care about your audience.
- Show the truth – believe what you say, live in truth (live what you say).
- Seek a response – the goal of all communication is action.

".... Developing excellent communication skills is absolutely essential to effective leadership. The leader must be able to share knowledge and ideas to transmit a sense of urgency and enthusiasm to others. If a leader can't get a message across clearly to motivate others to act on it, then having a message doesn't even matter ...."

- Gilbert Amelio

Pharaoh's Kamose and Ahmose drew on the power of their ancestral home in Nubia by routing out the rebellious tribes and neutralizing the Kerma Kingdom threat to Egypt. The army corps Nubian contingent was strengthened with ever more Nubian soldiers who were known in many lands as fearless to the death. The fortresses such as, Buhen was replenished and Medjay were conscripted once again to act as regional police and keep the peace. New monuments and stele were erected in and around Gebel Barkel; the holy mountain of AMUN RE (ANU) in Napata and the last royal pyramid was erected in the sacred city of Osiris, Abydos. The historians and the religious leaders of monotheism want us to forget our own glorious culture and ancestors, in favour of fabricated and unconfirmed fairytales and so called Holy Scriptures. I say to you all; *"Give them back their books of fiction! Give them back their false Gods and fake Messiahs".*

The House of Amunhotep: A Return to Splendour

Amunhotep I, was the 2nd Pharaoh of the 18th Dynasty and was also only a child when he ascended the throne, so it was another great Queen Ahmes-Nefertari, the main wife of Pharaoh Ahmose that took the reigns of power as his (Amunhotep's) co-regent while he matured. In later times, Amunhotep I and Queen Ahmose-Nefertari who are said to have founded the worker's village on the West side (bank) of the Nile in Waset (Thebes), called Deir El Medina and affectionately known as 'The Place of Truth'. This village of craftsmen and women was responsible for building monuments like the Pharaoh's 'Temple of a Million Years', and their 'Houses of Eternity' (tombs) in the Valley of the Kings/Queens, etc. This was a very important location and function which was located next to the Valley of the Kings and surrounded by a high wall for privacy and security from outsiders. Amunhotep I and Queen Ahmes-Nefertari carried on the great process of rebuilding and restoring which was begun shortly after the Hyksos war by Queen Ahhotep and Pharaoh Ahmose. Although there is not a lot of writings on Pharaoh Amunhotep I and he is usually shadowed by others such as, Amunhotep III, Akhenaton and Tuthmosis, we know that Queen Ahmes-Nefertari is one of the most venerated members of the royals in the annals of Khemetian history. These two were greatly adored and loved by the people.

Suten Djehutimose (Tutmosis) I

After Amunhotep I campaigned deep into Nubia, penetrating past the 3rd cataract unto Kerma to control the brewing threat and rebellion, Pharaoh Tutmose I took it further and destroyed the rebellious C-Group Kingdom (Kerma) and marched even further up to Kurgus, between the 4th and 5th cataracts. Pharaoh Tutmose I was a Pharaoh of conquest and began to create buffer zones by marching into and subduing neighbouring territories both south in Nubia and east in Palestine and Syria. The kings of the 18th Dynasty followed in his lead and began a process of greatly enlarging and expanding the Temple of Amun at Karnak, which was built by the Pharaohs of the Middle Kingdom. In essence, the whole of the Karnak complex (the oldest and largest temple complex in the world) was expanded and decorated with shrines for mainly Amun, Mut and Khons/Kush. Old Middle Kingdom buildings were often replaced with newer ones and builders constructed courtyards, rooms and gigantic gateways (Pylons) leading westward into the Nile. The temple of Karnak was connected southward by an 'Avenue of Ram-Headed Sphinxes', two miles long culminating at the next major Temple, the Temple of Luxor called affectionately - 'The Temple of Man', because of the knowledge of the human being (physical and spiritual) carved into its walls and the esoteric aspects of its design, the Temple of Luxor was a place where priests, sages, doctors, etc. learnt esoteric truths for 40 years before leaving a fully learnt master of Nuwaubu sciences. A good documentary on the subject is John Anthony West's 'Temple of Man', which can be watched on-line on YouTube for free.

His mother-in-law, Ahmose-Nefertari supported his (Tutmose I) claim to the throne being that he was not the son of Amunhotep I. This legitimized his rule in the eyes of the population. He further legitimized his rule by marrying Amunhotep I's sister Ahmose and also took a 2nd wife called Mutnofret who gave him the next Pharaoh, his son and successor Tutmose II. His first wife Ahmose gave birth to the famous Hatshepsut.

Another rebellion from the remnants of the Kingdom of Kerma in Nubia had to be put down by Tutmose II. He carried on the tradition of restoring the Kingdom to its former self by adding on to the Temple of Karnak and Luxor and reinforcing the buffer zones set up by his predecessors. His brief reign of 13-14 years achieved much and he too was honoured as a great ruler. His children were, Nefrura, mothered by Hatshepsut, who succeeded her mother as 'wife of Amun' and also a son with a lesser wife named Isis called Tutmose. This Tutmose would become his successor, Tutmose III.

Suten Tutmose III: Warrior-King, Military-Minded

When Pharaoh Tutmosis II died, the new Pharaoh Tutmosis III was still a boy, so the tradition of a royal woman from the previous generation acting as co-regent was assumed by Hatshepsut. Pharaoh Tutmose III did not rule singly until the 22nd year when and where Hatshepsut disappears from all records. In the 7th year of the co-regency, Hatshepsut took the Horus name Maatkara and ruled as a Pharaoh. Before this, she had always depicted herself as feminine in title and in depictions of herself. After her coronation, she began to depict herself as masculine appearing in male dress and depicting herself with masculine physique camouflaging her femininity. There has been much debate by Scholars concerning the reason for this all which has all been speculation because they just do not know what caused this all to happen. Hatshepsut ruled as Pharaoh for the next 15 years claiming to be the daughter of Amun, who appeared in the personage of Tutmosis I, her father. She was an able ruler who undertook many building projects including her mortuary temple at Deir-El-Bahri, which was inspired by the mortuary temple of Pharaoh Mentuhotep II at the same site. Hatshepsut sponsored many works of construction around the country and being that she had already acted the role of 'wife of Amun' with Pharaoh Tutmose II, her husband. At his side she already held all the strings of power concerning the running of state affairs. She later wrote that the God Amun declared her Pharaoh by way of Oracle.

In the role of 'Wife of Amun', the Queens of Khemet and Nubia exercised a powerful influence on the social aspects of the state. These illustrious wives had a far-reaching influence on political affairs of state also and worked in a sort of governing role at the side (not under) the Shekem Ur Shekems. Maybe she was ambitious and manipulative. Maybe she was not. What is fact is that she always acknowledged Pharaoh Tutmosis III, depicting him upon all her monuments together with his regnal years dated, but she always depicted him at the back of herself which gave him the appearance of inferiority. The most important fact about Hatshepsut is that she was actually born a Hermaphrodite (neutral gender), a fact not yet realized by Egyptologists and this accounts for her strange depictions and attitudes during her reign and lifetime. Pharaoh/Queen Hatshepsut is perhaps best known for her expedition to Punt (Ethiopia/Somalia) in which she was received by the rulers of Punt and given many spices, animals, ivory and other valuable goods and wealth which was commemorated on her temple at Deir-El-Bahri. Hatshepsut was an accomplished ruler who achieved much within her lifetime. One cannot speak of Pharaoh Tutmosis III, without mentioning Hatshepsut, his aunty. Pharaoh Tutmose III is most famous for his battles in Palestine on the field of Megiddo in c.1457 B.C.

Now Pharaoh Tutmosis III was definitely one of the strongest characters of the 18th Dynasty. His natural instinct as a military general was realized as a young man and he spent a lot of time away on military exploits, sometimes even years, while Hatshepsut was his co-regent. He led many campaigns into Palestine and Syria, even all the way up to the Tigris – Euphrates Rivers. When he assumed to lead the country without Hatshepsut as co-regent, Hatshepsut's administrators kept their positions and offices. This administration was split between Thebes and Memphis. Thebes was the heart of the administration, the Dynastic home of the 18th Dynasty, while Memphis was the administrative capital of the Kingdom. Being that Memphis was closer to the troubled northern delta region and strategically placed to react to any Asiatic (Indo-Aryan) invasions, the monarchs spent a lot of their time and energy there but the most important of the two was Thebes, which was the Heliopolis of the south (Upper Egypt). Palaces were also erected by the Tutmosids in the city of Avarice and the remains of these have been excavated and confirmed from surviving records and inscriptions.

It was Pharaoh Tutmosis III who achieved the most for Khemet's international prestige by extending its borders further than ever before; north, east, west and south. He is recorded in many campaigns engaging the Asiatics, people of Kerma, etc. and also brought back many plants which could be used medicinally and intriguing animals. What is most significant is that decades after his aunty, Hatshepsut passed on he decided to erase her name from all the monuments and destroy her statues in her role as Pharaoh. He replaced many of her royal names with his and seems to have taken a disliking to her memory and legacy.

The same was done with the courtier known as Senenmut, who was largely rumoured to be Hatshepsut's unofficial lover. The contemporary Khemetians seem to have taken a disliking to Hatshepsut's memory also and they omitted her name from all later king lists. The exception to this was Manetho. Her reign was later seen and remembered as a disruption to the natural order of succession which was sometimes tricky concerning the New Kingdom Pharaohs starting in the 18th Dynasty, but both Hatshepsut and Tutmosis III were powerful rulers. Pharaoh took Khemet into a New Age of imperial strength and was thus known as the Egyptian Napoleon by modern Egyptologists. He established many outposts.

So again, it was from the south, in Sudan, where the strength to carry on came, even for the house of Pharaoh. For the mother of Tutmosis III, his father's other wife Isis, was Sudanese, Meroitic Nubian. Tutmosis II's other children by Hatshepsut was again a daughter called Neferura. The fact that the high priest of Amun and the role of 'Wife of Amun' could only be fulfilled by full-blooded Kushites/Nubians, whether from Khemet or Kush is indisputable in every sense. The purity and importance given to these titles and roles becomes self-evident and unavoidable. Those Scholars who like to try to distinguish between Khemetian-Egyptians and Kushite-Nubians are only trying to confuse the abundance of evidence and interpret or misinterpret the facts to fit their miseducating Egyptological doctrine. The Khemetians never used the word 'Black' to distinguish themselves and the rest of Black Africa; for again, they called themselves Khemet-Nu – 'The Black People'. Any distinction between them and Sudanese-Nubians was tribal and not racial. When the kings of England went to war with William Wallace and Scotland, we did not say that means the English and Scottish are two different races. They are both Caucasians, with the same genetic roots. When Scholars try to use the fact that Egyptian Pharaohs campaigned into the south, into Nubia as evidence that them and the Sudanese-Nubians were a different race, it is nothing but a clever scheme to separate Egypt from the rest of Black Africa and its roots and connections to Black Africans as so many prominent and independent researchers have proved time and time again. The Nubians who remained in Sudan-Nubia, after the creation of the Pharaonic state of Khemet, were at times very warlike and not always as civilized as their northern counterparts. Many tribes constantly raided Upper Egypt and joined with Libyans from the western desert to achieve a takeover. The fact that countless Pharaohs, from the Old Kingdom to the New Kingdom, were constantly extending the southern border, building temples at Gebel Barkel (Meroe), erecting stele, etc. and putting down rebellions, in no way supports the claim that the Khemetians were a different race apart from Black Africans. Quite the contrary and even today, in many black countries, in and outside of Africa, we can still see the strife amongst different tribes and groups of Africans, fighting each other down. Let us use the civil war in Rwanda recently, between Tutsi and Hutus as one example.

The Amenhoteps and Tutmosids did extensive and considerable construction works in Lower (north) and Upper (Nubia). For some of the Pharaohs, their mothers were Sudanese. To the Pharaohs, it was important to marry Sudanese Kushite women to strengthen their connection to their ancestral, genetic roots from time to time, in order for the house of Pharaoh to retain its cultural and genetic identity. Any other theory on this reality is Egyptological bullshit and must be refuted robustly.

Amunhotep II was the son and successor of the brilliant Tutmosis III by way of his wife, Meryetre-Hatshepsut (not the aunty Hatshepsut) Pharaoh Amunhotep was also a military man like his father before him and presented himself as a great archer, huntsman and charioteer in his depictions. He carried on a brief campaign of solidifying his father's successes and foreign victories, creating diplomatic ties with the nations of the near-east. The military campaigns of Tutmosis III against Assyrians, Hittites and the likes never destroyed the threat but rather pacified them and stopped them for the time being. What his son and successor, Amunhotep II did was to begin diplomatic negotiations with certain nations in order to calm the growing chaos in the region and solidifying tributaries and alliances against Egypt's growing threats. It was a tense time for the near east and many formidable foes were on the rise, such as the Hittites and the brutal Assyrian warlords. They had been put down by the former Pharaoh Tutmosis III but the threat had not been eliminated permanently. Pharaoh Amunhotep II and his son and successor Tutmosis IV carried on the Imperial Age, more diplomatically than militarily and made efforts to have Egypt recognized as the supreme imperial power in the region with many Egyptian outposts in various areas like Palestine (Megiddo) and Mitanni (Northern Syria). A relative peace was reached with Mitanni whereby the reigning Pharaoh began the custom of marrying a Mitanni princess to solidify the peace achieved and alliance of the two nations. Pharaoh Tutmosis IV erected a stele between the paws of the Sphinx (the great Horemakhet), which he discovered buried under the sands when he was a prince. When he took a nap in Horemakhet's location it began to speak to him telepathically and told him that if he cleared away the sand, he would become the next Pharaoh (Shekem). He did as told and commemorates this with the stele he erected between its paws. There are also other inscriptions in which he states how Paut Neteru 'the company of the Gods' (Principalities of Nature) proclaimed him as Pharaoh when he was a youth. Pharaoh Tutmosis IV followed in his father's footsteps of prolonging and securing Egypt's future which was becoming less and less certain.

The Amarna Revolution: The Sacred Operation of the Sun

It is a well-known fact that the art, buildings, literature and otherwise of the New Kingdom was inferior to the Middle Kingdom and that of the Middle Kingdom was in many respects inferior to the Old Kingdom. In the 14th century B.C., the situation in which Egypt found herself fighting for her very survival against the growing threat of foreign enemies, after having to resurrect the culture after the heavy destruction of the Hyksos occupation, left her only a remnant of her former self. Although the Imperial Age of the 18th Dynasty extended her prestige and buffered up her borders, Khemet (Egypt) had lost so much of what had made her unique and mysterious that even the house of Pharaoh and the nobles were suffering a spiritual vacuum, a loss of the esoteric arts, an influx of foreign cultures, ideas and gods and even differences on the interpretation of the sacred and divine, a kind of nationwide amnesia. So much had been lost.

The sacred science of the sun (Nuwaubu), which is 'Right Knowledge, Right Wisdom & Right Overstanding (Sound Right Reasoning)' turned into Polytheism. The monotheist aspect of a unified pantheon, one Father/Mother creator which expressed itself in a myriad of Neteru (Gods) became confused and diluted. The secret operation of the sun as the manifestation of the creative power of Re was lost on the population and the esoteric knowledge of this had to be resurfaced and passed on to future generations. The mystery schools were failing to do this; then came Amunhotep III and Tiye.

7. Discernment: Put an end to unsolved mysteries

" .... Smart leaders believe only half of what they hear. Discerning leaders know what to believe ...."

- John C. Maxwell

Pharaoh's Amunhotep III, IV, Ura Tiye & Tutankhaten

Sons of the Sun God:

The mark of a good teacher is to be able to say and admit when they do not know something. With these Pharaoh's there is a lot of confusion and disagreement about the religious idealism and the new perspectives that they introduced and also implemented during their lifetimes. Many things said about them is a matter of opinion and conjecture and the effect of their religious reform can only be gauged by its effect on and reaction of the country and administration. I will not try to act like I know it all when I do not. But what I do know is that they were passionate about religion and philosophy, spirituality and their vibrant Kushite roots and culture, maybe even more so than many other Sutens that ruled before them. Many Egyptologists see only heresy in these religious ideals. Some see the roots of modern-monotheism and others still only see delusional sun-worship. Here we are going down the neutral road, in order to let the reader make up their own minds on the subject. We are going to do this by presenting the facts and looking at them from both sides of the fence. After much thought about it I think that this is the most effective way that I can present them and move us forward.

Pharaoh Amunhotep III: A Return to the Golden Age

The great Shekem Ur Shekem Amunhotep III was yet another Pharaoh who came to power as a young child. Some say as early as 2 years old, others say at as late as 12 years old. Following in the example of his fathers, he too married a Wasetian (Sudanese) wife who became remembered as the beautiful and powerful Ura – 'Female Leader', Queen Tiye.

Pharaoh Amunhotep was a vibrant, larger than life character who, like the Old Kingdom Pharaohs, did everything on a grand scale. For he inherited an Egypt which was in a healthy financial state due to the foreign conquest and offensive imperialist actions of the former 18th Dynasty Pharaohs beginning with Pharaoh Ahmose. Having the monopoly on gold and creating buffer zones in northern and eastern territory gave Egypt access to other precious good, such as lapis lazuli, other precious stones and metals like copper and the royal family and noble families lived lavishly advertising their wealth in a number of ways. During the glorious reign of Amunhotep III, the people of Egypt wanted for nothing and the royal couple were said to be the wealthiest monarchy in the world due to the tribute they received from the vassal states surrounding them and the wealth of the royal coffers. Thebes was benefitting from the revenue and Pharaoh Amunhotep III begun his building program which in terms of quantity outshone all other Pharaohs after himself with the exception of Pharaoh Rameses II later. Pharaoh Amunhotep III inherited an Egypt that was bordered in the north by Syria's coastline, stretching all the way down to the 3rd and 4th cataracts into what is today Sudan (Nubia). So he did not concern himself with trying to expand his Kingdom any further. His two brief campaigns into Nubia were more ceremonial, a show of pomp and strength. He followed his father's example of diplomatic relations with states, such as Mitanni and took two Mitanni princesses as wives to further extend the peace. With Shekem Amunhotep III, the imperial aggression against neighbouring countries ended resulting in an enormous empire which was flooded with wealth. The royals and elites, the noble families put this abundance of wealth into many building projects throughout the land that have stood the test of time and are still visible today.

The great Shekem Ur Shekem sponsored numerous building projects and left behind many architectural achievements and remains in the New Kingdom. As said, only Pharaoh Rameses II who reigned later, left behind more than himself, being that Rameses reigned 65 years compared to his 38 years and the fact that he (Rameses) renamed many of Amunhotep's monuments in his own name. Many of Pharaoh Amunhotep's buildings had a monumentality unseen since the glorious days of the Old Kingdom. The reign of this Pharaoh can be considered the Golden Age of the New Kingdom, albeit a short Golden Age. The most famous of his many colossal monuments were the Colossi of Memnon, which were located outside of his 'Temple of a Million Years' (Mortuary Temple). The 20 metre high colossus weighed a staggering 720 tons. These statues are exemplary.

Pharaoh Amunhotep III throughout time became associated with the Memnon of the Ethiopis and Iliad of the Greek writer Homer. He was indeed a Memnon of his time but he was not the Memna'un (Memnon) of legend and the hero of the Battle of Troy, which happened at a later time somewhere between the reigns of Pharaoh Meneptah and Pharaoh Rameses III. Still, Pharaoh Amunhotep III was a legend within himself during his lifetime.

The change in emphasis in his religious perspectives influenced his architectural works which expressed his vision. His connection to Paut Neteru was emphasised in a new way in the way he deified himself during his lifetime taking this deification further than any Pharaoh before himself. He was the first Pharaoh to do this during his lifetime and not after when a mortuary cult would've been formed within the traditional way. Some of his monuments contain displays of him making offerings to his own image. He included himself in the pantheon of Paut Neteru, claiming himself as the physical manifestation and personification of the Gods themselves. Some say in this way, he went back to how it was in the beginning when the Pharaohs claimed more divinity than contemporary times.

Some attribute this religious reform not to Amunhotep III, but actually to the influence of the wife, Queen Tiye. This so called 'Atenism' is said to be of Meroitic, Sudanese origin and was said to be the original monotheism of Old Kingdom Khemet repackaged. The Mother/Father creator energy was said to have manifested as Ra (pronounced Re), which was symbolized in the physical plane as the sun. In the Egyptian language Atun/Aten meant the 'Sun at its highest point', 'the Unique One'. Aten was one third of the 'Triad of Re', along with Atum – 'the Undifferentiated One' and Amun 'the Hidden One'. In Queen Tiye' and Pharaoh Amunhotep's 'Atenism', all aspects of Paut Neteru were contained within the Aten, symbolized as the 'Solar Disk with extended rays ending in hands'. This symbol represented the sun at its high point and not the Sacred Solar Barque (Nibiru) as some wrongly state. Queen Tiye' came from a military family of Wasetians, her mother and father being Yuya and Tuya. Yuya and Tuya were so important, they are the only non-royals buried among the Pharaohs in the Valley of Kings (tomb KV – 46). Pharaoh Amunhotep III commissioned many statues, some of them colossal, representing the powerful Queen Tiye at his side and his equal in size. This had never been seen before. Pharaoh Amunhotep III was very fond of her, having married her in his first or second year, they were inseparable. No earlier queen, save Queen Ahhotep and Ahmose-Nefertari received such status and official recognition, but in many aspects she out did even them and took Queendom to the highest level witnessed. Many reliefs and inscriptions partner her as the Pharaohs equal reflecting her and his strong Kushite principles. All Scholars worthy of the name, know for certain, that she exercised great influence over the Pharaoh and his court and was involved in the day to day running and decisions of the Kingdom both spiritually and politically. She, herself was deified along with Amunhotep as the personification of the Goddess, Het-Heru (Hathor), the companion of Re.

A'aferti Amunhotep III had two temples constructed in her homeland of Nubia around the 2nd cataract to commemorate their love. The one at Sodinga, was commissioned for Queen Tiye in the image of Het-Heru, companion of Re. It contained a beautiful canal for Queen Tiye and is an exquisite example of the love that bonds people together for eternity. 10 miles (15 kilometres) to the south, at Soleb, another temple was built honouring Pharaoh Amunhotep III as 'Nebmaatra' (his prenomen), meaning 'Lord of Nubia', which was constructed with several open solar courtyards. These temples were deep expressions of love for Tiye and Paut Neteru.

Pharaoh Amunhotep III celebrated three Heb-Seds, renewing his rule in the last decade of his life. He commissioned a gigantic palace city for the ceremonies and festivals in Malqata, western Thebes. This huge complex contained four palaces, residential palaces including an artificial harbour, a temple for Amun, residential areas and a palace for his love, Queen Tiye. He did not neglect eastern Thebes either, the religious centre of Amun. He expanded the legendary temple of Karnak, and connected it to Luxor, 2 miles (3 kilometres) to the south, with the processional road. His work at Luxor was significant and of special importance.

He dismantled the existing temple and elevated the new one in the form of which it can still be admired today. The Temple of Luxor encoded esoteric secrets that were sealed away from the uninitiated, enabling those secrets of creation to survive down to us descendants today. The representations on its walls contain hidden information which was kept away from the 'Servants of Serpent'. The temple also serves the function of the renewal of the Shekems divine Ka and birth. The complex was in use from the 29th through to his ascension (death) in year 38 of his illustrious reign, the complex was sublime, increasing Thebe's prestige.

So Pharaoh Amunhotep III identified himself with the Sun God Re, in his chief aspect as Amun, as well as Atun. He portrayed himself as the Son of the Sun God personified as his father Pharaoh Tutmosis IV and his mother Mutemwia. His Mortuary Temple was the grandest 'Temple of a Million Years' Khemet had ever seen, fronted by the two colossus of Memnon. It was completely dismantled through modern times but for the colossi, of which only foundations and fragments remain unfortunately. The ground plan shows how massive the building was. It held more statues than any other religious building complex in Khemet. His buildings show just how wealthy Egypt and Nubia was. It was the Imperial Age of Empire that made all of this possible for Khemet's New Kingdom.

Thebes was his religious capital, while the administrative capital was at Memphis. Many courtiers left behind inscriptions and there is an abundance of information left to us that attests to the entourage of the great Shekem Ur Shekem Amunhotep III in Thebes and in other locations. Ipet-Isut (Karnak) was a centre of spiritual energy and he added a great deal to that foundation. Although he adored Queen Tiye, Pharaoh Amunhotep III had many other wives. With Queen Tiye, the 'Divine Spouse', they had 4 daughters and 2 sons, who were also featured in royal representations. The daughters were Satamun, Henuttaneb, Isis and Nebetah. His son Prince Tutmose died before him and he was therefore succeeded by his other son Amunhotep IV. He may've had more children with other wives but the off-spring from Queen Tiye made up the core of the royal family. In the last 10 years of his life, Satamun the Princess inherited the role of 'Wife of Amun' from her mother, as Queen Tiye was elevated to the status of a Goddess.

Pharaoh Amunhotep had diplomatic marriages to two Mitanni Princesses which are well documented. They were Kelu-Heba and Tadu-Heba, two Babylonian ones and one from the Southern Anatolian state of Arzawa. He also requested female personnel from his vassals as well. He requested in a letter to King Gezer in Palestine, a tribute including *"40 female cupbearers, 40 shekels of silver being the price of a female cupbearer, send extremely beautiful female cupbearers in whom there is no defect, so the Pharaoh, your lord, will say to you 'This is excellent, in accordance with the order I gave you'."*

In the last 10 years of his life there is enough evidence to suggest that he took his son Amunhotep IV as his co-regent. Amunhotep III and Queen Tiye were legendary no matter what we may think of their religious reforms. A'se to the ancestors!

8. Focus: The sharper it is, the sharper you are:

- The keys are priorities and concentration.
- A leader who knows what his priorities are but lacks concentration knows what to do but never gets it done.
- If he has concentration but no priorities, he has excellence without progress.
- But when he/she harnesses both, he has the potential to achieve great things.

How should you focus your time and energy?

- Focus 70% on strengths.
- Develop them to their fullest potential.
- Focus 25% on new things.
- Growth = change.
- Focus 5% on areas of weakness.
- Minimize weaknesses as much as possible, delegate.

Suten Akhenatun & Ura Nefertiti: (Gods of Armana)

With the seed of religious reform planted by his parents, Pharaoh Amunhotep IV took the changes in religious ideals to its peak, as Pharaoh Amunhotep III had passed on at a relatively early age. Amunhotep IV still had the vast influence of his mother Queen Tiye to rely upon. In the first 5 years everything was as normal with the royal court still based at Waset (Thebes), but the views that the young Pharaoh was developing beneath the surface, would split the Kingdom into two factions over the next 12 year period and come to an abrupt and unfortunate end.

Pharaoh Akhenatun is how Amunhotep IV chose to be remembered in history. In the 5th year, influenced by his religious views he chose to rename himself 'Life of the Aten' to show his reverence to the God Aten, who he placed above all others including the 'God of Gods', Amun. This upset the traditionalists, especially the powerful priesthood of Amun at Ipet-Isut (Karnak), Thebes. The priesthood of Amun had been growing in influence and power since the Middle Kingdom Pharaohs empowered Thebes as Khemet's spiritual heart. By this time they had generated enough wealth and an estate to rival the Pharaohs and were seen to be becoming too big for their boots as a separate entity. It seems a feeling of mistrust was beginning to develop between them and the house of Pharaoh which even Pharaoh Amunhotep III and Queen Tiye had begun to realize. Some say that the priesthood began to abuse their power and manipulate the population with dogmas and superstitions, in the way the religious institutions of our modern times have be known to do. The superficial religious doctrine which they began to teach was said to have taken the divinity away from the people, increasing the importance, wealth and influence of a suspect priesthood. Egypt was dying rapidly.

Pharaoh Amunhotep III was trying to counteract this by presenting himself as the personification of Paut Neteru and therefore neutralize the priesthood's growing influence which was rivalling the house of Pharaoh. Pharaoh Akhenatun was said to be attempting to give this lost divinity back to the people, teaching that all of us were/are 'Sons and Daughters of the Most High, Re'. By taking the emphasis away from the God Amun, he was attempting to lessen the influence of the priesthood of the God. Was he right or wrong? He wasn't right or wrong? He did what he thought was the right thing to do, to preserve the culture within his own unique way.

Other Scholars claim that both Pharaoh's; father and son, Amunhotep III and IV, were delusional heretics; that they both lacked intellectual prowess and were men with unsound minds, but there is no evidence to suggest this. But if we look at it from this angle, one can argue that they both presented unorthodox ideas into the long running traditional view of the Pharaonic State and that after, Egypt reverted from these alien ideas back to the comfort zone of traditional ideals centred in Amun Re and a unified pantheon. This proves, say Scholars that the general population did not appreciate these religious changes initiated by father and elevated by son.

Another thing that did Pharaoh Akhenatun no favours in the eyes of the people was his unconventional appearance. For he too, like Hatshepsut before him, was neutral gendered. The Pharaoh Akhenatun was a he-maphrodite (leaning to the male) while Hatshepsut of earlier times was actually her-maphrodite (more towards feminine) and in their times they were both seen as anomalies. The fact that Pharaoh Akhenatun didn't hide from this fact, even changing the conventional artistic representations of the royal family in order to portray themselves as real as possible, added to the reaction of shock. Where before Pharaohs had portrayed themselves as flawless, masculine beings of divine perfection, Pharaoh Akhenatun depicted himself with all flaws present, wide hips, breast, elongated skull and head, pot belly, etc. This is known as Armana period art. He as second son wasn't meant to be the heir.

One of the biggest and boldest moves was to move his supporters in the royal court to his newly created capital, in the middle of nowhere, between Thebes in the south and Memphis in the north. His new city, said to be inspired by the Atun, was called Akhetaten – 'Horizon of the Atun' and was a grand and ambitious move which eventually failed to captivate the heart and spirit of Khemet/Egypt. This move, his religious reforms and his choice of main bride, divided the country deeply. It split the country's administration into two factions, the House of Pharaoh and the Priesthood of Amun at Thebes with the army and government bang in the middle. This created a climate of stagnation and battle of wills.

The quick construction of the new capital, the city of Akhetatun was an astonishing marvel which relied on new construction techniques. It was realized by using what are called Talataats - 'small blocks, 3 spans each', rather than massive blocks used conventionally. Even still, the building of this beautiful city, complete with palaces, procession roads, solar courts, living quarters and residential areas was an architectural miracle. Today the site is named Tel-El-Armana by local Arabs. Here the royal family lived an alternative existence in comparison to the traditional life of the Pharaohs. It is a period Egypt tried to forget about.

Pharaoh Akhenatun was his father's co-regent for up to 12 years, so there was a smooth transition and no challenge for the throne. Pharaoh Akhenatun gloried in himself as 'the Radiant Solar Disk'. Thus some say that in raising the Atun above all others, Akhenatun was actually glorifying the deification of his father, Pharaoh Amunhotep III. They say that the 'Cult of the Aten' was the simple admiration of his father, but I do not think so. I think there was a lot more to it than that if I'm honest. Some Scholars argue that there was no connection between the religious reforms of father and son, but of course there was. Her name was Queen Tiye. She was the power behind or rather at the side of both. The son, Pharaoh Akhenatun continued to honour the memory of his deified parents at Soleb, Sodinga and at Akhetaten where he is seen in depictions making offerings to them.

The main wife of Akhenatun is the famous Queen Nefertiti, who is often said to have been the most beautiful woman of her time, because of the fact that she is European looking and her bust has been retouched to emphasise this, she is often used as the standard of beauty for Black women, in a Vanessa Williams sort of way. The beautiful bust of Queen Tiye is way more sublime in my view but moving on, unbeknown to most, Queen Nefertiti was actually half Mitanni and the daughter of the High Priest, Ay, a government man before becoming Pharaoh Akhenaten's aid and later High Priest. A lot of people disliked the fact that she was made the main wife and the equal to Pharaoh Akhenatun over other lesser wives, such as Kiya, mother of his successor, the famous Pharaoh Tutankhamun. Similar to his mother and father, Pharaoh Akhenatun and Nefertiti were inseparable and were nearly always portrayed together doing various activities, embracing the rays of the Atun, engaging with officials and the people, appearing at the 'Window of Appearances', etc. Most controversially, they were depicted being intimate (kissing) which was not the usual way royalty portrayed themselves.

The couple ended up having six children, all girls. Nefertiti was heavily involved in the religious reforms of the Pharaoh, the artistic revolution and general state ideology as can be seen from the numerous representations and inscriptions from the period. Together they seem to have had an unusual attitude towards the glorification of Amun over the other Gods. They commissioned a temple to Atun to the east of the temple of Amun in Karnak and they seldom represented or even mentioned Amun throughout their reign, but they still gave reference to the Most High Re, of whom Atun and Amun were just other aspects. The aspect of Atun dominated the reign of Pharaoh Amunhotep IV (Akhenatun) and Nefertiti. Interestingly, the Pharaoh did not include AMUN's name in any royal titulary outside of his birth name but uniquely ATUN's appeared in two, proclaiming him Pharaoh. Queen Nefertiti renamed herself Neferuneferuaten and an area within the temple of Atun was dedicated to her. Later, the city of Akhetatun was dismantled block by block and the names of Pharaoh Akhenatun, Queen Nefertiti and even Tutankhamun were removed from all of their monuments. This was begun by Pharaoh Horemheb, head of the army.

Between his third and fifth years, Akhenaten's religious changes went into overdrive and he began to have the name of Amun and other God's removed from monuments. He was relentless in this area and no other God was tolerated by him. Where before Atun was elevated above Amun in status, now the God Atun was alone. There was no other God besides him, not even a spouse. No longer the local Khemetian falcon headed deity with the sun disk on top of his head (Re-Horakhty), Atun now became represented as the sun disk with numerous rays ending in little hands. His changes were of an ideological nature and effected every aspect of life; spirituality (religion), language, art, politics, foreign policy and economics. He closed down the temple of all of the traditional Gods, having their priesthoods re-educated to the religion of the Atun. He imposed these changes under the compulsion of the army. His reign was a period of minimum military activity although he continued international correspondence with other nations from his new capital.

The Pharaoh and his Queen distanced themselves from the traditional elite of Memphis and Thebes who previously controlled all the strings of power in the courts of previous rulers. He used up a lot of the state's wealth to achieve his ambitions and colourful plans. Because of his intense persecution of the pantheon of Neteru (Gods), it even had an effect on writing. Old and Middle Egyptian writing became replaced with Egyptian phonetic writing. Ideograms symbolizing other Gods were banned throughout the entire Kingdom. In his showcase of a city, where he paraded himself conspicuously in public, he began to pen religious hymns and other writings, such as the 'Hymn to Aten'. It was all an innovation in Egyptian cultural history begun by his mother and father. Many people see this shift in emphasis as the root of all world monotheism, especially Judaism, Christianity and Islam. Some say Judaism is an extension of the Aten cult.

The general population did not favour these profound changes and secretly carried on worshipping in the traditional ways. Behind closed doors, in people's houses of the period, many household family Gods images were found; God's, such as Hathor, Tawaret, Bes, Isis, Osiris and Horus, etc. The general population and large parts of the country's administration did not buy into his new ideology.

Within his stylized art revolution which was taught by the Pharaoh himself, many people see feminine features. His effeminate looks and elongated neck and body cause Scholars to seek an explanation in the form of diseases and conditions, such as marfin syndrome. Some suggest that he was a sexual deviant and speculate upon a number of things. I don't know of any Scholars admitting that he was a hermaphrodite; apparently, they see no evidence of this.

The story of Pharaoh Akhenatun does not end well. After year 17 of his unorthodox reign, he disappears from records. His last 5 years from year 12-17 were a time of turmoil. Nefertiti disappears from all records during this time and is replaced with a new female partner using various titles. Some say he was murdered and others that he died in his city, after his powerbase began to diminish but he never abandoned his beliefs. In his mysterious story, there are many unanswered questions which have caused more debate than arguably any other Pharaoh. During his reign, Egypt lost much of the territory it had won through conquest.

The Esoteric Perspective

I am sure that you can appreciate how difficult it is to put the lives of Amunhotep III and his son and successor, Akhenatun into a working context. During my deep research into the truth of his reign, I have come across many different perspectives of his life and times and what he was trying to achieve. One of the most intriguing views on this particular enigmatic individual is that he was a student and transmitter of divine knowledge concerning the 'Secret Science' of the Neteru and the 'Secret Operation of the Sun'. According to Noble Dr Malachi Z. York 33°/720°, Pharaoh Akhenatun received a holy scripture from the Anunnaqi/Neteru and was in communion with them on an interdimensional level. Thus, he was a divine supernatural, androgynous being who was way ahead of his time and was thus rejected by his people because they were not ready for that deep degree of knowledge. The holy scripture that he was said to have received was none other than El's Holy Tehillim (The Psalms), which is usually associated with the Hebrew King David of biblical fiction. Indeed Psalms 104 is a direct plagiarization of Pharaoh Akhenaten's 'Great Hymn to Atun', which was discovered inscribed upon the walls of the Temple of Aten. The only difference being the word 'Atun' is replaced by 'God' within the pages of the myth made Bible, which was put together by Jewish authors.

More to the point, Pharaoh Akhenatun was said to have been introduced to the Emerald Tablet and the Science of Alchemy. Having gained all of this information at a time when Egypt was experiencing the dilution and death of Kushite culture, he and his family tried in vain to transmit this divine information to the nation, not just elites, priests or nobles, but also to the common people in general. Seeing the polytheism, the result of the breakdown of Nuwaubu, he tried to unify the pantheon of principalities of nature into the Atun, the personification of the Neteru 99^{+1} attributes and elemental forces. He knew that in this solar system, the sun was the centre of and 'father of fertility' in this solar system. As a student of the 'Secret Operation of the Sun', he tried to preserve and transmit the alchemical aspect of the 11.5 year radiation cycle with its 96 micro cycles. Each of the 5 great Kushite nations were keepers of this divine and sacred, esoteric knowledge. Due to the invasions of these nations the knowledge was forced underground into mystery schools and when those mystery schools were infiltrated and therefore destroyed by the Servants of the Serpent, the knowledge was hidden away and even in some regions lost. This is what happened in Ancient Sumer and also in Egypt during the chaos of the Hyksos wars. The knowledge had to be kept out of the hands of those who would use it for malevolent purposes, as is being done today. The Pharaoh was said to be one of those the knowledge was given to, to try to preserve the teachings through his time so that it could survive into the future; today.

As a young child, it is known that the young Amunhotep IV was not particularly interested in becoming the next Pharaoh, but he was preoccupied with spirituality and devoted much of his time to religious ideology and philosophy. Only because of the death of his elder brother, Tutmose V, did he become reluctantly the successor of Amunhotep III. It was a responsibility he had to take and one which gave him the position of influence to try to change things. Being who he was, he took steps to encode and seal up the information, hidden from the uninitiated to inevitably resurface during the last days and times due to the intellectual growth of humanity and the technological age of information.

Pharaoh Tutankhatun: The Messiah Child

In 1922 A.D., an undiscovered tomb was found and excavated in the Valley of Kings by Howard Carter and his sponsor Lord Carnavoron. It is the greatest archaeological discovery of all time, complete with all of its exotic grave goods and ancient artefacts which was undiscovered by tomb robbers. The Pharaoh in the tomb was called King Tut and after a surge of interest, European archaeologists and the likes swarmed into the Valley of the Kings, funded by the same illuminati bloodlines.

This was Pharaoh Akhenaten's son and successor, not by the chief wife, Nefertiti, but by Kiya. Akhenaten's successor was Pharaoh Tutankhatun. He came to the throne at the age of 9 years old, after his father's turbulent end. He ascended the throne at a time of chaos, after having being heralded as 'The Messiah Child'. At the end of his father's failed attempt to raise the spiritual awareness of the masses, every negative that befell Egypt was blamed on Pharaoh Akhenaten's abandonment of the traditional values and ideology of the Kingdom. Akhetaten, his father's new city was rapidly abandoned to the sands of the desert, said to be cursed by the Gods and the capital was moved back to Thebes. The temples of the Gods were quickly re-opened and the powers behind the throne compelled the young boy-King to change his name to Tutankhamun to reflect the reinstating of the old ideology with Amun at the head of the Pantheon.

During Tutankhamun's brief reign, he was controlled by both government and the army. The two people who held the most sway were Ay, the Vizier and Horemheb, General and Head of the Army. The Amun priesthood also regained their influence, wealth and prestige and people lived with the fear that Pharaoh Tutankhamun would revert to the catastrophic religion of the Atun. When, at 18, Tutankhamun became a man capable of making his own decisions, the administration feared the worst, as the young Pharaoh reminded them of his father. Pharaoh Tutankhamun died at 18 years old after a brief 9 year reign and many speculate that he was murdered by the Vizier, Ay, who was keen to take power being that Tutankhamun and his wife, Akhenesenaten (whose name was changed to Ankhesenamun) daughter of his father and Nefertiti, did not produce any heirs. Their children were stillborn and mummified, entombed with Pharaoh Tutankhamun. Pharaoh Tutankhamun was hurriedly buried with all of his belongings in a makeshift tomb haphazardly, as if the people couldn't wait to get rid of the memory. What's interesting is that all of these hazardously stored goods symbolized the 'Secret Operation of the Sun' and weren't so randomly thrown in after all. The burial was performed by Ay himself, acting as High Priest. Both he and General Horemheb are chief suspects with the most to gain.

Some say that Pharaoh Tutankhamun was a wicked child, who went against his father and sided with the Amun priesthood after Queen Nefertiti smuggled him out of the city of Akhetaten and took him to Thebes. They say that he was set up in Thebes as a rival to Pharaoh Akhenatun. The priesthood used Nefertiti and then turned their back on her, after which she tried to seek forgiveness from Pharaoh Akhenatun but he never forgave her and she was banished from his city and replaced. Her name and image was thus removed from many of the monuments in the city by the Pharaoh and this may explain her sudden disappearance. Some say she was replaced by one or another of the other five daughters; either Meritaten or Neferuneferuaten and was co-regent with Pharaoh Akhenatun.

After their untimely deaths, both Pharaoh Akhenatun and Pharaoh Tutankhamun were removed from the king lists, their names were erased from off of most of their monuments along with their images. Pharaoh Akhenaten's city was taken apart and the talataats were used within other building projects by Pharaoh Horemheb who succeeded Ay and was the Pharaohs of the 19th Dynasty. Ay and Horemheb were rivals for the throne and after two brief reigns Horemheb choose Rameses to be his successor, who became Rameses I.

Pharaoh's Amunhotep III, Akhenatun and Tutankhamun were enigmatic and revolutionary to say the least. They dared to do what was unthinkable in Egypt for whatever reasons. They had powerful female counterparts to assist and influence them in a time when Egypt's supremacy was being challenged by the rise of other international kingdoms, such as Babylonia, Assyria, Hatti, Mitanni, Minoan-Crete and the threat posed by the growing strength of the Indo-Aryans who inherited these Kingdoms. Egypt was forced to acknowledge a fast-changing world which threatened its very existence culturally, economically and politically. The memory of the Hyksos occupation and the impact that this had on the state psychologically, the threat of another Asiatic (Indo-Aryan) invasion and occupation and the dilution of the Kushite culture and ruling classes changed New Kingdom, Khemet (Egypt) dramatically and profoundly underneath the surface. So whatever we may think of this family, they did what they thought they had to do. I will leave it to my readers to research further and make up their own minds on this family and their intentions, for my job is not always to give you the answers, it is enough to point you in the right direction using references. One more thing, compared to what was stored within the tombs of other Pharaohs before their tombs were discovered and robbed, Pharaoh Tutankhamun with all his glorious and beautiful belongings was broke. Imagine that! During Pharaoh Tutankhamun's time ascending the throne, other persons of political significance rose up too like the mysterious Smenkhare whose identity remains elusive. Most importantly, don't let the media fool you into thinking these rulers looked Middle Eastern. They were not Shashu (mixed). They were full blooded Nubian Kushites that looked like the average Black person today. We are their direct descendants – Children of the Sun; please wake up from the amnesia.

In 2015, channel 5 ran a documentary called 'The Secret of King Tut's tomb', which claimed that there was a hidden chamber behind one of the walls in the tomb. It was claimed that the 'experts' speculate that the sarcophagus of Queen Nefertiti, her body and tomb never having been found, resides inside of this hidden chamber. The suggestion has been made that the tomb was never really meant to house the body of Pharaoh Tutankhamun, but rather was the intended tomb of Queen Nefertiti. Because the Pharaoh Tutankhamun died earlier than expected, his 'house of eternity' was never significantly begun or finished and so he was hastily buried within the tomb that he was found in but so far, it hasn't been confirmed. Another tomb found in the Valley is said to contain the bodies of Pharaoh Akhenatun, Tuya, Yuya and others, hidden away in a secret tomb.

The death of Pharaoh Tutankhamun, who did not produce an heir to the throne, ended the rule of one family which spanned 400 years since the reign of Pharaoh Seqenenre-Taa. This powerful family did much to prolong the miracle called Egypt by rescuing and preserving its unique culture, they rebuilt, defended, extended the international prestige of the civilization, adding another 1,500 years to its lifespan. Although Egypt never regained its former splendour in full and lost many facets of its uniqueness, through the diffusion and dilution of Kushite spiritual principles, these powerful rulers did the best that they could do to hold on to our legacy and counteract the 'Spell of Ignorance of Racial and Spiritual Amnesia', cast over our cultures by the Serpent Race (Indo-Aryans and Black Cainites).

The infiltration of the mystery schools was opposed for as long as possible before the death of the state, with esoteric secrets hidden away from the unworthy but the 'Children of Malevolence' did manage to steal away bits and pieces of sacred knowledge which branched out into the various religions, orders and secret societies of today. All spirituality and religion originates in Egypto-Nubia.

Far from being puppet kings, most of the Pharaohs were absolute monarchs with far reaching vision and mastery of their times and situations. They were the Servants of Ma'at 'Truth, Justice and Reciprocity', with the exception of a few rulers of insignificant reigns. Like goal-keepers on the football pitch, the great Pharaohs of Khemet (Egypt) became the last line of defence against the growing darkness (shadow) which was trying to dim the 'Light of Civilization'. The history of history is culture and it was the Kushite culture who propagated the Light of Civilization into the world as beacons of Paut Neteru, not Reptilian Nephilim.

The 18th Dynasty Pharaohs achieved what must have seemed impossible. Indeed, many knew the prophecy and were aware that the writing was on the wall for Egypt in a rapidly deteriorating world. But rather than roll over onto the backs and surrender, the great Shekem Ur Shekems fought unto their last breaths to preserve the teachings, the principles and memory of a utopian heaven on earth, so that us, their descendants and heirs, would real-eyes what we are capable of, our legacy and potential as Children of the Sun, the Flock of the Gods, Without the efforts they made, we would not know who we really are beyond modern slavery.

9. Vision: You can seize only what you can see.

".... A great leader's courage to fulfil his/her vision comes from passion, not position ...."

- John C. Maxwell

Vision is everything for a leader:

- It leads the leader.
- It paints the target.
- It sparks and fuels the fire within and draws him/her forward.
- It is also the fire lighter for others who follow that leader.

Close of the 18th Dynasty

The murder or death of Pharaoh Tutankhamun only 18 years old and with no heirs, led to a power struggle between rivals Ay, who was the father of Nefertiti and Vizier to Pharaoh Akhenatun. When Ay took power after Tutankhamun's death, he was already an old man. His reign was brief and insignificant. Many, people speculate that Ay, who took on the role of High Priest to conduct Tutankhamun's hasty burial is the culprit who murdered the young Pharaoh in his sleep, with a sharp blow to the back of the head.

During this tragic time, General Horemheb was away with the army in Syria. When he took the throne he erased the name of Akhenatun, Tutankhatun, Nefertiti and Ay from off of royal monuments. He was appointed second-in-command under Pharaoh Tutankhamun and is the other chief suspect in the murder theory of the young Pharaoh's death. With the inauguration of Horemheb, the Amarna period comes to an end and the 19th Dynasty begins. He quickly restored Egypt to its traditional values, art, religion, language and began the process of erasing the memory of the so called heretics, the reigns of Amunhotep IV (Ankhenatun) and his son Tutankhamun. All visible evidence of their times were removed. The long standing fragmentation of the civil administration and army was patched up, the elite families of Thebes and Memphis, side-lined for so long, were re-empowered along with the priesthood of Amun. Though the 'Cult of the Aten' survived and definitely inspired other monotheistic religions, it was just one in many ideas. Amun was returned to prominence and the Kingdom moved on.

Pharaoh Horemheb chose Paramesu as his Vizier. Paramesu was another army man like Horemheb and after the few years Horemheb spent on the throne of Egypt stabilising the country, appeasing the Gods and erasing the names of the three rulers before him.

Paramesu mounted the throne of Egypt as Pharaoh Rameses (Ramesu) the first. He was the first Pharaoh of the 19th Dynasty who was also already an old man when he came to the throne. He ruled only one year before his son, Seti I, the only Pharaoh brave enough to name himself after the God of Storms and Chaos, 'Seth', came to the throne. The 19th Dynasty was in full swing. It was the time of the famous Ramessids – 'Sons of the Light'.

Suten Ramesu II: Great Sun of the Light

Seti I: The Sparkplug: Khemetian Renaissance:

One cannot speak about Ramesu II without first briefly speaking about Pharaoh Seti I. Pharaoh Seti I was a serious man and leader who concentrated and focussed on restoring Egypt's equilibrium and balance, internally and externally. This concern was serious business after the deterioration caused by the confusion of the Amarna period. Due to the apathy of the priest ruler, Akhenatun, Egypt's foreign territory and thus borders contracted and rival states among the world powers of the time began to build in strength and confidence and entertain delusions of grandeur. In a time when neither Egypt nor any one single nation reigned as the supreme superpower, nations began to blatantly challenge the authority of each other: Elam, Babylonia, Amurru, Hatti, Assyria, etc.

One of these rising powers which began to undermine the sovereign image of Egypt was none other than the sons of Heth, the northern nation of Hatti. These Indo-Aryan Hittites exploited and overran the nation of Mitanni, penetrating further south into northern Syria and Palestine. They threatened and overpowered many Egyptian outposts including the buffer zone of Kadesh and the surrounding area. It was Pharaoh Seti I who took the responsibility of restoring order to this Egyptian territory which was a very important piece in the territorial jigsaw. He ended up having minor skirmishes with the warlike Hittites which cost the lives of many on both sides. War was not in the best interest of either nation at this particular point in time, so the decision for regional peace was not taken lightly, with brief military campaigns

Pharaoh Seti I was an able, intellectual and well-loved leader under which Egypt began to prosper again. He brought back political solidarity and unity to the central administration, sponsored many monumental building projects once again, such as the Osirion in the sacred city of Abydos. He honoured the Pharaohs who blazed the trail before him and the ancestors and made sure that the Egyptian economy was once again flourishing with abundant riches. He led campaigns into Syria, the western desert and Nubia. The strengthening of the kingdom was Seti's main objective.

From year 7 onwards, he involved his son and successor Ramesu II in all of the royal functions without having to make the young Ramesu co-regent. Many depictions of Pharaoh Seti I, include the young Ramesu at his side. This made sure that Pharaoh Ramesu was well prepared when he took over and came to power, demonstrating what a great mentor his father Seti I was. It was Pharaoh Seti I's building project that Pharaoh Rameses II continued and expanded upon. The massive project involved the restoration of many temples and monuments that had been neglected in the reign of Pharaoh Akhenatun. Still, one of the most exquisite pieces in his building project was the Osirion temple in Abydos which served as both a sanctuary and mortuary temple honouring Osiris and the main Gods of the Pantheon. The place soon became a place of pilgrimage for the cult of Osiris. It contains a depiction of himself and the crown Prince Ramesu making offerings to 75 Pharaohs tracing back to Pharaoh Menes, the pioneering founder of Pharaonic Khemet and ending with his father Ramesu I. Still Queen Hatshepsut and the four Amarna Pharaohs were omitted as illegitimates.

He also ignored the reigns of suspect rulers of the two intermediate periods placing the focus on the reigns of earlier Pharaohs. He paid homage to his ancestors and returned Khemet to its grandeur in the most beautiful ways. His reign can be considered another period of renaissance during the New Kingdom. Most importantly, he continued to recognize the supremacy of the God, Amun-Re and much time and effort was spent on Thebes and Ipet-Isut (Karnak), where he expanded the Temple of Amun, constructing the splendid hypostyle hall in front of the third pylon. He filled an area large enough to fit Notre Dame of Paris with rows of columns which supported a gigantic stone roof, an amazing feat of architectural engineering. The two rows of six columns of the central nave are (21 metres) 70 feet high with their top parts designed in the form of open papyrus plants, with diameters of 18 feet. One hundred and twenty two columns, 40 feet (12 metres) high with closed bud papyrus plant designs as capitals, flank the central rows. The aesthetic effect is mind bendingly beautiful, even as ruins.

Pharaoh Seti's tomb in the Valley of the Kings is also one of his top achievements. It is one of the most sublime and exquisite ever discovered (KV 17). It was a watershed in tomb building, having every surface covered with painted reliefs. Being the longest and richly decorated tomb in the Valley, it contained pictorial reliefs of the Pharaoh praying and making offerings to the Gods and hieroglyphs, excerpts from the Book of the Coming Forth By Day (Into the Light). Pharaoh Seti I was indeed a great and accomplished Pharaoh who achieved incredible things during his reign, left the Kingdom in a rich and healthy psychological state and produced the most worthy of heirs to carry on and expand upon the great work. Enter Ramesu II – 'The Great'!

Ramesu II: The Great: Sara "Son of the Sun (God)", Son of the Light:

10. Response-ability: If you won't carry the bull, you can't lead the team.

" .... *Success on any major scale requires you to accept response-ability ... In the final analysis, the one quality that all successful people have is the ability to take on responsibility...*"

- Michael Korda

Are you on target when it comes to responsibility?

"*When an archer misses the mark he turns and looks for fault within himself. Failure to hit the bull's eye is never the fault of the target. To improve your aim, improve yourself....*"

- Gilbert Arland

This Shekem Ur Shekem set the standard for the 19th Dynasty and by raising the bar in the way that he did, many other Pharaohs chose to call themselves Rameses in emulation of him throughout the 19th Dynasty. In the eyes of many, Pharaoh Rameses II, was the greatest Pharaoh to sit on the Khemetian throne of all time and was also of the greatest of warriors, along with Pharaohs Tutmosis III and Sesostris.

As aid, Pharaoh Rameses was mentored by his father Pharaoh Seti I since he was a young child, which developed in the young Rameses a thorough overstanding of the running of the Kingdom and his responsibilities to his people. He was prepared for the throne arguably better than any other Pharaoh due to this. The dynamic reign of Pharaoh Seti I, initiating the renaissance was the perfect example of the potential of the new era, 19th Dynasty. Pharaoh Rameses expanded on his father's great building programme and began to erect and restore monuments all over the Kingdom. There is no part of the Kingdom which wasn't touched by Pharaoh Rameses, The Great's, building programme and he did this by usurping many of the buildings of other rulers under his name, especially the buildings of Amunhotep III. He also completed several projects under Seti's name, including works at Abydos and Karnak. His own personal building project was gigantic and there is no time in his reign where the Pharaoh was not active in some way. He left a treasure-trove of monuments for archaeologists to study; more so than any other Pharaoh. Although many of his constructions used the talataats of the derelict ruins of Pharaoh Akhenaten's failed utopian city and are considered inferior to the marvels produced during the Middle and Old Kingdoms, his architecture was still carried out on a monumental scale and many of his buildings were sublimely beautiful, the most famous of which are his temples dedicated to himself and his main Queen Nefertari at Abu Simbel, Nubia. Its rooms are cut 60 metres deep into the rock face with shrines dedicated to Re-Horakhty, Ptah, Amun and himself. In this way, he emulated Pharaoh Amunhotep III by deifying himself as a God during his lifetime. So in subtle ways he carried on the innovation of Amunhotep III and the Amarna period rulers without going too far to offend the Amun priesthood and the traditionalists. The four colossal statues that front the Temple of Abu Simbel gives it its fame. At 69 feet each, these fantastic depictions of the Pharaoh have the effect of the Colossi of Memnon on the viewer. Sailing down the Nile through Lower Nubia, the presence of the Pharaoh cannot be missed. At their feet, smaller statues of his mother, Muttuya and Queen Nefertari complete the masterpiece.

Perhaps the Pharaoh's most elaborate achievement in architecture was the construction of Pirameses, his military city in the Niles eastern delta. The city was not realized for religious purposes like Pharaoh Akhenatun, but rather for military purposes, the defence of the Kingdom from the Indo-Aryan threat posed by many, not least the threat of the growing power – the Hittites of Hatti. The city affectionately called 'The Turquoise City' included the former Hyksos city of Avaris. The city of Rameses was a strategic formation complete with army barracks and horse stables and even a garrison was excavated.

During the illustrious reign of Pharaoh Rameses, the Great, war with the Hittites escalated and reached crisis point. During the reign of his father Pharaoh Seti I, brief campaigns were mounted in Palestine and Syria (Amurru). The area was involved in a tug of war between Egypt and Hatti, who were both keen to bolster their defensive territory. The age of imperialism had ensured that Pharaoh Amunhotep III had not had to engage in any military campaigns in the region and the same situation was inherited by Pharaoh Akhenatun but due to his apathy concerning the situation, much of the Egyptian territory switched sides due to the intimidation of the region done by the Hittites southern advancement. This was seen as a declaration of war by Pharaoh Rameses who thought that there was no choice but to react to the situation when the Hittites advanced into the strategic, fortress stronghold of Kadesh.

In his fourth year, the Khemetian army marched up the Lebanese coast to the city of Byblos. The situation built up into the most famous battle of Kadesh in 1275 B.C., one of the most famous battles in Ancient Egyptian history. The memory and commemoration of this great battle made Pharaoh Rameses a living legend and also amplified his claim of divinity. The Pharaoh himself depicted and described the battle many times using his own words. Two narratives survive poetically glorifying the heroic deeds of the monarch, along with a more basic version in numerous different places throughout the Kingdom. As well as these, pictorial commemorations were recorded on five different monuments, the details of which are now all known to Egyptologists and the likes. They claim that the story is a fabrication from the Egyptian point of view and refuse to believe the 'supernatural' story recorded by the Shekem Ur Shekem, Rameses II. The Hittites themselves were mostly silent about it until the reign of Muwatallis's brother who claimed that the Hittites defeated the Khemetians.

According to Pharaoh Ramesu, the Great, his army consisted of four divisions named after the Gods: Ra, Amun, Ptah and Seth. Pharaoh was at the head of the Amun division as his army approached the site of Kadesh and he was met by two cunning Hittite soldiers who claimed to be deserters giving the Shekem false information, claiming that the Hittite army had chickened out and gone into retreat. After leading his division to high ground, Rameses set up camp to wait for the other divisions. His soldiers caught two Hittite scouts who revealed the true situation to Pharaoh after being beaten. The core of the Hittite army hadn't gone into retreat, but was waiting behind of Kadesh. The Pharaoh had been led into a dangerous trap. The Pharaoh urgently tried to dispatch a message to the rest of his troops to hurry up revealing to them the danger of the situation, but the Hittite chariots attacked the Ra division by surprise, from the side while they were still in march formation. The Khemetians panicked and fled to Pharaoh Rameses with the Hittites in hot pursuit. When the Shekem heard from them that he was surrounded and his cowardly army were dropping like flies, he single handed engaged the enemy, slaughtering vast numbers from his chariot. It is said that Pharaoh became empowered by the spirit of Amun-Re.

This is the description:

" …. Then, his Majesty advanced in a gallop and he charged the forces of the enemy from Hatti, being alone by himself, none other with him. His Majesty proceeded to look around him. He found 2,500 chariots encircling him on his way out, the fast troops of the enemy from Hatti and the many countries who were with them – Arzawa, Masa, Pidasa, Keshkesh, Irun, Kizuwatna, Aleppo, Ugarit, Kadesh and Lukka, three men to a chariot acting together.

No officer was with me, no charioteer
No soldier of the army, no shield bearer;
My infantry, my chariotry yielded before them,
Not one of them stood firm to fight with them.
His Majesty spoke: "What is this, my father Amun?"
Is it right for a father to ignore his son?

What are these Asiatics to you, O AMUN,

> *These wretched ones, ignorant of God?*
> *Have I not made for you many great monuments,*
> *Filling your temple with my plunder?*
>
> *I sacrificed to you thousands of cattle,*
> *And all kinds of sweet scented herbs.*
>
> *Now, though I prayed in the distant land*
> *My voice reached to southern On (= Thebes)*
> *I found that the God Amun came when I called Him.*
> *He gave me His hand and I rejoiced!*
> *He called from behind as if nearby:*
> *"I am with you,*
> *I am your Father and my hand is with you.*
> *I prevail over 100,000 men*
> *I am Lord of victory who loves courage!"*
>
> *One called out to the other saying:*
> *"No man is he who is among us,*
> *It is the God Seth, Great of Strength, Baal Himself.*
> *The deeds of man are not his doing,*
> *They are of the One who is unique,*
> *Who fights hundreds of thousands without his army and chariotry!*
> *Come quick, flee before him,*
> *To seek life and breathe air …."*

The Pharaoh continues that he continued to slay the Hittite, sons of Heth until the Hittite King sent a letter begging surrender and suing for peace. Scholars try to find excuses to explain how Rameses could have achieved this victory. Experts claim that the battle was a draw, a stalemate. But consider how one man who is apparently surrounded by 2,500 chariots without his standing army didn't die but fought, with the power of his God, Amun, until the enemy begs for surrender. This was a supernatural – superhuman being. The psychic powers of the Uraeus is a reality not a fabrication and Pharaoh Rameses II is one of the best examples to prove that this power was still accessible to the Pharaohs, even in the New Kingdom 19th Dynasty. Still, even though Pharaoh Rameses 'the Great', won the Battle of Kadesh, Egypt had lost the war and lost much of her influence in the region of Kadesh and northern Syria to the Hittites. In saying that, Pharaoh Rameses II achieved what seemed impossible. He pacified Hatti and nullified the Hittite threat of invasion in Egypt and laid the foundation of peace between the two warring and competing nations. In this way, he spared the lives of many and from then on was referred to as Pharaoh Rameses 'the Great', for the Hittite cowards broke many of the rules of engagement. They did not attack from the front, nor did they issue any formal challenge to Khemet. In a letter to Hattusilli III, the Shekem states that he was deceived and cheated by the Hittites and single handed achieved his victory by the power of Amun. The evidence shows that the warlike Hittites took his words very seriously because they did not engage the Khemetians again. Even when the Khemetians led other military campaigns into Palestine and Syria, the Hittites did not get involved or interfere, because both sides were weary of the other. The Battle of Qadesh signalled the breakdown of diplomatic and military protocol of the time, but in many ways solidified a lasting peace between Hatti and Khemet (Egypt).

In Pharaoh Rameses II's twenty first year (1259 B.C.), a peace treaty with Hatti was concluded. The treaty was sealed complete with defensive alliance and was special to both Hatti and Egypt. Each country engraved the details upon a silver tablet. The Khemetian version was sent to the capital of Hatti, where it has survived in cuneiform script on several damaged clay tablets. The Hittite version was sent to Egypt, translated into Egyptian and carved into the walls of the Temple of Amun at Karnak and also the Ramesseum. The details stressed that the two Kingdoms wanted a lasting peace and would assist each other if any of the two were threatened by any other nations. Correspondence between the two nations was begun and in Pharaoh Rameses II's 34 year, a diplomatic marriage was arranged, which was honoured with several inscriptions. The Hittites felt compelled to seek such alliances because to the east of them, the rising threat of the Assyrians was developing, a nation even more warlike than the Hittites themselves. The Assyrians were more of a threat to Hatti, their neighbours, but as history would later show, a threat to the power structure of the entire region, including Khemet. In this way, Rameses was an expert diplomat and planner.

During these times the Khamites (Egyptians) intensified their presence in the region, with residences for officials and military garrisons. They converted strategic cities and locations into fortresses to further buffer up Egyptian borders. The Shekem also shored up the borders in Nubia between the 1st and 2nd cataract and established fortresses along the border of the western desert. The western desert was infamous for Libyan incursions.

The famous Queen Nefertari was the love of Pharaoh Rameses' life, similar to the love shared by Pharaoh Amunhotep III and Queen Tiye. He deified Nefertari as a God in the same fashion, also dedicating a most beautiful temple to her at Abu Simbel, portraying her as the Goddess Het-Haru (Hathor). Nefertari was very special to Rameses even before he mounted the throne and she died in his 24th year of reign. Many times Queen (Goddess) Nefertari was depicted as the equal of Pharaoh and observed him in war and helped him administer the Kingdom. She also actively participated in the correspondence with Hatti, with the Hittite Queen, Putuhepa. Pharaoh Rameses II's 65 year reign included many wives and many children. It is claimed the Pharaoh had 150 sons (that we know of) and at least 40 daughters. He was very proud of his offspring and mentions many of them in his inscriptions. His wife, Isetneferet mothered his successor, Meneptah. Queen Nefertari gave him Meryet-Amun, a daughter and his oldest son Amunhirwenemef. His other son by Isetneferet was Khaemwaset who left many monuments and was the High Priest of Ptah in Memphis. He died before his father, but was fondly remembered.

The death of such a strong Pharaoh as Rameses II signalled trouble upon the horizon and a breakdown in not only Khemet, but the entire region. The reputation of this long reigning and powerful monarch had travelled to the four corners of the planet and discouraged many would be rebels from fomenting any trouble with this formidable character and leader of men. This death had a psychological effect on Khemet and the daily lives of the people. Pharaoh Rameses was the rock of Egypt and was loved and admired by the entire nation down to Gebel Barkel in Nubia. It is easy to overstand why many consider him to be the greatest Shekem Ur Shekem to occupy the throne and crowns of Khemet, for Egypt prospered in every area and dealt with every challenge under his hawk like watch. He achieved more than any other Pharaoh in terms of international peace since the exploits of Tutmosis III and extended the prosperous renaissance of Pharaoh Seti I. Under Rameses the economy prospered because of the security he established from his marvel of a military city in the eastern delta. His name became legendary, his feats heroic and his achievements and deeds immortal.

For the rest of the 19th Dynasty, others tried to emulate him, for the rest of Egyptian culture, the people remembered him as 'Rameses, the Great'.

Steady, steady your hearts, my soldiers!
See me victorious, me alone
For the God AMUN is my helper, his hand is with me
How faint are your hearts, my charioteers
None among you is worthy of trust!

- (Rameses II to his soldiers)

*Kushite Reality Vs Scriptural Mythology:

Eye have been forced to engage in many heated debates with religious zealots, Imams, Priests, Rastafarians, Scholars and even New Agers and those, such as David Icke followers upon the questioned authenticity of the so called 'Holy Scriptures': Bible, Qur'aan and the topic of Extraterrestrials made famous by those, such as Eric Von Daniken and the late Zecharia Sitchin, among many others.

Many times I have tried to make clear to people that story of the Gods (God) has two faces; One Agreeable and Benevolent and the other Disagreeable and Malevolent. Indeed I have sited many evidence which proves that the Kushite, especially Khamite and Sumerian realities were the sources of much of the twisted information contained within the Babylonian corruptions, the Indo-Aryan Ramayana and Upanishads, the Vedas, the Greek and Roman legends and of course the Jewish Torah (Old Testament and books of the prophets), which fathered the Christian Bible and the Arabic Qur'aan. The Plagiarization of the ancient tablets, such as the Enuma Elish, the Epic of Creation, the Epic of Gilgamesh, the tablet of Etana, the Egyptian Book of the Coming Forth (Per Em Heru), the 42 Negative Confessions of the Neteru of the Tribunal, the Litany of RE' and many others of the Khemetian Mysteries formed the foundation of all spiritual and religious concepts.

Again it is the reality of Paut Neteru/Anunnaqi from which the world received its obsession with Gods (God) and His Angels. The Most High ANU who is The Amen, and Paut Neteru referred to as Anu and the Anunnaqi by the Sumerians, became the Olympians and Titans of Ancient Greece and Greco-Rome, the Eloh (Yahuwa/Yahweh) and the Elohim of the Torah, the Allah and Allahumma (Aalihaat) of the Qur'aan, or simply the Theo and Theos (God and His Angels) of the Bible. Religious people don't want to accept these facts.

These melanated Gods known as extra-terrestrial Supreme Beings from another star constellation and dimension are known to institutions like N.A.S.A. as the ancient astronauts and most people today have no difficulty verifying this for themselves with a little research. The problem is that most authors confuse the Nephileem – 'Fallen Angels' with the Agreeable Anunnaqi. They report the Neteru/Anunnaqi as the Draconian – Reptilians from the constellation of Draco and claim that these same Neteru/Anunnaqi are in fact the 'Serpent Gods' of those, such as the Babylonians and others, such as the Maya. The fact is that the Anunnaqi (Giboreem) 'Mighty Ones' are not the same group as the Nephileem 'Fallen Angels', who both groups are in a conflict up to this day. This war will result in Armageddon inevitably.

The Disagreeable among the Anunnaqi – 'Those who Anu sent from the Heavens to Earth', are referred to as Anaqi and are those who mixed with the Draconians at a particular stage in the war, be they Rizqiyans, Pleiadians, Zeta Reticulans, Greys, Alpha Draconians, etc. These malevolent beings were led by Tarnush the father of Nakash, better known as Lucifer and Satan. These Alpha-Draconian sympathisers; those that disagree, having made war on ANU, AL'YUN AL'YUN, AL "THE MOST HIGH, THE HEAVENLY ONE" and his commander MURDOQ, interfered with the genetic-engineering experiments of the Adamites (Humans), passing themselves off as the Gods Paut Neteru to the beings of the Kosmos, and our ancestors on earth. The Archons, (Nephileem) manipulated the human (D.N.A) genetic code to manipulate hybrid human reptilians (shape-shifters) onto the planet. The Serpent – humans have bred in with every race and are currently controlling The Matrix. They have been in control for the last 6000 years. It was these bloodlines who manufactured the Caucasian into existence through the genetic conditions known as Albinism, Vitiligo, and Leprosy (Canaan/Libana 4004 B.C.E) and encouraging him to mix with the Neanderthal (Flugelrod, Cavemen). This was done by way of the Pleiadians influencing the Neanderthal's mixing with the son of Ham named Canaan in the Bible, the cursed race (Genesis 9:25). As far-fetched as this may sound, the Black Devils bred the Lepers (both reptilian) to advance their agenda of fear, war and bloodshed. Again, this is not to condemn all white people and condone the behaviour of all Black people; quite the contrary, for Good and Evil go beyond racial boundaries. Also this is not to condemn all snakes or snake symbolism as bad. Here I am referring to the space-junk called Alpha Draconians. The fact is that this particular group of reptilians, Pleiadians and Caucasians (Indo-Aryans) set out from 4004 B.C. to control the planet and its resources by working from the lower fourth dimension in the shadows - The Servants of the Serpent, and they have been very, very successful to date.

As fantastic as this all sounds to many of you, the evidence is there for you to confirm it all for yourselves. It is these malevolent forces who have gained control of the planet and are now using mass-mind control techniques to keep you away from the truth. These same devils fabricated the Jewish Torah, Christian Bible and Mohammadan Qur'aan to imprison your mind. Whoever controls your thoughts also controls your actions as a consequence. The world is slowly being introduced to the fact that we are not alone in the universe or even on the planet Earth. The hollow earth has Extraterrestrials that live within the earth in many of the numerous caverns like Shamballah and Agartha. Many authors have written about this.

The (Draconian) Reptilian bloodlines and their network of secret societies which penetrated the mystery schools since the 15th Century B.C., ensure that any esoteric knowledge which exposes their sinister origin is taken out of public circulation. They alone wish to access the sacred knowledge in order to control the world and its inhabitants. Your royal families, politicians and bankers, your scientists and religious leaders, at the top level, are all involved in the 'Reptilian Agenda'. All the war and disease, the unnecessary bloodshed is caused deliberately and not by accident. It was this hidden force that the benevolent Kushites, such as the Shekems were fighting against and we kept them at bay for 3000+ years.

Now the stories of the scriptures, the prophets are composite characters largely based on real Kushite people, such as Pharaohs Menes, Khufu, Sneferu, Djoser, Ahmose, Tutmose, Rameses, Seti, etc. and other Kushite such as, Sargon, Gudea, Gilgamesh, Etana, Memnon, Utnapishtim, Aset, Osiris, Horus, Dammuzi, Tammuz and many others. The alleged and fictitious Temple of King Solomon was based on Pharaoh Rameses II, the Queen of Sheba, based on Queen Nefertari, King David based on Pharaoh Seti I, Enoch based on Pharaoh Sneferu, Noah – Pharaoh Khufu, the story of Abraham was taken from Pharaoh Djoser and Imhotep, Moses from Pharaoh Tutmose I, II and III and Pharaoh Ahmose and Pharaoh Akhenatun and on and on. Research that for yourselves. I am only here to point the way towards the evidence which can be found within the story and 'Glory of the Black Race', in all its various forms. The truth of the Holy Scriptures is in the legacy of the Kushites of the ancient diaspora. Know the Truth and the Truth will set you Free. KNOW THYSELF!

As for the White Martian theme popularized by David Icke, these extra-terrestrial Indo-Aryan White people are none other than the Pleiadians from the constellation of Pleiades, who were bred by the Malevolent Draconian Reptilians. It was during the genetic engineering of the Adamites that the reptilians and Pleiadians interfered before this Lulu Amelu – 'Primitive Worker' Project was completed. They reactivated the Shimti Laboratory in the region of Cydonia on Mars, and then from manipulating the inherited project, proceeded to introduce the 'Recessive Gene/Germ' into the planet Earth which was kick-started with the 'Dominant Brown Gene/Germ' of the Anunnaqi – Melanin, and grafted down, or regressed.

These White Martians, therefore, were not in an eternal war with the Draconian – Reptilians, but are involved in the war against the Anunnaqi. These two wars in the skies, mentioned within El's Holy Injiyl 'The Book of Revelation' involved the mixing of the Anunnaqi with other disagreeable beings, such as the Draconians, Alderbarans, Pleiadians, etc. in order to produce warriors with the capacity to fight disagreeable wars like Enki, Marduk, and many others. Marduk becomes Mikay'El (Angel Michael) through the wording of the myth made Bible and its cousin, the Arabic fusha Koran. I know you don't like to hear it. But the only people who will not like the Truth in these words are those living a lie, the unlearnt. Claiming that the White Martians are responsible for Cydonia and its pyramids on Mars and Egypt and its pyramids is misguided, and just another attempt by white people to claim another black reality. As we have also shown, the Phoenicians were Kushites. When Icke makes the claim that Egyptian advanced civilization is the result of the Phoenicians he becomes again a misinformer. Excavations of the earliest Phoenicians prove that they began as Hamite – Ethiopian/Nubian Kushites before the region fell victim to Indo-Aryan occupation. In this way the only difference between Phoenicians and Egyptians was location and name.

After 4004 B.C. with the sons of Canaan the leper and the movement of mass groups of Indo-Aryans from the Caucasus region, 4 out of 5 of the Great Kushite nations were over ran and usurped by the Caucasians. Even across the Atlantic in the Americas, the Indo-Aryans eventually replaced the mother culture of the Xia (Olmecs) civilization. The same pattern was repeated all over the planet, as the 'Mankind' replaced the original man (Kushite). The last Kushite civilization standing out of the 5 great nations was Egypto-Nubia (Khemet and Kush). If as claimed, White Indo-Aryans were responsible for the 5 advanced civilizations, then the question remains, *"Why is there no pyramids or evidence of these high civilizations in the Caucasus or Northern Europe dating back to these same periods of antiquity (40,000 B.C., 10,000 B.C., etc.)?"* Yes Britain was settled by Maritime Phoenicians but they were first Kushite-Phoenicians. Only later did lighter and lighter Phoenicians take over after mixing with the peoples of the north of Europe, such as British groups. The Indo-Aryans then sailed as far as America where they encountered the mother culture, the Xia people, Chinese and East Indians.

The Indo-Aryans never gained a strong foothold in Egypt until the 21st Dynasty of the New Kingdom and onwards. Only upon the breakdown of Pharaonic Egypt did the so called White race inherit the throne. Before this, there is absolutely no evidence to suggest even one single Indo-Aryan/Asiatic Pharaoh ruled in Khemet. Furthermore, the Egyptian Kushites did not depict their Gods with blond hair and blue eyes or White skin as Icke and others falsely claim. They, and even (Indo-Aryan) Greco-Romans after them, depicted their Gods as Black like the Kushites themselves. The legendary 25th Dynasty was our last respite before the Persian and Greco-Roman (Indo-Aryan), reptilian bloodlines ran riot in our beloved Egypt. With the establishment of Alexandria, the famous city of Alexander the Greek (reptilian bloodline) and the Ptolemy (reptilian bloodlines), did the Indo-Aryans steal enough of the lower mysteries to advance their agenda of world domination. From this sacred knowledge the Abrahamic faiths and contemporary secret societies were manipulated into existence by the bloodlines.

History was thus falsified to cover the origin and tracks of these Caucasians (Indo-Aryans) and the sacred texts and all esoteric knowledge was taken out of the public and hoarded by bloodline institutions like the Vatican, for their use only. The destruction of the knowledge began with the destruction of the 'House of Wisdom' in Egypt and even the Indo-Aryans own creation, the famous Library of Alexandria. This pattern was also repeated all over the world, even later on in Europe with the witch hunts and inquisitions of monarchs, such as King James, the Arabs falsified their history in the same compulsory way.

History (His-Story not Ourstory) painted the Black people as barbarians, while painting the faces of Egypt, Sumeria, etc. as White Indo-Aryans. Religion fabricated lies to portray these great men as idolaters, Satanists and the likes to stop you from studying the African Origin of Civilization and Spirituality which is the Stolen Legacy and Glory of the Black Race. Many of our major contributors were written into the Bible and Koran to make them seem authentic when the truth is none of the so called prophets are real but rather composite fabrications. This is how they mixed truth with falsehoods. Again, no concrete evidence has ever been found to suggest that any of these prophets ever existed, other than the prophet Muhammad Mustafa Al Amin (570 – 632 A.D.). This does not mean that the Arabic (Fusha) Koran is any more authentic. It is built upon the same foundation of lies as the Bible, using the same unconfirmed persons. They perpetuated the lies and created newer ones. They, for instance, also claim that Pharaoh Rameses 'the Great' persecuted the Jews in Egypt and in the fabricated Exodus was drowned by Yahweh/Allah in the Red Sea. History proved that lie wrong when the body of Pharaoh Rameses and his records were found, showing that he ruled for 65 years and died at a ripe old age. They then said it was Meneptah, Seti I, and even Akhenatun, none of whose records mention any Moses or mass-Exodus. It's all lies for the real Exodus was the expulsion of the Hyksos brutes under Pharaoh Ahmose. Research will prove me right and still, the Scholars will still live in denial of historical facts and so will Jews, Christians and Muslim sheeple. They are mind controlled and they just cannot perceive the Higher Truth more times than often.

The purpose of this book is to point you all in the right direction so that you could not just simply believe, but confirm the facts for yourselves and separate the truth from the falsehood. The time for doing that is now. Our youth are depending upon us and so is the world at large because the bloodlines won't stop until we take back the power and start to right the wrongs and heal the world. Discovering the truth of our real human potential is where it starts, for Blacks, Asians, Whites we are all children of The All. So, let us continue with the truth of the Shekem Ur Shekems and the gargantuan efforts to preserve Maatian principles and instruct us correctly - For we are their descendants, heirs to the Kingdom; 'The Flock of the Gods – Paut Neteru'.

11. Security: Competence never compensates for insecurity.

".... No man will make a great leader who wants to do it all himself or get all the credit for doing it ..."

- Andrew Carnegie

- You don't follow the crowd, you make up your own mind.
- Stand for conviction in leadership.
- Maintain the confidence of the people.
- Effective, great leaders attain great honour.

Suten Meneptah: Mould of his Father

The Shekem Ur Shekem Meneptah was a worthy successor to his father Rameses 'the Great', but for the fact that he was already an old man when he succeeded to sit on the throne and wear the crowns. The country that Shekem Ramesu II left behind was in a healthy and prosperous state, still when Rameses II passed on from old age, it signalled the end of an era and the end of an empire. Khemet's buffered and fortified borders were secured, the country was benefitting from an extended peace with the nations in its region and the economy was prospering.

The fact that 150 years later, the country was in crisis, near breaking point as the house of Pharaoh lost control of the Kingdom. Neighbouring nations no longer respected Egypt's sovereignty, politically the country was falling apart, over the long period of 150 years, conditions were up and down like a rollercoaster and it is a wonder the New Kingdom even survived for so long. There were many brief pockets of recovery, but the amount of problems and challenges Egypt had to face was non-stop and relentless, as crisis after crisis erupted frequently. There were civil wars, robberies of tombs, temples, embezzlement of the Kingdoms resources and a whole lot more. Before looking deeper into this period, we will have a look at the last few great Pharaohs of this time of Ramessids. Pharaoh Meneptah was one of them.

When Shekem Meneptah took to the throne trouble was already brewing in Palestine and in Libya. Meneptah, being mentored well into adulthood by his father and being well experienced in military pursuits did his best to maintain his father's greatness and govern the Kingdom with a strong arm. Imagine the kind of pressure this Shekem had on his shoulders after the illustrious 65 year reign of Rameses, his father! The kind of expectations the people might have debated; whether or not he could be half as effective a leader as Rameses and especially at such an advanced age.

History shows us that during the reign of Pharaoh Meneptah, Khemet faced one of the gravest situations it had ever faced. The Germanic Sea peoples were penetrated into the

Balkans and the southern Mediterranean basin had joined forces with the ever rebellious Libyans and was advancing to attack Khemet on two fronts. It was left to the son of Rameses 'the Great', Pharaoh Meneptah to intercept and diffuse the ticking time bomb. The security of the country was now severely jeopardized.

Added to that, the Kushite authority from the southern Wasetian region was being rivalled from the city of Pirameses in the northern delta. Though Thebes, at this time, had still retained its importance, its power of influence began to wane, as the position of Kushites at the top of the political, military and administrative structure began to be compromised by foreigners. The new city of Pirameses had become a magnet for migrating Asiatics (Indo-Aryans) who were assimilated into society more and more, diluting the purity of Khemetian culture and thought.

It was at the height of this atmosphere that the Shekem Meneptah emerged with the weight of the near-eastern world upon his shoulders. The potential for all chaos to break lose, due to the death of Pharaoh Rameses, was serious. The threat posed by the Libyans and their alliance of sea peoples was paralyzing. Any lesser character may have crumbled under the pressure that Pharaoh Meneptah was forced to bear. His destiny and that of New Kingdom Egypt was written in the stars. Egypt was now on borrowed time.

In 1209 B.C., four years into his brief ten year reign, Pharaoh Meneptah defeated the 'Sea People' and the Libyans and secured extra time for the Kingdom of Kham (Egypt). Just how he managed to defeat them, only the God's can know, but history is the witness. It is a fact that the Shekem totally hammered the Indo-Aryan enemy and set up a stele to celebrate his great victory. Because of its mention of the people of Israel, it is referred to as the 'Israel Stele'. It refers to Israel as a people, not a country or a city. This is the earliest mention of Israel in history. The people of Israel were none other than the expelled Hyksos – Syrian, Palestinian hoards who were kicked out of Kham by Shekem Ahmose and Queen Ahhotep in the 1500's B.C. Their resentment fermented and added to the great coalition of Tamahu forces that had made a mighty alliance and gathered up to surround and attack Khemet. This shows how much of a tactician and military mastermind Shekem Meneptah must have been. It says so much of his formidable, unbreakable character clearly inherited from his legendary father, Rameses 'the Great'.

The only flaw in the illustrious rule of Shekem Meneptah was the civil war that erupted between his son and successor Pharaoh Seti II and his grandson Amenmessu, son of Pharaoh Seti II. A civil war erupted between them for the throne of Khemet lasting 3-4 years. Amenmessu challenged Pharaoh Seti II for the throne, basing himself in the southern

Theban region. Here and in Nubia, Amenmessu gathered support in an effort to legitimize his claim to the throne but the Shekem Ur Shekem Meneptah himself had chosen Seti II as his successor before his death. The civil war sent Egypt into decline, politically, spiritually and economically. There was a general breakdown of order among every level of society which eventually undermined the sacred institutions and even the authority of the great house of Pharaoh. Maat was jeopardized and injustice ruled in its place. Pharaoh Seti II eventually captured Thebes and erased the overlapping rule of his son Pharaoh Amenmessu. This was the end of an era.

With the end of the civil war, the face of Ancient Kham (Egypt) had profoundly changed and was never again to be the same. The influx of foreign persons within the court of the immediate successor, Pharaoh Saptah betrays the breakdown of Kushite rule and the natural order and authority of the House of Pharaoh. After the death of Pharaoh Meneptah, many insignificant rulers sat upon the throne of Egypt, naming themselves Rameses and trying, in vain, to emulate the great man himself. There were in total 11 Rameses known to us. After Pharaoh Rameses I and his grandson, the great Rameses II, 9 more of them came to sit on the great throne. All but one of them failed to meet the criteria of a great leader in the image of Rameses II.

The Illustrious Suten Rameses III: Last of a Dying Breed

His name was Pharaoh Rameses III of the 20th Dynasty started by Pharaoh Sethnakht. It was a time in which the House of Pharaoh failed to provide for the administration and people in the way that it had been doing for the last 400 years of the New Kingdom. The damage that this had done to the sacred and royal image was a devastating blow to Khemetian theocracy. The ideology that the Pharaoh was the source of all prosperity and wealth for the people had dramatic consequences when the people watched the authority vanish. The respect and order of Ma'at had been severely compromised at all levels of society.

Pharaoh Rameses III had hoped to follow in the footsteps of Rameses II, but other than building one of the greatest mortuary temples of western Thebes (Medinet Habu), which was based on Rameses II's, he built few other major monuments. The loss of Egyptian foreign territory, the tributary and revenue that came with it, the corruption and breakdown of order, amplified and quickened Egypt's downward spiral and decline. The resurgence of the AMUN priesthood and the shift of power from the House of Pharaoh to themselves were accompanied by a transfer of resources. The donations which the Pharaohs made to the temples to appease the Gods were astronomical, as the state feared the coming of another age of uncertainty. The misuse of oracles by the superficial priesthood only made matters worse as they interfered in all aspects of official life. The loss of the Pharaoh's status began to accelerate in the reign of the Shekem Ur Shekem Rameses III and the rulers of the 20th Dynasty were incapable of stopping it. They being mostly, middle aged men, who ruled only for a few years, were fighting a losing battle trying in vain to reassert their declining power and authoritative image of sacredness.

What set the Shekem Ur Shekem Rameses III apart was his victories against the same coalition of Sea Peoples and Libyans who Pharaoh Meneptah defeated in 1209 B.C. The great Aha – 'Warrior', Pharaoh Rameses III defeated them on three separate occasions at a time when Khemet was a declining power and only a remnant, a shadow of her former self. The Pharaoh defeated them three decades after Pharaoh Meneptah, in his fifth year (c. 1180), his eleventh year (c. 1174) and his eighth year (c. 1177) respectively. He celebrated these victories, most elaborately in his eighth year with lengthy inscriptions and beautiful reliefs and sculptures depicting battles on land and on sea. Just as in the reign of Pharaoh Meneptah, the Sea Peoples consisted of various Tamahu groups, such as Philistines (Palestinians), Syrians, Hyksos, Libyans, Armenians, Germans, Canaanites, Turks, Greeks, Mysians, Lycians, Dardanians, Achaeans, Tyrrhenians, Sicilians and Sardinians, etc., all Indo-Aryan people who changed the face of the near east forever at the end of the Bronze Age. They sacked the colonies of Troy, Cyprus, Crete (Minoa), Ugarit, Hatti, Amurru, etc. They desolated these Kushite colonies and massacred the people and the land. Indeed, the 1200's B.C. was a time of monumental change in the history of our planet and its inhabitants. Pharaoh Rameses III, like Pharaoh Meneptah halted the Indo-Aryan invasion into Khemet and bought us Kushites some more borrowed time to preserve that which is kept sacred and record 'our story' (not his-story) which is the story of the planet earth in its entirety.

The mass movement and attack of the Sea Peoples into the Mediterranean basin was sudden and unforeseen. From the north east, they penetrated into the south complete with women and children, carts and household goods, as can be witnessed through Pharaoh Rameses III's depictions. The disruption that this brought to the near eastern region can never be overstated. Scholars like to act as if they do not know who the Sea Peoples were and from whence they came because it betrays the Kushite origin of Egyptian and near eastern civilizations, such as Sumer, Elam, China, etc., by showing how the region reacted to those Indo-Aryan (Caucasians), the ancestors of the White Canaanites and modern Europeans. They know full well that this mass movement of the Russian Steppes peoples, culminated in this wave of Sea Peoples who resented their harsh nomadic lives in the northern hemisphere and coveted the glorious Kushite Kingdoms of the southern hemisphere, a case long proven by the late great Cheikh Anta Diop and many others.

Before the mass movement of the Sea Peoples, they had been trickling in to Libya and Egypt's delta from before Pharaoh Rameses II. Rameses employed them as mercenaries in his army, as did the Hittites and others. Many Kushites saw this as a grave mistake on the part of the Pharaoh because they knew that these people could not be trusted. The Wasetians saw the situation as a powder-keg, a ticking time bomb waiting to go off. After their defeat, Pharaoh Rameses II also employed great numbers of these Sea Peoples in a mercenary role, this of course included Libyans. With the defeat of the Sea Peoples, many Libyans, along with their families, were allowed to settle in the western delta and many Sea People were settled by the Pharaoh in Palestine and Syria. We (Kushites) won the battles but lost the war, as in time (the third intermediate period), the Libyans in the delta would gain disastrous political influence.

So the reign of the Shekem Ur Shekem Rameses III ended in the same condition in which it began. It was an atmosphere of turmoil for Egypt and its inhabitants. The miracle known as Kham/Khemet, like the rest of the Kushite ancient kingdoms, was now at breaking point. The world was now on the brink of losing one of its greatest kingdoms ever known. The Temple and Light of the world, the rule was at its bitter and tragic end in the ancient world.

During his reign, Pharaoh Rameses III faced challenges to his rule, even from amongst members within his own court. One such incident which is recorded is referred to as the 'Harem Conspiracy', in which persons sought to disgrace the Pharaoh but the plot failed and the perpetrators were severely punished. This goes to show how much the Pharaoh's image, the sacredness and respect of which had fell into disrepute and the corruption that had replaced Maatian principles. During the 20th Dynasty, this led to the fragmentation of the kingdom into the north and south once again. The north was ran from Tanis, the foreign capital in the delta which was peopled by foreigners, while the south was ran from the old foundation of Waset, 'Thebes', still and always, the spiritual capital. The border between the two lands, as always, was 60 miles to the south of Memphis. This situation manifested after Pharaoh Rameses XI. The sons of Pharaoh Rameses III were Rameses IV, V, VI and VIII and Rameses VII, was the son of Rameses VI, all of whom failed to make their mark in history. All of the evidence point to a dying kingdom in crisis and total breakdown.

The Shekem Ur Shekem Rameses III, for all his failures, achieved victory over the biggest coalition of Indo-Aryan forces Khemet ever seen and what's more he did this at a time when Khemet was fragmented and weak. He achieved the unthinkable when everything was in decline and against him, with all the political problems and inner chaos of a dying civilization. The man behind the mask must have been a determined and innovative thinker, a doer rather than a dreamer, as with most of the other men behind the funerary masks mentioned within this section of the scroll. How exactly they achieved the unachievable for so long will remain a mystery to most admirers. The example of these God Kings is second to none, especially those of the earliest dynasties. Pharaoh Rameses III endured hardships that would've sank most second rate leaders of the world today, with their fickle politics and obsessions of wealth and self-interest. Therefore, he too, must be remembered, revered and honoured as one of the great men of the Kushite – Khemetian Stolen Legacy. In my view, he was the last great Pharaoh born of the land of Egypt. From Pharaoh Rameses VI to XI, Egypt was upon its last breath. The Khemetian Shekem Ur Shekems, from the time of the great founder Pharaoh Menes (Narmer) could buy us no more time. From Shekem Menes, the Pharaonic state, the miracle named Khemet/Kham (Egypt) had lasted for more than 3,500 years, but now with the third intermediate period, it was staring at its tragic end. There was one last ray of hope. It came from the south as always. As with the beginning, these Pharaohs came from Kush (Nubia). They closed the third intermediate period as the 25th Dynasty.

The Glorious 25th Dynasty: The Last Line of Defence:

In 715 B.C. Khemet was still holding on, gasping its last breaths. The Assyrians, the dreaded enemies of the late New Kingdom Khemet and the Persians had risen to power and threatened the entire region with tyranny. These Indo-Aryan usurpers were having their way, crowning themselves Pharaohs in Egypt. This began with the 26th Dynasty and continued with the 27th, but before this happened, salvation for Kushite-Khemet came from Kushite – Kush/Nubia.

It began with Pharaoh Alara and his son and successor, Kashta, who began by leading campaigns from Nubia into Egyptian Thebes. Alara was the first Pharaoh of the 25th Dynasty. His son and successor Pharaoh Kashta penetrated into Thebes also where he was accepted and crowned as Pharaoh of Upper and Lower Egypt. Both he and his father Alara came from El-Kurru in Nubia/Kush and Pharaoh Kashta left a stele in the Khnum Temple at Elephantine on the first cataract. It was Pharaoh Alara who restored the Temple of Amun at Gebel Barkel, Napata which became the new Kushite capital when the Libyans began to rule as the 21st Dynasty from Bubastis and Tanis. The alliance of the cities of northern Egypt was accomplished by Tefnakht to rival the southern Kushite alliance of Thebes with Napata.

This caused a response from the successor of Pharaoh Kashta in c. 747 B.C. This successor was the formidable Pharaoh Piankhi or simply Piy. From his stronghold in Napata he ruled over Upper Egypt (Thebes) where his sister was installed as 'Wife of Amun'. Here in Thebes the Pharaoh positioned troops and the soldiers and officials assisted his sister Amenirdis I in running the Theban region. The Scholars like to remain silent on the fact that, throughout Egyptian history, the 'Wife of AMUN' role, along with the 'High Priest of AMUN' role had to be filled by Kushite – full blooded Nubian (Sudanese/Meroitic) stock. None but Kushites could fulfil these most important positions from the beginning of the Pharaonic state, to its end. European Egyptologists and the likes try to ignore the significance and cultural impact of this but they no longer can if we reclaim our 'Stolen Legacy'. Pharaoh Piankhi set up a stele detailing his response to Tefnakht's alliance and advance in his 21st year at Napata. After sending his troops which were stationed in Thebes, he personally led his army in c. 728 B.C. He defeated his opponents and captured several fortified towns in succession, sometimes without even having to fight for the enemies surrender. This was not a Pharaoh to take on. Enemies took one look at this force to be reckoned with and quickly surrendered begging forgiveness. After taking the fortified stronghold of Memphis, he accepted the complete surrender of the northern cities and alliances who knew that it was futile to resist any further. His stele of commemoration lists them in specific details, including King Osorkon of the 22nd Dynasty. Tefnakht sent emissaries but dared not come to Memphis himself. He returned Egypt to its natural order and left returning to Napata which he preferred. In Napata, he decorated the Temple of Amun with reliefs detailing and depicting the submission of the northern rulers and his Heb-Sed festival. Although he did not change the political situation and conquer the whole of Egypt, he laid the foundation for Pharaoh Shabaka to do so, only ten years later.

12. Initiative: You won't leave home without.

".... Success seems to be connected with action successful people keep moving. They make mistakes, but they don't quit ...."

- Conrad Hilton

Qualities leaders possess to make things happen:

- They know what they want.
- They push themselves to act.
- They take more risks.
- They make more mistakes.

The Hawk Shabaka: The Regenerator & The Falcon Taharka, son of Piankhi: The Mighty Crown

".... In 712 Shabaka ascended the throne of Egypt, after routing Bocharis, the usurper. The enthusiastic welcome accorded him by the Egyptian people, who saw him as the regenerator of the ancestral tradition, attests once again in favour of the original kinship between Egyptians and Negre Ethiopians. Ethiopia and the African interior have always been

considered by Egyptians as the holy land from which their forebears had come. This passage from Cherubini indicates the reaction of the Egyptians to the advent of the Black Dynasty from the land of Kush (the Sudan):

In any event, it is remarkable that the authority of the King of Ethiopia seemed recognized by Egypt, less as that of an enemy imposing his rule by force, than as a guardianship invited by the prayers of a long suffering country, afflicted with anarchy within its borders and weakened abroad. In this monarch, Egypt found a representative of its ideas and beliefs, a zealous regenerator of its institutions, a powerful protector of its independence. The reign of Shabaka was in fact viewed as one of the happiest in Egyptian memory. His dynasty, adopted over the land of the Pharaohs, ranks twenty fifth in the order of succession of national families who have occupied the throne.

This King of Egypt and Nubia, of Mesraim and Kush, both sons of Ham, is revealed by many events in Egypto-Nubian history. After Cherubini, it is Budge's turn to note: "Observing at Semma that the temple of Ti-Raka was dedicated by this King to the spirit of Osorta-Sen III, addressed as a divine father", Budge expressed the opinion that the local Ethiopian Kings considered the Egyptian conquerors as their ancestors ..... Nevertheless, Budge takes into account the Egyptians conviction that he was united by close bonds to the people of Punt, that is, to the Ethiopia of today ...."

- Cheikh Anta Diop: The African Origin of Civilization: Pg 146 (In Part)

Shekem Ur Shekem Piankhi reaffirmed the status of the House of Pharaoh throughout the Kingdom and was recognized as Supreme Ruler by all of the local lords of Libyan and Tanite stock in Lower (northern) Egypt. All of the usurpers were forced to recognize this Kushite as the highest authority in the land. Tefnakht was succeeded in the north by his son Bakenrenef (Bocchoris to the Greeks), who was burned alive by Pharaoh Piankhi's brother and successor, Shekem Ur Shekem Shabaka c. 711/706 B.C. Where before Pharaoh Piankhi had left the country nominally independent, with power divided by local lords – the Libyans, Pharaoh Shabaka took a different attitude towards them with his army and asserted full Kushite control of the state.

Bakenrenef had followed in the footsteps of his father, triggering a response by trying to broaden the north's sphere of influence. The severity of Pharaoh Shabaka's reaction shows how seriously this action was taken. The worst kind've death one could experience in the eyes of Khemetians/Kushites, was to be burnt alive, to ashes, with no body left to mummify and entomb (bury). This deprived the person of an afterlife. Pharaoh Shabaka did not hesitate to burn this heretical usurper, sending a serious message to the rest of them. The rise of the Assyrians and their total domination of Mesopotamia, Hatti, Syria and Palestine, rang alarm bells for the Kushites of both Egypt and Nubia. This was the right moment to take action in Egypt, be strong against the enemies, pull together and stand firm against all threats like Pharaohs of before, such as Tutmosis III, Seti I, Rameses II, Rameses III and Meneptah. The Kushites had been supporting coalitions against the Indo-Aryan Assyrians for decades; both Egyptian and Nubian (Sudanese) forces were sent.

Pharaoh Shabaka unified the lands of Khemet and Kush when he was crowned Pharaoh at Memphis. Because of these deeds, he is seen as the official founder of the 25th Dynasty by Manetho and many contemporary Egyptologists. The 25th Dynasty ruled the unified Egypt for approximately 50 years ending the 3rd Intermediate Period. White Scholars try to ignore the significance of the 25th Dynasty or explain it away as 'foreign' and insignificant. Many of them try to claim that the 3rd Intermediate Period ended with the 26th Dynasty, which is ludicrous. We all know by now why they do this. The Pharaohs of the 25th Dynasty ruled Kush at the same time as ruling Khemet, a vast empire with Memphis and Napata 1000 miles apart. They amazingly split their time between Napata, Thebes and Memphis and records make it clear that whenever the Indo-Aryans (Asiatics) attacked northern Egypt, the Pharaohs from Kush were personally in lead of their armies.

Wars with Assyria dominated the period. For the first 25 years we Kushites kept them off through military action and diplomacy, at times even sending troops into Palestine. Pharaohs Piankhi and Shabaka sparked a powerful movement of cultural revival and national resurgence. Shabaka proceeded to restore the great Egyptian monuments. The Pharaoh also served as first priest of Amun and therefore the 25th Dynasty revived theocratic monarchy and spread it over the whole of the country.

".... Until the close of the Egyptian Empire, the Kings of Nubia (Sudan) were to bear the same title as the Egyptian Pharaoh, that of the Hawk of Nubia. Amon and Osiris were represented as coal black. Isis was a Black Goddess. Only a citizen, a national, in other words, a Black could have the privilege of serving the cult of the God Min. The priestess of Amon at Thebes, the Egyptian holy site par excellence, could not be other than a Meroitic Sudanese. These facts are basic, indestructible. In vain, has the Scholar's imagination sought to find for them an explanation compatible with the notion of a White race ...."

- Cheikh Anta Diop: The African Origin of Civilization, Pg 147 (In Part)

A'aferti Shabaka switched the capital back to Memphis, then to Tanis, displaying his determination to annihilate the independent feudal lords of the Delta. After he burnt Bocchoris alive, he made Necho, the son of Bocchoris his vassal. When Pharaoh Shabaka passed on circa. 701 B.C., he was succeeded by his nephew Pharaoh Shabaka. One of Pharaoh Shabaka's archaeological relics is the famous Shabaka Stone, found in the Delta, which he conquered. It is a basalt slab with an inscription revering the city of Memphis, re-emphasizing the Memphite Theology of creation by the Neter (God) Ptah. In it, the original creator God Ptah engenders other Neteru through thought and speech (Hika & Sia). In such ways Shabaka and other 25th Dynasty Pharaohs restored the very spirit of Khemet that had been trampled and broken for so long since the 20th Dynasty. These rulers of the 25th Dynasty cherished all the writings, monuments and teachings of the past and they were given great authority. Thus, the Sudanese monarchs emulated the grandeur and divinity of Menes and the past.

War with the Assyrian enemy broke out in Palestine. The Khemetian army marched against the forces of King Sennacherib. They (Khemet) were led by the mighty Taharka, the youngest son of Piankhi. The Kushite – Khemetians were initially pushed back after Pharaoh Shabaka was betrayed by the alien vassals of the Delta cities, who turned their backs on him against the foreign forces. These usurpers in the Delta refused to aid him, but the native people rallied to his cause and formed a militia saving Khemet. Artisans and shopkeepers from the Delta cities volunteered to form the militia and repelled the Assyrians. The peace then lasted for 25 years. Taharka then assassinated Pharaoh Shabaka and ascended the throne in 689 B.C., proclaiming himself the son of Mut (Queen of the Sudan) and constructed a temple to honour her. The policy of centralization continued under his mighty reign and he imposed his royal authority even more intensely than his predecessor Shabaka. Exactly why he assassinated Pharaoh Shabaka is unknown but history has recorded that this ruler was a no nonsense leader. The twenty feudal lords of the Delta lived in fear of his determined will. To break their resistance, he did not hesitate to deport their wives to Nubia, in 680 B.C. Records say that the formidable army of Pharaoh Taharka penetrated into Europe as far as the 'Pillars of Hercules'. The Pharaoh made such a mark among the Indo-Aryans (Asiatics), that they recorded him into their myth made Bible in the Book of Kings. This is a man who knew how to make his presence felt as a seasoned warrior.

The cultural, economic and especially architectural renaissance begun by Pharaoh Shabaka, was amplified by Pharaoh Taharka who constructed new monuments worthy of Khemet. Many of his relics remain and monuments, such as the Column of Taharka in the Karnak Temple, the statues of Mentuemhat and Amenirdis. Taharka restarted foreign campaigns, intervening in Asia Minor in an attempt to regain Khemet's (Egypt's) international prestige achieved by the early 18th Dynasty. For a short time, he nearly achieved that goal.

The coward rulers of the Delta eventually betrayed the Kushites – Egyptians again as soon as the Assyrian army penetrated Egypt's borders. The flagrant actions of Necho, son of the slain Bocchoris sold out the Delta to the Assyrians and his son, Psammiticus took over from his father as Assyrian vassal – King of the Delta. Taking refuge in Thebes, Pharaoh Taharka had the full support of the priesthood clergy, which refused to recognize the sovereignty of the Assyrians and their vassal as legitimate. Thebes and its people remained loyal to Taharka. Not one to roll over and accept defeat easily. Pharaoh Taharka determinedly returned to the battlefront in 669 B.C., re-capturing Memphis and remaining there until 666 B.C. Once again, he was deceived by the feudal bums of the Delta and was forced to flee to Napata. In his homeland he died only 2 years later. His sister, having been adopted by Amenirdis, succeeded her as 'Wife of Amun'.

Shekem Ur Shekem Taharka was an intense character and is seen as the greatest Pharaoh of the awesome 25th Dynasty. He never gave up the fight to liberate, restore and defend Kushite sovereignty, even when time and the whole world was against Egypto-Kush. The strength of the will of the 25th Dynasty rulers was remarkable and their contribution to the legacy of Ancient Egypt should not and will never be forgotten. The odds that they faced should not be lost on the reader, knowing the terrible state in which they inherited Egypt. The deeds of Pharaoh Piankhi, Shabaka and Taharka go down in history, for they are the preservers of the culture.

2 Kings 19:9 (In Part)

9. But when the King learnt that Tirhakah, King of Cush was on the way to make war on him, he sent messengers again to Hezekiah, King of Judah to say to him, How can you be deluded by your God on whom you rely when he promises that Jerusalem shall not fall into the hands of the King of Assyria? Sure you have heard what the Kings of Assyria have done to all countries, exterminating their people; can you then hope to escape?

13. Servanthood: To get ahead, put others first.

".... I don't know what your destiny will be, but one thing I know: The ones among you who will be really happy are those who have sought and found how to serve ...."

- Albert Schweitzer

- The true leader serves, serves people.
- Serves their best interests and in doing so will not always be popular, may not always impress.
- But because true leaders are motivated by loving concern rather than a desire for personal glory, they are willing to pay the price.

- Eugene B. Habecker

The biblical quote refers to the battle of El-tekeh in support of the Judaeans. King Sennacherib claimed victory, but the coalition of Egyptians, Sudanese and Judaeans prevented him from capturing and sacking Jerusalem. Pharaoh Taharka also constructed a large pyramid nearer to Napata at Nuri, which became very important to many later Nubian Pharaohs. During the years of war fought against the brutal Assyrians, Pharaoh Taharka lost his heir and several other family members to Esarhaddon.

Shekem Ur Shekem Taharka was succeeded by Tanutamun, son of Shabaka. He replenished the army in Sudan and was acclaimed at Thebes as the legitimate heir of the Pharaohs by the Amun priesthood and clergy. Pharaoh Tanutamun then attacked Memphis, waging war against a new coalition of all the northern feudal lords. The Shekem managed to defeat them and Necho was killed in the battle. All of the northern alliance surrendered humbly, except for Psammiticus, son of Necho, who remained loyal to Assyria, fleeing to the court of Nineveh.

Lights Out:

".... In 661 B.C. Ashurbanipal attacked Egypt and pillaged the city of Thebes. Tanutamun escaped to Napata. The fall of the most venerable city of all antiquity aroused deep emotion in the world of that time and marked the end of the Nubian – Sudanese or twenty fifth Ethiopian Dynasty. That date also marked the decline of Black political supremacy in antiquity and in history. Egypt gradually fell under foreign domination, without ever having known a republican form of government or secular philosophy, throughout three millennia of cyclical evolution.

Such authors as Malet and Isaac, in their standard French textbook for Sixieme (seventh grade), used to train the younger generation since 1924, have systematically ignored the extraordinary epic of the 25th Dynasty and have tried to play up the reign of 'Psammiticus – Nahu – Shezib Anni, the unworthy Libyan usurper who disguised his name to please the alien invader. It would be difficult to imagine a history at France (or Britain – my emphasis) written according to those criteria. The reign of Psammiticus served only to pave the way for foreign rule ..."

- Cheikh Anta Diop: The African Origin of Civilization

Psammiticus brought in the 26th Dynasty, whose greatest ruler was arguably Amasis. Under the reign of Amasis is when and where Khemet (Egypt) lost its independence and its lights went out as a power. The Persians under King Cambyses conquered the land and Amasis was executed, after the Persians brought an end to the Assyrian Empire, along with a resurgent Babylonia.

Bullet point recap:

- Pharaoh Menes inaugurates Pharaonic Egypt coming from Nekhen in the south (Nubia) with the Nubian – Kushite A-Group and the culture. The centre of this Black culture in the region was Sennar (Nile Junction) and Meroe. The elements of this culture political, spiritual, architectural, artistic and otherwise, were already fully developed but perfected and mastered to new levels by Khemetians. With this the enhancements travelled back south. Pharaoh Djoser takes nation to pinnacle (3rd Dynasty).

- At the end of the 6th Dynasty, Memphis was sacked by the rebels. With this, royalty gradually took refuge in its ancestral southern region (Upper Egypt), which happened repeatedly in times of trouble.

- The city of Heracleopolis, in Middle Egypt, became the temporary capital during the 1st Intermediate Period (between the 9th and 10th Dynasties). Parallel reigns occurred throughout the troubled period of anarchy. Thebes never failed as the guardian of Kushite tradition and legitimacy and its princes were the founders of the redeeming 11th Dynasty, which took on the responsibility of national rebuilding.

- After two centuries of struggle (civil war) and efforts to reunify Egypt, the southern monarchy reunified the country. The 11th Dynasty, under Pharaoh Mentuhotep II brought back administrative centralization which was achieved by Pharaoh Zoser and the 3rd Dynasty Rulers, with all its glories and effects. The 12th Dynasty brought this administrative centralization to its fullness.

- The sudden rise of the Heka-Khasut (Hyksos) population in the Delta (c.1730 – 1550 B.C.) ushered in another Intermediate Period of chaos. They introduced the horse and war chariot into the country. They only ever managed to overpower the Delta from Avaris, their capital. Their barbarism was indescribable. Royalty again found asylum in Thebes, Upper Egypt.

- During the Hyksos atrocities a movement of liberation began under Pharaoh Seqenenre-Taa and Queen Ahhotep, representing the people's will to free Egypt from (Asiatics) Indo-Aryan, foreign rule. After the martyrdom of Pharaoh Seqenenre-Taa, the struggle continued under Queen Ahhotep. Pharaoh Kamose and Pharaoh Ahmose, bringing in the

18th Dynasty. The Hyksos were evicted out of the country in c. 1550 B.C., by Pharaoh Ahmose and the period of Egyptian imperialism began with the New Kingdom.

- After the death of Queen Hatshepsut, the great reign of 18th Dynasty imperial campaigns was brought to its pinnacle. This was achieved by the army man Suten Djehutimose, Tutmosis III, another southern ruler of a Sudanese mother. He annexed all of the states of western Asia and the islands of the eastern Mediterranean, making them vassals paying Egypt tribute. The whole of the region including Assyria and Babylonia was integrated into the Egyptian Empire. The fleet of ships was built under Queen Hatshepsut who sailed famously to Punt (present day Ethiopia). At this time, as of the time of Pharaoh Sesostris I, II, III, Egypt was the foremost technical, military and imperial power in the world. Foreign vassals competed with each other in submissiveness; each tried to flatter the Pharaohs addressing them like, "I am your footstool, I lick the dust from your sandals. You are my Sun", a Syrian vassal wrote to Pharaoh Akhenatun (Amunhotep IV)

- After the 18th Dynasty, the Khemetians began to take the sons of their vassals in Asia and the Mediterranean, training them in the Pharaoh's court in the hope that they might later govern their countries as good vassals. This was one of several reasons and causes of the extensive, profound and almost exclusively Egyptian influence on western Asia and the Mediterranean. The 18th Dynasty also saw a return to administrative centralization. Administrative posts again, were no longer hereditary.

- The 18th Dynasty then turned back to absolutism under Pharaoh Amunhotep III and his Wasetian (Sudanese) wife, Queen Tiye. This was amplified by Pharaoh Amunhotep IV (Akhenatun), who placed the religious traditions strictly on the monotheist aspect, making it the universal religion of the Empire. Though his religious reforms eventually failed, his absolutist policy survived and was consolidated under the 19th Dynasty with the deification of Pharaoh Rameses and Queen Nefertari. Pharaoh Rameses began settling Hittites and other Indo-Aryans in his city of Pirameses and the Delta region once again. The policy was continued under Pharaoh Meneptah. Social conflicts of great implications had begun under the reigns of Pharaohs Akhenatun, Tutankhatun and Ay. Horemheb succeeded Ay and implemented a series of laws to protect the common people against fraud and the excesses of bureaucratic agents. The laws were designed to protect the weak and improve the living conditions of the poor, but under Pharaoh Rameses II, royal absolutism reappeared. The God Amun who had suffered under Pharaoh Akhenatun and his priesthood re-emerged as the supreme in the land and among the clergy. A period of reconstruction ensued as temples and monuments had suffered under Akhenatun. Fierce imperialism ended. Suten Rameses II was the son of an officer of the 'foreign' war chariot corps.

- The end of the reigns of Pharaohs Rameses and Meneptah witnessed massive migrations of Indo-Aryans and others, which upset the cultural balance in the region, c. 1230 B.C., after the Battle of Kadesh (c. 1275) Pharaoh Meneptah defeated the first coalition of Indo-Europeans allied with Libyans. These Indo-Europeans included Etruscans, who settled in Italy. Many of the survivors followed the coasts of Cyrenaica as far as Queen Dido's Carthage. According to Herodotus, these Asiatics were probably survivors of the Trojan War and the great Dorian Drive.

- From here on, Egypt continually had to defend its borders against relentless thrusts of White skinned people, north, and east and from the sea. The borders had been continuously fortified by Pharaoh Rameses II. After victory, Meneptah begins a campaign to pacify Palestine, as Pharaoh Ahmose began before him. In the time of Pharaoh Meneptah, the first wave of 'Sea People' had arrived in Palestine. He records that the vassals begin to rebel. White survivors of wars were given to Egyptian temples as branded (with a hot iron) slaves who were used either in farming or as 'mercenaries', a policy began by Rameses, his father. This saw an expansion of feudalism after his death. With the collapse of central power, local militias began to assume local security.

- Libyan, Syrian and Palestinian slaves begin to rebel under the leadership of military officers and foremen. Aramean slaves captured by Rameses II, took advantage of the brief period of anarchy and turmoil to revolt. Salvation, once again, came from the south in the form of the viceroy of Sudan, Seti who marched on Thebes to re-establish order. He gained the support of the priesthood, married Queen Tausert and became Seti II. The peace was only temporary.

- Khemet (Egypt) sank bank into anarchy and chaos under the feudal rulers. The 20th Dynasty is begun by Sethnakht which ends the anarchy. After two years his son Pharaoh Rameses III succeeds him on the great throne. Suten Rameses III inherits an Egypt facing extremely challenging conditions, as he is forced to face a new invasion of 'Sea Peoples' by land and sea. He reinforces the Egyptian fleet assigned to defend the mouths of the Nile. The most formidable coalition ever formed against Khemet in antiquity, comprising the whole group of White skinned, Indo-Aryans, unstable since the first migrations in the 13th century, set up their immigration camp north of Syria. Due to superior organization, the Khemetians achieve a dual victory on land and on sea, over the second alliance. They were completely destroyed having the invasion route cut off and then a third coalition was assembled in Libya, against the Kushites, which Pharaoh Rameses III smashed. He also defeats another coalition in c. 1191 near Palestinian coast. He defeats a fifth coalition at Memphis in 1188 B.C. The defeated are settled in the region and also employed in the army's auxiliary foreign corps called Kehek.

- The iron branded White skinned prisoners of war (slaves), who were used as farmers and mercenaries and sometimes made notables by law and freed, began to rebel against authority especially under Psammiticus. This northern Delta population would become the ancestors of the mixed (Shashu) coptics which today are mistaken as the descendants of the Kushite – Wasetian Khemetians. Their true origin has never been forgotten by the true Nubian (Sudanese) Egyptians.

- The drafting of these foreign elements began under Pharaoh Rameses II, who kept a careful watch on this population of around 30,000. To prevent their flight he had them branded with the seal of administration. The Egyptian population could easily absorb this group without losing its identity, but the army began to lose its national Kushite identity, only the high command and a few detachments of archers remained Egyptian. To guard against this Pharaoh Rameses III began a process of conscription drafting one Egyptian national out of ten. In times of peace the foreigners were used as farmer and in times of war auxiliary mercenaries. The situation reached its climax under Psammiticus.

- The end of the reign of Pharaoh Rameses III witnessed the disintegration of the central administration as anarchy disorder and corruption took root and grew into wide spread chaos. Royal authority was lost to the feudal lords of the Delta up to the reign of Pharaoh Rameses XI, who appealed to the south (Upper Egypt and Lower Nubia) reinforcement of the priesthood - clergy's administrative autonomy intensified and created a separate clerical state within Upper Egypt. The high priest of Amun centralized power in his hands as a system defence against the northern chaos. This system was used to select the Pharaoh and other officials and to make governmental decisions. The end of the 20th Dynasty saw massive social conflicts all over the nation. This was a time of corruption, insecurity, tomb robbery and desecration of the temples.

- The Kingdom was saved for the fifth time by the south, the Nubian Sudan. The Viceroy of Nubia, who responded to Pharaoh Rameses XI, destroyed the city of Hardai, centre of the insurrection. The Kingdom reached a point similar to the end of the 6th Dynasty but Egypt's prestige abroad was still intact, though hanging by a thread.

- Pharaoh Piankhi battles the northern warlords at Heracleopolis and Hermopolis as the unity of the Black Egyptian and Sudanese (Nubian) nation overpowers Libyan feudalism in the Delta. Pharaoh Shabaka reunifies the nation and Pharaoh Taharka re-initiates Kushite imperial conquests throughout Asia Minor. A cultural renaissance ensues lasting until the sacking of Thebes.

".... During the reign of Psammiticus, when the Egyptian army was mistreated, some 200,000 of them, led by their officers, went from the Isthmus of Suez to the Nubian Sudan to

place themselves at the service of the King of Nubia. Herodotus reported that the Nubian ruler settled the entire army on lands that it farmed and its elements were finally assimilated by the Nubian people. That happened at a time when Nubia civilization was already several millennia old. Consequently, we are amazed when historians try to use this fact to explain Nubian civilization. On the contrary, all the earliest Scholars who studied Nubia, even those to whom we owe the discovery of Nubian archaeology (such as Cailliaud) conclude that Nubia had priority.

Their studies indicate that Egyptian civilization descended from that of Nubia, in other words, Sudan. As Pedrals observes, Cailliaud bases this argument on the fact that in Egypt all the objects of worship (thus, the essence of sacred tradition) are Nubian. Cailliaud assumes then that the roots of Egyptian civilization were in Nubia (the Sudan) and that it gradually descended the Valley of the Nile. In this, he was merely rediscovering or confirming to some extent the unanimous opinion of the Ancients, philosophies and writers, who judged the anteriority of Nubia to be obvious.

Diodorus of Sicily reports that each year the statue of Amun, King of Thebes, was transported in the direction of Nubia for several days and then brought back as if to indicate that the God was returning from Nubia, the centre of which was Meroe. In fact, by following data provided by Diordorus and Herodotus on the site of that Sudanese capital, Cailliaud (c. 1820) discovered the ruins of Meroe; 80 pyramids, several temples, consecrated to Amun, Ra and so on. In addition, quoting Egyptian priests, Herodotus stated that of 300 Egyptian Pharaohs, from Menes to the seventeenth Dynasty, 18 rather than merely the three who correspond to the Ethiopian 'dynasty' were of Sudanese origin.

Egyptians themselves – who should surely be better qualified than anyone to speak of their origin – recognize without ambiguity that their ancestors came from Nubia and the heart of Africa. The land of Amam or land of the Ancestors (man = ancestor in Wolof), the whole territory of Kush, south of Egypt was called land of the Gods by the Egyptians ...."

- Cheikh Anta Diop: The African Origin of Civilization, Pg 149-150 (In Part)

Nubia continued after the advent of the 25th Dynasty too. Pharaonic Nubia began before Pharaonic Khemet, as it was the starting point of the culture. The Kingdom of Nubia (Sudan) lasted until the British occupation. Right after the end of Egypto-Nubian Antiquity, the Empire of Ghana rose like the Phoenix out of the ashes from the mouth of the Niger to the Senegal River, circa the 3rd Century A.D. Viewed from this perspective, African history proceeded without interruption. Nubia remained the single source of culture and civilization until about the 6th Century A.D. and then Ghana seized the mantle from the 6th – 12th Century A.D and my brothers and sisters, 'the rest is history' as they say;

Namastu'.

Conclusion

Though I have fully enjoyed sharing this knowledge, wisdom and history with my dear readers, all good things must come to an end. I did the best that I could do to re-write the history of the Kushites from a new perspective and although for myself it has been very emotional, I feel a great sense of achievement deep within. In answering the call of Paut Neteru 'the Company of the Gods', any mistakes made within this writing are completely my own. After all, like the singer 'Rag & Bone Man', says, 'I'm Only Human', after all.

Think about what you have been taught, officially about the Ancient Kushites; be they Sudanese (Ethiopians), Khemetians (Egyptians), Si-gag-ga (Sumerians), Elamites, Nabateans, Anu, Xia (Olmecs), Phoenicians, Xi and Shang (Chinese), Harrapans (Dravidian – Puntites), etc., etc. How misinformed we have become due to the so called 'official history' of the educational institutions. Contemplate what you have been told by monotheistic religion about the ancient people of the world and their civilizations. I hope now you all can 'real-eyes' the character assassination that has been done, the lies that have been perpetuated upon our ancestors. The fact that so called Scholars either hide the Black origin of the world and its civilizations by attributing the source, wrongly, to Greco-Rome, or by painting the faces of those, such as the Khemetian Egyptians White.

Now that you have been forced to unlearn all the nonsense that they put onto your predecessors, it is time to reclaim your stolen legacy, replenish and embrace it and return the planet to the rule of Ma'at, the original and pure spirituality which was the Right Knowledge, Right Wisdom and Right Overstanding (Nuwaubu) of the Anu – Ptahites, given to the sages to record and hand down through the generations. For it is time for a new spiritual 'Golden Age', a modern day utopia reality, whereby we take the power away from the 'Royal Court of the Dragon', the Servants of the Serpents. The 13 Draconian Reptilian bloodlines who are the 'Illuminati (of the amber light) are relying on us to reject all information, such as this, that is different from the 'official line'. These Satanist – bankers who have imprisoned the world tried to hide their true origins from out the shadows of history, by taking the esoteric knowledge out of circulation, because it exposes exactly who they are.

Now is the time to research deeper into the origins of religion, to see for yourself that all of the monotheistic faiths plagiarized the ideologies of Egyptian and Sumerian realities while labelling our culture pagans. All of the spiritual concepts now lying dormant within Jewish, Christian and Muslim creeds, originates within Kushite theology and there is no denying it. Give them back their 'isms and schisms and be brave enough to question everything that you are told as truth. Begin to think for yourselves again critically and the search for the ultimate truth will lead you all back to Kush, the light of the world and the font of all civilization and science. Given all the political conflict and self-interested materialism in the world today, the threat of war, financial corruption, poverty and disease, sexual perversion, climate change, racial tension and fear mongering, a return to Maatian Principles is the only solution to the impending nuclear Armageddon (World War III). It may be inevitable, but that doesn't mean that humanity cannot come through it to the other side. More spiritually inclined and aware of just who and what we all are, 'Eternal Consciousness'; for we are all (Black, White, Asian) Children of The All (Ba Kuluwm).

If we do not pass this information on to those who need it the most, then what is the point of anything else? It is our natural purpose to help each other to free the planet from the malevolent imprisonment it has fallen victim to. Our children are worshipping in the new religion of ignorance (celebrity), the religions of the heart such as, money, greed, self-gratification, fame, vanity and promiscuity – sex. They are out there killing, stabbing and shooting one another because the false contemporary Gods and their religions of fear cannot protect them. Neither Moses, Jesus nor Muhammad are coming back to save them. We have been sold a lie. Only true spirituality can save the world, humanity, from itself. It's either a new cataclysm (extinction – level event) where we start from scratch, like times before or a new utopia, beginning with the spiritual awakening of the people against a satanic elite of bloodlines interbreeding to keep the power of the world in a few hands only.

Stop fearing your own knowledge and culture because it's not the knowledge that is good or bad, but the person using it or how it is used. Let the ancients be the example for you in how to be an effective leader of people and how to exercise the Rule (Maat). Boycott those that are upholding the lies; Hollywood, the music industry, the political industry, fashion, banking and let's start to rebuild the planet. Your satanic leaders today have proved themselves, as have the terrorists. They are all senseless, fanatical murderers in disguise, child molesters, rapists, paedophiles, robbers, manipulators – devils in the flesh, how much more do you want for them to expose themselves.

My only hope is that this book goes some way into helping the planet, especially Black people (Kushites) to wake up, stand up and be counted like in the days of old. To challenge all that is wrong and confront injustice anywhere that one may find it. Because millions of people are still suffering in 2017 A.D. Mass mind control is still the order of the day, while society is glued to their phones, online and social media. Peel yourself away from the sleep walking trance of technology and take a good look at yourselves in the mirror and the world. Find the divine spirit of God, whatever name you want to call Him/Her within yourself. The ancestors are relying upon us to personify Paut Neteru once again. Too much blood has been spilled which is keeping the earth locked into this low density vibration (John 10:34, Psalms 82:6).

The further that humanity has come from the Zep Tepi – 'First, Beginning Times', the more that has been lost, spiritually. Thus, you will find that the newest religions are the most spiritually empty. They have been manipulated by the bloodlines into dogmatic shells lost to spirituality. Why do you think religions, such as 'Islam' are so intolerant and no longer about 'the peace' they were founded upon? The true universal religion, Maat, will rise again whether you like it or not. That is, 'Truth, Justice, Reciprocity, Uprightness, Balance, Harmony with all humans and all of creation. Long live the memory of the ancestors. Long live the true memory of the Shekems.

Jewels of the Nile: Black Renaissance-Awakening

The Islamic snakes, sorry, state, cannot be fought in the military way that the political West is doing. One cannot battle against their fanatical ideology in this counter-productive way and they are too aware of this on both sides. What we are currently witnessing is two sides of the same coin: heads and tails. All wars are first won mentally, by way of the mind. Thus, the correct way to fight this war is through the mind, not with weapons of war, because the more bombs dropped, the more people are brutally killed, then the more grief and terrorists are created by way of the emotionally imbalanced ideology, of brain washing.

At the top level, all of these people are working for the same masters, be they politicians, Jews, Muslims, the West, Russia, China, North Korea, Israel, etc. As far-fetched as this may seem, this current situation has been planned and been developing on the 'Reptilian Agenda' for many thousands of years. Once the mystery schools were infiltrated and overtaken and turned into today's network of secret societies, such as Jesuits, Freemasons, Templars, Rosicrucians, etc., they covertly penetrated into all the world institutions that mattered, to contract the world's power structure and manipulate the infamous 'New World Order' into its existence. We are now at the point where their cunning and diabolical plan has been realized. The only thing stopping them is the few minds that are resisting in pockets all over the planet; For the mind, not space, is the last frontier.

This is why we must engender and usher in a spiritual and cultural renaissance among humanity. The bloodlines depend on invisibility to continue in carrying out their Luciferian Conspiracy. By raising awareness and shining the light of the sun upon these Draculas (Dracos), we will consume them to ashes. To do this, humanity must travel back to their roots, individually and collectively, in a conscious effort to exercise our divinity, take back power and control of what is occurring. Collectively, we can reverse this nightmare, hell on earth. All of this religious compulsion perpetuated by Islam (Muhammadism) needs to be disposed of first and foremost; the compulsion to force religious views on others and labelling those who disagree with their self-righteous indoctrination as 'Kuffers – Unbelievers'. The same goes for Jews and their 'Anti-Semite' game and the Evangelical Christians viewing others as 'Infidels'. Rather than have a return to the Crusades and Dark Ages of Inquisition, the Kushites of the modern era need to rediscover the principles that made others see us as blameless. The knowing by which we did not have to believe in unconfirmed beliefs because we know better. The tried and tested formula of the facts (Haqq) kept us going for more than 3000 years and never failed us. We failed Maat!

How anyone can still believe in Muhammadism and Politics while witnessing what is taking place on the planet is beyond me, but I know that anyone who takes an unbiased look into Kushite spirituality and philosophy will come out on the other side – Enlightened, Awaken One. The wisdom of the ancients, such as the sage Ptah-hotep, Imhotep, Amenemhet I, the Book of the Coming Forth by Day (Into the Light), the Holy Tablets, the Emerald Tablet, the Sacred Records of Atum-Re, the Sacred Tablet of Tama-Re, the Egyptian Book of Light, etc., will be transfigured by the love and light within those powerful teachings. The simplicity and beauty of those works will render the Torah, Bible & Koran obsolete. I challenge the people to take that look, compare it to the over complicated dogmas of the mainstream faiths and their conflicting interpretations and violent sectism. If you are a pure potential being of light, a truth seeker, you will not be able to carry on in any false beliefs, blind devotion and/or spiritual amnesia.

Re-embracing our glorious culture will render us 'astute individuals' once again. We will become the parents of applied scientists, atomic theorists, mathematicians, architects, philosophers, sages, poets, alkhemists, physicians, astronomers, engineers, and other fields of intellectual passions, rather than just the parents of musicians, comedians, actors, sportsmen and women and drug dealers. It is on us to teach our children about the NUN and cosmic egg of AMUN RE (the Big Bang Theory), the Goddess Neith – the Weaver of Matter (Torsion and String Theory), Ptah and Memphite Theology, the Rashunaat and Sedjet, the Secret Operation of the Sun (the radiation cycle) and the 4 Laws of the Universe, the 99^{+1} natural elements and attributes, etc. All of which our Kushite ancestors knew (not believed) already. Together with the rediscovery and re-activation of the spirito-sciences via the re-mastery of the chakra system and the kundalini energy, we will become what we were created to be once again. Only then will the Anunnaqi-Elohim - 'the physical Gods' intervene and guide us beyond this dimension. Only when we become worthy will they quarantine and expel the malevolent entities holding humanity captive and re-locate the earth to another galaxy and dimension.

In order to achieve all this, you must expand your minds and change your way of thinking, replacing the atmosphere of fear with one of love. It's not about getting revenge or pointing the finger of blame but embodying the solution which is all mental. To erase the false 'ism ideologies of capitalism, socialism, communism, Mosism, Christism and Muhammadism, among others, we must educate the world to the eternal, universal principles of the Rule (Maat) living by, and for, one another once again. We must counteract the hate with love. Neither the western democractic corruption nor ideologies, such as I.S.I.L. and Al Qaeda, can survive through it, because as their own Qur'aan says in Surah Al Nasr, originally the last chapter, 'When the truth comes, then all falsehood must perish'.

Re-establishing a reciprocal relationship with each other, the planet and all of nature and creation, is the only positive way forward. Only then will we stop allowing the Illuminati from exploiting and destroying our planet. When (not if) we learn to construct pyramids once again, we can focus on the re-balancing of the earth's magnetic field by way of its meridians and leylines, therefore cleansing the energy grid and creating love, peace and happiness. It all begins with reverence and gratitude for nature and the glorification of the Most High, ANU AL'YUN AL'YUN, AL and Paut Neteru without whom, nothing would exist. You are the universe and the universe is you; Black people, humanity in general, 'Please wake up!' Hotep Lukum Kosmosans.

Personal Message of the Scribe: Final Message From the Kosmos

Let us pay homage to the ancestors. May they continue to light our way, guiding us along the path of Righteousness. May our deeds be fuelled by the creative power of our predecessors, who are reborn among the stars and are always present among us.

A perfect word is hidden better than a precious stone, and yet it is found among serving girls who work at the grindstone. The totality of Paut Neteru 'The company of the Gods' is both unified and multiple. You must ponder upon the greatness of the Gods. We must continue to make them offerings which have been made since the time of the Shekem Ur Shekem Menes. What we must offer is the greatest and best part of ourselves; the part of us all that is greater than birth and death. It is the eternal that will again bring the hieroglyphs to life. We must make our ancient and cultural religious rites sacred once again, just as in the days of old. This is all in taking back and reclaiming our stolen legacy. The togetherness will disempower the Illuminati (sons of the Amber Light). Realizing our own divinity and power within is what they most fear, for they know that they are on borrowed time.

A good man will always put purpose before pleasure and as a soldier of Maat, knows that he must never abandon discipline. This is the key to achieving 'The Great Work'. Live in the infinite now and concentrate on the gift which is called the present. In this way will we guarantee our future. From the present one can project the mind into the past or future, while remaining in the now, so let it be the default, know that evil happens only when good people fail to act.

All of this is very important because we have not been in control of our history for so long and the time has come for us to write it ourselves. Others must follow the example set out in this book, in rewriting the history of the Kushite race. For if we do not, others will continue to dictate their own biased view upon us and our forebears and we cannot allow this to continue any longer. We cannot allow unconfirmed beliefs to cast our ancestors in the shadow, by imposing their religious dogma upon our ancient culture. We should not be made to feel guilty for challenging their distorted and prejudiced views on our predecessors, because the religious views have only proven to be misguided and unfounded and based on nothing but conjecture and speculation. Views which come from a racist and covetous agenda to assassinate the character of Black people, while usurping the glory of the Black race. I think we have proven, beyond the shadow of a doubt that all spirituality originates in the Ancient Kushite culture and its awe inspiring civilizations which have been imitated, but never replicated by any others. The cosmic (alien) origin of Ancient Khemet and Sumer speak for themselves and this knowledge was dissipated throughout the near east, becoming the foundation of all religious ideals, faiths and esoteric secret societies. African (Kushite) spirituality was and is the origin and source of all world spirituality and your contemporary institutions want to blind you from this basic fact. Do not believe me go do the research for yourselves. Use this book and the many other great works of other authors to assist your research and point you in the right direction, the purpose of which is not to indoctrinate or convince you, but to show you where to look. Only you can convince yourselves from the inside, others cannot convince you from without, for knowing is better than believing.

Religious institutions wish to use fear to stop you from seeking the truth; Fear of hell fire and its punishment for transgressing 'God's' commandments, sinning and breaking His laws. This paralyzing fear stops us from looking into anything other than what we have been programmed to believe. This is all done deliberately, because they can never get rid of the ultimate truth, only blind you to it so that you cannot recognize it. Therefore, the truth is and has always been staring us in the face, carved six inches into the hardest stone tablets and monuments upon the planet - Immovable as the pyramids themselves. Erase the fear with love and 'seek the true face of God(s) and ye shall find it. Knock and the door to the temple shall be opened to you. Ask and the answer will be revealed, for the time is now and always has been and will be'.

Believing, is not knowing and when you know something then you do not have to have faith and believe. Believing by way of the facts is best. Blind belief is blind devotion which is ignorance; 'ignoring the fact', as so many religious people do. Not knowing is worse than idol worship, for it is 'worshipping in idle'. Learn to think critically and ask the right questions and we will erase religious indoctrinations, such as I.S.I.L. and Al Qaeda and the likes. There ideology will die out along with all others of a similar nature, Islamic or otherwise.

Good news should always be celebrated with a feast because life is meant to be a celebration, not a burden. Food is a blessing, nourishment for the heart and soul, so share it among you, especially with the less fortunate - Since giving is receiving. I give these words of love, light and wisdom to the truth seekers, if only to implore the favour of Paut Neteru and nothing else in return. For when we find the favour of the benevolent Gods, we will real-eyes that we need nothing else because we will have all that we will ever need. So, as the ancestors did, look at the earth as an extension of yourself. Everything is connected by the same ground, the same ether.

A real man must spend time educating his woman and vice-versa if needs be. Spend time reading, teaching and studying together and passing that knowledge, wisdom and overstanding to your off-spring. Cherish this wisdom as jewels and precious stones. Absorb the transformative writings of the sages, in whatever form you may find them. Support your woman; help her to secure her future. Pleasing a spouse is an achievement that deserves a reward. Keep each other happy; invest in your love until you return to the realm of Osiris.

In this world of perpetual conflict, true brotherhood/sisterhood is a rare quality. You must real-eyes that the 300 years of Willie Lynch Syndrome is past, put away the postcode wars and Black on Black violence and once again become each other's keeper, for the 'bond between brothers is the sword that defends the nation'. The bond between sisters is the medicine that heals the population. Change the way you look at things and the things you are looking at will change. Matter is malleable and in this way you have the power to create your own reality.

Let the unifying of northern (Lower) and southern (Upper) Khemet be symbolic of the need to unify the physical and spiritual aspects of the self. Especially in today's secular world, the separation of the physical and spiritual self is a recipe for disaster. Only by bringing the two aspects together can we find balance. The dark and the light, both forces are needed. This is the mastery. The Masonic man must square off all of his actions and then circumscribe that square with the circle. This will keep us from sinking into lawlessness.

Infinite love unites all forms of life within the boundless universe(s). The highest expression of this alchemical, infinite love is the union of mind, body and soul. The quintessence of this is the Nun, which brought the universe(s) to life and is the source of all creative forces. When we create things in the spirit, intellectually or artistically, the Nun will make it manifestly real. As soon as your mind crosses the boundaries of the visible world, we enter (reconnect) with it. We are situated within the Nun, which is the one thing. The earth is situated within the Nun, an island which has manifested from it temporarily. This unlimited energy envelopes us and nourishes our entire being, both physical and spiritual. Artists live within the Nun and have the privilege and power of creating, expressing its limitless power. Without it, our creations would amount to nothingness. In the spirit of the Nun have we brought this work to you dear readers.

The role of destiny is to present us with surprises. The disappearance of our ancestral values has been a disaster for the world over the last two millennia. The present has given us the honour of re-establishing them and changing the world by first changing ourselves. This alchemical transformation begins within the self, within the household, and within families and so on, into the world at large. This awakening is already begun, within and around us. The secret of the alchemist is the power to transform matter, the matter of self, first and foremost - mind, body and soul. Admire and give reverence to the appearance of the Sun's rising and setting, for it's the Sun that is the true father of Alchemy, transforming day into night and night back into day. In this, we become its children; Children of the Light, capable of listening to the voice of our ancestors.

Steering a ship as Titanic, as Khemet was a greater burden than most men could bear. Few men could handle the role of Shekem Ur Shekem (Pharaoh) without becoming corrupted by that degree of power or folding under the immense pressure. He who courts violence rebels against Maat. No event, happy or sad would ever weaken the resolve of a servant of Maat or cause them to stray from the path the Gods had shown them. The transmutation of the soul (Ba) depends upon the strength of this resolve, which grants the soul the power to fly up to celestial paradise.

There is nothing more binding and precious than a person's word. When one's word is kept it enables us to sail upon the ocean of strength – giving energy (Nun) nourishing our Ka (spiritual essence) with power. This is the true and pure reverence of the Divine Light. This is the legacy of yesterday, today and tomorrow – the infinite now – the Gift. Stay true to your word my dear readers, for your word is your bond in sincerity.

14. Self-discipline: The first person you lead is yourself.

"A man without a decision of character can never be said to belong to himself. He belongs to whatever can make captive of him ...."

- John Foster

".... Don't quit, because once you're in that mode of quitting, then you feel like it's okay..."

- Jerry Rice

A Pharaoh who abuses his power is unworthy of his office. It is the voice of Maat that we must heed, at every moment and in all circumstances. And it is precisely because we cannot do so that we must continually build her temple within us and fight against our natural tendency to injustice and greed. Those who give in to these tendencies may gain a small victory today, but will suffer a heavy defeat tomorrow. Those who flatter you will betray you. It is in their very nature, just as it is in a predator's nature to devour its prey.

The power of Maat has the power to tame matter and to overcome time. In order to hear the call - the voice of the light, your heart must not be deaf. Like the Sun which (symbolically) dies in the evening, you must cross the shadow (night), confront fearsome trials and strive to be reborn in the morning. You must possess the strength and courage to see the light shining within the darkness. In this way, one can find the path of the coming forth by day (into the light). This is the voyage that the ship of the sun undergoes through the underworld each night, in which the light of Ra and Osiris are united and Osiris vanquishes the darkness. I sincerely hope my hands have successfully translated what my spirit has perceived to my readers, within the book of life. Its words are written all around us, we read through its pages together. Remember these words of power, because life sets us trials which make us fall from great heights and for some the fall is more severe than it is for others

It is better to die than to betray one's solemn oath. Especially in the world today, sincere and honest people are rarer than precious stones. Words are sacred and those that know do not squander their words easily. The higher the social status and influence of a person, the more impeccable their character must be. The spirit of Maat must dwell, not in a person's head but within the thinking heart. Generations pass and all that endures is the word of the Gods, which is embodied in light or in stone. Be wary of those who only pray/worship to be seen of men. They only wish to be admired by other people and not by God(s). When they are behind closed doors, in the privacy of their own homes they worship not. The same can be said for those who fabricate and twist words only to look and sound as if they know much, when in fact they know only little. These kinds of teachers are addicts of conjecture and speculation. These are they who are always looking for debates to enforce their views on others, mentally or otherwise. They detest critical thinking and the freedom of thought. In their misguidance, they only bring down the wrath of the God(s) upon themselves. Their rigid belief systems only kill the remnant of spirituality.

15. Teachability: To keep leading, keep learning

".... It's what you learn after you know it all that counts ...."

- John Wooden

Why should you keep growing?

- Your growth determines who you are.
- Who you are determines who you attract.
- Who you attract determines the success of your organization.
- If you want your organization to grow, you have to remain teachable.

".... A true teacher always remains a student ...."

- Anonymous

The thoughts of the spiritual man/woman drift in a universe beyond the hours of night and day, beyond time and space in which mortals dwell. They are like the stone in the Valley of the Pharaohs, feeding off the invisible. By this means they gain access to what is inaccessible to most others. Although unseen by the physical eyes, these are those that live on the light. They are constantly reborn of the creative power that was born of itself, through their works. They embody the transformation that is never fixed, reconciling the One with the many, wholeheartedly devoted to the wisdom of the sages. Their works turn matter into light.

The ancients already overstood that time and space, are aspects of the same thing long before the advent of Western science. That the radiant void is ever alive and constantly creating the building blocks, which the universe breathes in and out, itself contained within Ba Kuluwm 'The All'. This is the knowledge of many thousands of years which we must explore further and further, passing on what is learnt. The wisdom of the ancients can enable us to see aspects of reality which elude most others, perceiving the invisible world and the eternal laws of harmony. When the flame of enlightenment ignites within us and dispels the shadow, we must never let it go out.

Idleness is the worst of all vices men prone to small talk say many words which rarely hold any value. The noble among you may say few words, but those few words weigh heavy with value. These few nobles who guard both their mouths and their private parts are those few who are capable of going beyond themselves and their own faults. They know that this world is only an unworthy portion of reality. That this life is not at all the pinnacle of existence and that this realm dulls in comparison to the higher.

Seek to establish brotherhood. For brotherhood is stronger than death. Become an Akhu 'useful being' and strive to become illuminated. When you truly enter the light, you shall see as its sees, practising the Rule of Maat is to know its radiance. To become a Being of light you must transform the mortal into immortal, by generating the astral body. All of the base elements are already within you. By assembling all of the materials, you will form an unchanging body. Your hand will know God's designs and your mouth will speak the words of transfiguration. Thus, you will achieve The Great Work, through your own personal legend. Always remember that the light of Maat grants life to those who embrace it. Take apart your own inner elements and put them back together in a different way to create the self-transmutation, as long as you overstand that all energy comes from the heart of the universe. Carry this light within the centre of your Being, because when you carry the Kingdom of God within, everywhere you go, you take the Kingdom of God with you. 'When there is no enemy within, no enemy outside can harm you'. The initiate is as a rough-hewn stone, when you enter the brotherhood/temple, you become a refined block able to help build the temple. This is how the ancestors built the Land of Light in which the Rule was celebrated by way of the Rites. The radiant souls of our predecessors maintain the power of the Rule. He who is deaf to the voice of Maat has no brother and there is no feast day for the greedy men.

It is only when we do not seek power that true power is given to us. When pursuing our dreams, we may falter, but only when we give up on them, do we fail. A man's main concern under the guidance of Maat should be to be a worthy husband and father, a woman's is to be a worthy wife and mother. See what must be seen, what is hidden and what is clear, in the subtle and the gross. Do what is right and just, be clear and calm and may your character be firm and capable of bearing misfortune and happiness, may your heart be vigilant and your tongue sincere. These are the customs of the ancestors that we must cherish until the end of time.

The ancestors will never leave us, their silence will become words if we listen for their voice. Living with their life blood in our veins, our hands will continue what they began and through us all, they shall live on. This is the mystery that unites past, present and creates the future in Hathor's creative love. It is the duty of all Kushites to cultivate their ancient culture once again, thus ending the current identity crises. My brothers, know that the greater a man's abilities, the greater the trials he must face. You must always respect the Rule impartially, even if certain decisions may feel discomforting. You must ensure to always conduct yourself and do things correctly. Let this rediscovered brotherhood unite us like the stones in the pyramids and our resolve will stand the test of time.

I took on this Great Work in order to allow the truth to touch your very soul and awaken it to unseen realities. This is not coming from me, but through me. For all of this is the wisdom of the ancient ancestors, rediscovered and passed on to this generation, a lost and found culture. The last 3000 years akin to the Sun going on its night journey through the underworld, to re-emerge reborn after the 12th hour. Let these words of the divine speak to the centre of your Being, reconnecting you with the seen and unseen, the gross and the subtle, back to the source. Thus, we will renew the pact between Paut Neteru and humanity. It is urgent! We cannot let what's left of righteousness vanish from the earth. We must instead use the spirit of Maat to create a new world, fit for everyone to live harmoniously in. In building this work I pay homage to Ptah, Patron God of buildings, Tehuti, God of Knowledge and the Sacred Word and Amun-Re, the Most High Supreme.